Digitalization and Social Change

Digitalization is shaping our everyday lives, yet navigating the changes it entails can feel like trekking into the unknown, where both the possibilities and the consequences are unclear and difficult to grasp. Exploring how digitalization affects all aspects of our lives, from health to culture, this book aims to develop and strengthen the reader's ability to think critically about such developments.

Written in a clear and concise manner with reference to science fiction and pop culture, this book presents potent theoretical perspectives for understanding digitalization processes as societal change. Various exercises are included throughout to encourage readers to critically explore digitalization in their own lives.

Replete with illustrations and examples, this book is an accessible guide to digitalization in the modern societal context, appealing to students at the undergraduate level as well as general readership.

Kristine Ask is an Associate Professor in Science and Technology Studies (STS), at the Department of Interdisciplinary Studies of Culture, Norwegian University of Science and Technology (NTNU) in Trondheim, Norway. She researches emergent user practices and communities online, spanning from games to social media and memes. Dr. Ask has a particular interest in internet culture that is dismissed as frivolous or mundane.

Roger A. Søraa is an Associate Professor in Science and Technology Studies (STS), at the Department of Interdisciplinary Studies of Culture, Norwegian University of Science and Technology (NTNU) in Trondheim, Norway. His research focus is on automation, robotization, and the digitalization of society—how humans and technology relate to each other. Dr. Søraa is especially interested in the social domestication of technology and how different groups are impacted by technology.

Digitalization and Social Change
A Guide in Critical Thinking

Kristine Ask and Roger A. Søraa

CRC Press
Taylor & Francis Group
Boca Raton London New York

CRC Press is an imprint of the
Taylor & Francis Group, an **informa** business

A CHAPMAN & HALL BOOK

Designed cover image: Nienke Bruijning

First edition published 2024
by CRC Press
2385 NW Executive Center Drive, Suite 320, Boca Raton FL 33431

and by CRC Press
4 Park Square, Milton Park, Abingdon, Oxon, OX14 4RN

CRC Press is an imprint of Taylor & Francis Group, LLC

Library of Congress Cataloging-in-Publication Data
Names: Ask, Kristine, author. | Søraa, Roger A., author.
Title: Digitalization and social change : a guide in critical thinking /
Kristine Ask and Roger Andre Søraa.
Description: 1 Edition. | Boca Raton, FL : CRC Press, 2024. |
Includes bibliographical references and index. | Identifiers: LCCN 2023031626
(print) | LCCN 2023031627 (ebook) |
ISBN 9781032267036 (v. 1 ; hardback) | ISBN 9781032258911 (v. 1 ; paperback) |
ISBN 9781003289555 (v. 1 ; ebook)
Subjects: LCSH: Social change—Technological innovations. |
Information technology—Social aspects. |
Information technology—Psychological aspects.
Classification: LCC HM851 .A785 2024 (print) | LCC HM851 (ebook) |
DDC 302.23/1—dc23
LC record available at https://lccn.loc.gov/2023031626
LC ebook record available at https://lccn.loc.gov/2023031627

ISBN: 9781032267036 (hbk)
ISBN: 9781032258911 (pbk)
ISBN: 9781003289555 (ebk)

DOI: 10.1201/9781003289555

Typeset in Myriad Pro
by codeMantra

Contents

PART 2   Analytical Tools

PART 4 Conclusions and Handouts

Preface

For years, our students asked for a textbook that took a broad approach to digitalization and societal change. Something to help them connect the various technologies, actors, and futures they read about in journal articles, in news media, and on social media. This book is our answer to that request, and we hope that you, as a reader, find it useful as you navigate digitalization both in your studies and in everyday life.

Making sense of digitalization can be challenging. Not only is it a process of change that occurs in all areas of our lives, but it's also something ongoing and fast-paced. Because of this, we need analytical tools that persist beyond the latest trend and remain useful after today's platforms, services, and apps are replaced. Consequently, in this book, we present insights and theories for thinking critically about the relationship between technology and society, the role of users in shaping digitalization, and how digitalization affects society.

The version of this book you are holding in your hands is a revised English translation of the original Norwegian-language edition. To make it accessible for an international audience, we considered toning down the Nordic focus and many local examples in favor of a more global story about digitalization. However, after considerable contemplation, we decided to not only keep but also *lean in* on our own Norwegian context.

There are several reasons for this. Firstly, digitalization is such a large and complex phenomenon that any general book on the subject would be big enough to sink a ship and highly unpractical to acquire and carry around. Secondly, we do not want to omit how the Nordic STS tradition has shaped us as researchers, especially our orientation toward user studies and everyday life. Finally, reading about examples and case studies that are outside of your own culture can help put into focus important aspects of digitalization practices that are closer to you. While we, as Norwegians, consider many of the selected cases both mundane and obvious, they might appear exotic and strange to you: nurses in Norway navigating fjord roads, goats grassing in arctic climates, and flowerpot robots caring for older adults in rural villages prone to winter storms. We have, however, added more explanations of phenomena that can sound alien to foreign readers but can otherwise reassure you that the different language editions are more or less the same.

A textbook is always more than "just" dissemination of facts. A textbook is also an assertion about a field and what the next generation of students should take with them. In this selection process, we are shaped and influenced by our own education in the field of Science and Technology Studies (STS), not only through research but also through our affiliation with the Department of Interdisciplinary Studies of Culture at NTNU: Norwegian University of Science and Technology.

We wish to thank our wonderful colleagues at our department, who have been generous with both knowledge and support. A special thanks goes to our supervisors and mentors, who have made it possible for us to develop our own critical sense and our disciplinary work—Margrethe Aune, Nora Levold, Knut Sørensen, Stig Kvaal, and Per Østby.

We wish to thank our editors and translators at our publisher, Routledge, as well as our Norwegian publisher, Fagbokforlaget, and *The Norwegian Non-Fiction Writers and Translators Association*, for their support of the first Norwegian version of this book. A special thanks to Jennifer Duggan for her work in translating the English version and Jin K. Hurum for indexing.

We thank in particular our eminent and talented illustrator Nienke Bruijning, who has made this book stunning, and Martine Meen Hobæk and Mark W. Kharas for their help cleaning up the references. A large thank you also goes to the critical readers of an early draft of the manuscript, who have given us necessary and useful feedback underway: Jenny Bergschöld, Jennifer Duggan, Håkon Fyhn, Bård Torvetjønn Haugland, Stig Kvaal, Nora Levold, Artur Serrano, Ingvild Kvale Sørenssen, Gunhild Tøndel, and Jostein Vik.

We would also like to thank our supporters at home, Mark, Håvard, and Magnus, who have helped us to keep up our motivation and encouraged us to write, as well as reminded us that there are more important things in life than work. Both authors contributed equally to this book, and it can be referenced as follows:

Ask, K., & Søraa, R. A. (2023). *Digitalization and Social Change: A Guide in Critical Thinking*. Routledge.

We wish you an enjoyable reading experience and hope that this book can be both useful and inspiring in your studies and research linked to digitalization.

Happy reading!

Kristine Ask & Roger A. Søraa
Department of Interdisciplinary Studies of Culture, Norwegian University of Science and Technology (NTNU), Trondheim, Norway

PART 1
A Critical Perspective On Digitalization

CHAPTER 1

Getting Lost in the Digital

What if you woke up tomorrow to a world without digital technology? If, overnight, there were no more mobile phones, computers, or internet? If we presume this abrupt change was *not* caused by an alien or zombie invasion (which would of course affect your priorities), what would you do? Would a sudden shutdown of all digital infrastructure and services be scary and disorienting, like losing a part of yourself—the way many people feel when their mobile phones are unavailable? Or would you, perhaps, experience it as a relief to be free of the many digital artifacts in your life or even exciting to try to find non-digital solutions?

Let the thought experiment begin in the morning. What would your day look like? There would be no alarm on your mobile

DOI: 10.1201/9781003289555-2

3

phone to get you out of bed, no news on social media to consume with your morning coffee, no access to your digital calendar to find out where and when you have appointments, and no mobile games or podcasts on your way to school or work. Already, the day is quite different from a normal day which includes digital technology, and we have just barely left the house, let alone arrived on campus or at the workplace where most of us are dependent on emails, educational platforms, digital ordering systems, and numerous other digital technologies to fully function well in society. To take it further, you would no longer have access to your health data, submit taxes online, or send electronic applications for student loans or mortgages. Communication would go slowly since messages would need to be physically moved between one place and another—with so-called "snail-mail."

There would, however, be many things we wouldn't miss. Like pop-up ads, scamming attempts, program updates, synching issues, and other more or less harmful time- and attention thieves. Without digital technologies, annoyances would be gone, and you could even find yourself more focused or calm.

Without digital technology, both our individual everyday lives and society in general would look very different. The fact that one can identify dozens, if not hundreds, of situations and relationships in our lives that are formed by digital technology is an indication of how strongly digitalization shapes the time we live in. Consequently, the question "Why study digitalization?" is in many ways superfluous. Digitalization is something that affects everyone. Today, there are virtually no arenas, processes, or people who are not influenced by digitalization. It can be challenging to understand which changes digitalization entails precisely because digitalization represents so many different technologies, services, actors, and processes.

On the cover of this book, you see an adventurer in a deep forest of technology. The illustration captures that life in a digital world can feel like being lost in the wild, surrounded by technologies that you are unsure are friends or foes, and where the path forward is not clear. The cover image and metaphor of learning as a journey point together to how digitalization can be experienced as moving into a world that is disordered and unclear, with possible dangers around every corner. At the same time, the forest is here used as a metaphor for the unknown—a place still not entirely understood, still able to invoke great fear and excitement, and in need of exploration. However, in the unknown, there is also potential for new knowledge, perspectives, and resources. Maybe some great opportunity or innovation is waiting behind the next bend? By reading this book, you will be better able to understand and navigate the unknown forest that digitalization represents, equipped with a theoretical backpack to help you navigate and a set of analytic binoculars to sharpen your gaze.

This book is written around three core themes: social change, user perspectives, and critical thinking. Digitalization is seen primarily as a form of *social change* where our society's behaviors, relations, norms, and institutions are being shaped by the development and implementation of digital technology. The *user perspectives* provide us with information needed to understand digitalization as it describes the technology in practice, and *critical thinking* refers to the required nuanced perspectives on the relationship between technology and society. Throughout this book, we will explore what digitalization involves, what meanings it holds, and how digitalization forms society and the individual. Nevertheless, the aim is not for you to acquire some quick facts about digitalization that can be regurgitated on your next exam and then promptly forgotten. Rather, the aim of this book is for you to develop the necessary cognitive tools to be able to assess digital technology that is being introduced into society, to consider the consequences of digitalization processes, to critically evaluate the premises on which digitalization is based, and to question what is usually presented as the inevitable effects of digitalization.

1.1 Limited or Liberated by Ubiquitous Digital Technology?

As the thought experiment above suggests, digital technology is everywhere (as a multiplicity of objects, systems, and practices) and can thus be described as *ubiquitous*—something that is around us all the time, including when we sleep (Levold & Spilker, 2008; Ling & Donner, 2013). The ubiquity of digital technology causes many of us to have an ambivalent relationship with digitalization, as we are experiencing both its possibilities and its constraints. We have to relate to many different technologies and have experienced both positive and negative consequences.

Some argue that digital technologies, particularly digital media, are taking up too much space in their lives. Counter-movements like "Digital detox" aim for people to periodically stop using screens or to reduce screen time. It advocates a balanced approach to the use of media technologies and is motivated by the idea that reducing screen time will lead them to a more authentic, happy life. While an admirable goal, it is worth noting that such movements tend to idealize what it means to be "offline"—and may be understood as a commodification of authenticity and nostalgia (Syvertsen & Enli, 2020). Regardless of how you personally feel about the time you spend with screens, if you decide to completely cut off digital technology from your life, you might find it challenging due to digital technology's ubiquity. Since most of us have bosses, clients, and commitments that require digital presence, an everyday life without established platforms like Zoom, Slack, Facebook, Microsoft Office, or Android/iOS is nearly impossible in practice (Matias, 2018).

There are many instances where digitalization feels forced upon us. Even when the goal is to get out in nature, and away from our screens, the digital is still present through apps to pay for parking or hiking trail maps published online, not to mention the more-or-less obligatory trail summit selfie. We can also feel fairly powerless and at the technology's mercy when it doesn't work; for example, if a server goes down, a website is being updated, or a teacup overturns onto your keyboard at a critical moment, such as 10 minutes before a deadline. In these instances, digitalization can feel limiting, like something we didn't choose, cannot opt out of, and simply have to deal with.

At the same time, we are acutely aware of how digital technology has improved many people's lives. Digital technology opens up possibilities by connecting us to people, information, and cultures far out of our physical reach. Our lives are extended by digital surfaces and platforms for education, communication, learning, work, and self-actualization. Digitalization give access to streaming services that offer content from the entire world, we can have conversations and play with people across borders and time zones, and we can save time and money when working digitally from home offices. Archives that used to require resources and approvals are now accessible with the click of a mouse (although this requires access to technology, which is not equally distributed across the globe). Those connected to the internet can express and explore identities and relationships in new ways through digital formats like selfies, games, memes, and dating apps. Digitalization can also give us increased security and belonging, as we can keep in contact with each other digitally, both while traveling and by sharing the ups and downs of our (mostly mundane) everyday lives. Society can also be made more transparent when registers, databases, or archives become digital and accessible to all. However, digital technologies also have grimmer sides to them that affect society, many of which will be explored in the remainder of this book. An important takeaway to already be aware of is that technology in itself is neither good nor bad.

That digitalization can *simultaneously* be experienced as limiting and liberating is central. Our relationship to "the digital" is both contradictory and complex; a single digital technology can be experienced as both useful and useless, as a source of joy and sorrow. The book you are holding in your hands now explores this tension and attempts to explain how processes of digitalization can have both positive and negative consequences at the same time. The aim is to make you equipped to navigate the complex, paradoxical effects of digitalization and thus help you to distinguish friend from foe, and useful from useless, when you fumble about in the metaphorical dark Norwegian woods. This book's purpose is to strengthen your ability to think critically about digitalization. This requires awareness of what values and norms are linked to technology, how digital technology forms our lives, and how digitalization processes can have different effects in different places, at different times, and for different people. To think critically means asking questions about what is "normal" and taken for granted, including your own relationship with digital technology and your perspectives on how digitalization affects your own life. Consequently, we begin this book with a "digital detox" exercise that encourages you to not use digital technology for one day (see Box 1A). The goal is for you to become more aware of your own relationship to digital technology. Throughout this book, you will find orange boxes containing various exercises and activities that will help you explore the consequences of digitalization.

Box 1A.   Exercise: Digital Detox

An effective way to make yourself aware of what technology does or doesn't do in your everyday life is to cut it out for a period of time. Instead of a thought experiment, you can try it in practice. How will your day look if you cut out digital technology for 24 hours? Try a "digital detox," during which you turn off all your digital devices for a period of time. Reflect on what this does to your everyday life: Which tasks become difficult? Are some things impossible to do? Are some things easier? What alternative solutions did you find? Not least, how did it feel to be "offline"? What did you miss? What didn't you miss? Reflect with pen and paper.

1.2 It Could Be Otherwise (ICBO): The Foundation of Critical Thinking

It is tempting to turn the story of digitalization into a story of continued progress in which technology is only getting better, faster, and more important for society. However, the effects of digitalization on society are not predetermined, nor is it clear whether these effects can be considered progress. What we consider "good" digital solutions are dependent on time and place, and even small changes in the legislation, policy, interpretations, and designs of a technology can have big consequences for its impact on society.

The thought experiment at the beginning of this book asked you to imagine a day *without* digital technology, prompting you to think of a radically different daily life. This time around, we want you to imagine your digital everyday life if it was just a *little different*. If digital technology was still ubiquitous but not quite the same. What would social media be like if smartphones never caught on and everyone posted and "liked" content from their laptop? What if everyone just mocked the recommendations of algorithms because we thought of them as notoriously untrustworthy and the idea of receiving advice from an algorithm was absurd? Or if nobody ever thought of putting a camera in a mobile phone, so it remained a single-use tool to call people with? Such questions are worth reflecting on because they allow us to consider how things could have turned out differently. This type of reflection also draws our attention to the variety of factors that affect digitalization, which goes far beyond technical specifications and technological trends.

In short, critical thinking is dependent on the ability to consider how the world could be different. By rejecting the idea that a technology's developmental trajectory and consequences for society are predetermined, we create space for the unknown to be recognized as a possibility. Moving through the digital "deep forest," there are many possible paths forward, and we have to make continuous decisions about which to follow. Occasionally we can find ourselves retracing our previous steps, falling off a cliff, or discovering that we had been following the tracks of a dangerous polar bear all along. This way of thinking is called "It Could Be Otherwise" (ICBO) (Latour & Woolgar, 1979; Star, 1988; In some ways, this concept is self-explanatory; you should be aware that things could have been different. In practice, the concept can be challenging to apply because we are so used to the world being as it is. That which seems normal appears just that—normal—like the world is as it should or must be. To open a space where alternate developmental trajectories are possible requires us to first become aware of what we see as normal and why. ICBO meddles with what we take for granted and pushes against the limits of what we think is possible, acceptable, or desirable. You can read more about ICBO in Box 1B, and you will find more purple fact boxes that elaborate on certain concepts, themes, or phenomena throughout the book. You may perhaps already know some of this information, but as this book aims to give a broad introduction to readers at varying levels, we have opted risking saying too much rather than too little.

Box 1B.   Recommendation: It Could Be Otherwise (ICBO) as Seen through Speculative Fiction

ICBO is about showing awareness that there is no predetermined direction for how society and/or technology develops. We can easily see this through different countries' modes of government—for example, how Germany or China have chosen different strategies when faced with technology and systems developed in the US. China has chosen to develop and produce its own technologies and literally build a wall around its internet ("The Great Firewall of China"), while the EU has developed legislation and regulations like the GDPR (General Data Protection Regulation).

To develop your ability to imagine alternative worlds and societies, we recommend viewing/reading/playing/ exploring fictional alternatives through science fiction. Whether the story is set in the past, present, or future, in space or on Earth, is not important. The point is to play with ideas about what "different" can be, get used to the thought that normality can be more than what you already know, and meet alternative ways of creating a society. When you sit down with a science fiction story, you should reflect on which technologies exist in this world and which effects they have. How is society organized, and how does it compare to yours? Why don't these fictional technologies exist in reality, and what do you think would happen if they did?

We will also draw on fictional examples throughout this book to further explore how It Could Be Otherwise.

ICBO rejects the idea that the way the world is ordered is somehow predetermined, inevitable, or necessary. Instead, it welcomes a perspective where technologies can be interpreted in different ways and have different consequences, agendas, or possibilities depending on their contexts. Not least, ICBO stresses a critical lens through which we no longer think of today's technology as resulting from evolution, where the best and strongest technologies survive, but rather as the result of a process affected by coincidence, mess, and unforeseen consequences. This invites us to think about digitalization as driven by more than just "technological innovation."

Take module-based mobile phones, for example. Module-based mobile phones are designed so that the user can switch out different parts based on their needs, including installing a better camera, more storage space, or a longer-lasting battery. Several large producers, like Google and LG, launched variants of module-based mobiles around 2016, but they were a total fiasco and were pulled from the market, and the projects were discontinued (TechAltar, 2017). If we dismiss module-based mobiles as simply "inferior technology" (though we do not deny that these phones had problems), which naturally gave way to "better models," we omit how other interpretations of or infrastructures around the technology could have created a different outcome. Maybe these technological challenges would have been solved if the producers had attempted another few models. Or maybe small changes in the cultures surrounding mobile phones would have been enough. For example, if we, as mobile users, valued flexibility over other qualities or if it was seen as high status to have an individualized phone, it isn't certain that the module-based phone would have flopped.

Being able to identify alternative ways technology and society could function together, other than what we currently have, is the foundation of critical thinking about digitalization. If you can consider how things "could be different," you acknowledge that digitalization's effects are not predetermined and are instead complex sets of identifiable and changeable factors. Many institutions and companies see digitalization as a linear journey from A to Z, in which technology is introduced and either succeeds or fails. With such a perspective, digital technology is introduced into society with only two alternatives: it will either be accepted or be rejected. This underestimates the many ways in which things could be different and suggests we do not have the power to influence the digitalization process.

1.3 Opening the Black Box

Turning digitalization into a simple input–output model where new digital technology is "inputted" and consequences are "outputted" is to turn digital technology into a "black box" (Rosenberg & Nathan, 1994). Black boxes are characterized by knowing the "before" and "after" but not the "during." In this book, with the help of theory and empirical examples, we will open black boxes and show digitalization as a process comprising identifiable and influenceable factors. Digitalization consists of both technical and social elements, and it is our wish to make you, the reader, able to identify these elements and, through them, open black boxes. To do this, you need a critical understanding of how digitalization happens and an awareness of how the final product is in no way predetermined but rather a consequence of choices and coincidences that you can influence.

The ability to critically evaluate the process of digitalization can be considered a component of digital literacy. Digital literacy is increasingly important and includes both being able to use digital technology and being able to exercise digital judgment, including following privacy rules and considering others online. However, in order to think critically about digital technology, we need to consider its role in society and how it shapes our lives in specific ways. We must be able to criticize and problematize not just the technology itself but also the premises for the development and implementation of digital technologies. In addition, we need to evaluate the consequences of implementing new technologies based on how technology is used and how it affects our everyday lives, such that our evaluation is on the basis of technology's actual role in society (Levold & Spilker, 2008; Nye, 2007; Pinch & Bijker, 1984; Lie & Sørensen, 1996). If we want to know what opportunities for change exist—and, through them, find ways to create better, more sustainable, and ethical technologies and societal solutions—we must understand how technology forms our lives.

1.4 A Response to Political and Corporate Solutionism

When you, the readers, are given the responsibility of developing a critical perspective on digital technology, it is because history has shown us that we cannot leave the job of evaluating and regulating digital technologies to developers and politicians. Developers are often too concerned with money and success, while politicians generally know too little about technology and are concerned with short-sighted, election-focused promises.

We do not mean to dismiss the many innovations that have come from Silicon Valley and similar technological milieus. However, it has become clear that a desire for profit steers technological development at the cost of utility, user friendliness, and fairness—with high costs for exploited workers, the environment, and end-users whose lives and habits have become highly valued by data companies. Take, for example, "Juicero," a "smart" Wi-Fi-connected juicer that, surprisingly, did not juice fruit. Instead, its only function was to squeeze drinks out of prepackaged juice bags (inadvertently adding another function: creating plastic waste). Another example is image-recognition algorithms that have been trained on datasets with primarily white faces and thus fail to identify individuals of color, all because ethical considerations have been subordinated in the development process (see also Chapter 10). A more recent example is how AI systems like DALL-E and Midjourney are made possible through the world's largest art theft, where the AIs are trained on copyrighted images without permission from artists. Together, these examples—a small selection from many—give little reason to believe that the solution to our societal problems will be made in Silicon Valley. Even technologies that explicitly seek to solve societal problems (as opposed to only generating profit) are all too often affected by "solutionism," where codes, algorithms, robots, and technology are presented as complete and friction-free solutions to the world's problems (Morozov, 2013).

Politicians, for their part, are notoriously slow to respond to new technological developments and rarely show the foresight or efficiency required to regulate the introduction and use of digital technologies (Elish, 2019). From a lack of legislation and resources regarding privacy, which makes it possible for personal data to be sold for profit against our will, to political and legal downgrading of online threats and harassment, it is clear that (needed) political regulation of technology often comes long after the technology has been integrated in society.

Political leaders also lead with ill-conceived prestige projects that look good on paper but create chaos in practice. For example, the Health Platform project in mid-Norway was supposed to create a shared patient record but is facing machine criticism from health practitioners; Digital Audio Broadcasting (DAB) radio, which was supposed to replace FM radio but is not terribly popular; and Smittestop, a government-created app that was supposed to monitor Covid-19 infections in Norway but had security holes and was not universally designed. That many experts warned politicians about these problems both before and during development is a reminder that these outcomes were not unavoidable or impossible to predict. Finding digital solutions that benefit society is thus also about political will and competence, not just what is technically possible.

The consequence of a profit-based technology sector and politicians' lagging behind is that we, as students, researchers, and citizens, need to do the work of learning critical perspectives and strategies. Critical perspectives are needed if we want to prevent digitalization from being reduced to solutionism or prestige projects—where the consequences of bad design, ethical shortcuts, and lacking regulatory decisions are put on us. Part of this responsibility is to ensure that digitalization does not become a process that further entrenches power and money in the hands of a few, which is neither fair nor sustainable and would lead to further marginalization of vulnerable groups. We must equip ourselves with critical thinking skills and knowledge about the changes digitalization entails so we may understand, evaluate, and influence the digitalization process in desired directions.

1.5 Digitalization as a Topic for Science and Technology Studies (STS)

Digitalization is not something one discipline or one example can elucidate. To understand the complexity of digitalization, it is important to have an academic foundation that emphasizes nuances, tensions, and complexities and rejects simple, surface-level explanations. To achieve this, this book combines perspectives from *Science and Technology Studies* (STS) (see Box 1C) with case studies, that is concrete examples, from fields like internet and game studies, organization and health research, artificial intelligence, and social robotics. STS examines the relationship between people, science, and technology, and has developed a series of perspectives that help us analyze complex ethical aspects of technology, as well as risks, possibilities, and negotiations linked to science and technology. Because of the field's interest in and nuanced understandings of technology, change, and users, STS is a suitable theoretical entry point into studies of digitalization processes.

Box 1C.   Fact: Science and Technology Studies (STS)

Studies of knowledge, technology, and society, also called Science and Technology Studies (STS), is a relatively young field of research with a diverse focus on the relations between scientific knowledge production, technological systems and innovations, and society and its many actors (Kuhn, 1962; Bijker et al., 1987; Jasanoff et al., 2001; Latour, 2005). For this book, with focus on digitalization, this includes asking, Who makes technology? Who uses it? Why is one technology developed and used rather than another? How are technologies developed and used, and what implications does this have for diverse groups in society? For an introduction to STS, see Sismondo (2010).

The case studies in this book cover the following themes: health, work, control, culture, and the self, each thematized in its own chapter (8–13). Together, they show digitalization as a diverse process with a multiplicity of technologies, users, and consequences. As digitalization takes place at many different levels, in different arenas, and with different actors, the case studies showcase how digitalization isn't a linear process nor a phenomenon that can be easily summarized. A shared characteristic of these case studies is (in addition to their focus on digital technology) an empirical perspective on *users* where technology is understood in light of how it is used (see Box 1D). In addition to presenting select case studies, we will also show that there are analytical tools that function across contexts and users and that the sociotechnical perspective can just as easily be applied in studies of digitalization in the health sector as when trying to make sense of the advent of influencers.

This book is particularly relevant to undergraduate and graduate students in STS, media studies, medical humanities, and other social science and humanities fields that work with digitalization. Yet, we hope this book will also find readers outside of these fields. As we have suggested, everyone should be able to undertake a critical assessment of digitalization processes—irrespective of discipline—since digitalization is ubiquitous and occurs in all arenas. If you are a health worker put under ever-stricter optimization demands from your reporting platform, a caseworker who keeps being introduced to new and "better" administrative systems, a teacher who must evaluate which digital teaching aids actually work, or a student who is exposed to "innovative" learning systems, you need to be able to evaluate how digitalization is shaping your day-to-day life. Whether you are trying to build opposition to a technological solution that isn't working or you want to learn how to get a technology to function in the best possible way, the ability to critically evaluate technology is crucial.

Box 1D.   Fact: Empirical Research

Research based on what can be experienced or sensed, for example, observations, interviews, experiments, and text analysis. Both qualitative and quantitative research can be empirical. Empirical research is different from research based on theory or logic. For example, in this book, the first chapters clarify various points through thought experiments and reflection activities (not empirical), while Part 2 of this book is based on factual studies and concrete situations and technologies (empirical).

This book does not, however, cover the technical skills needed for digitalization (e.g., programming), and if you are planning to start a digitalization process, you won't find any checklists or flowcharts to follow here. This book is nonetheless relevant for those of you who wish to develop and implement technology because the key to successful technology lies in understanding the interaction between what technology can do and how it is actually used. It is not just about the technology itself and what it can do, but also which *contexts* it will be used in, *how* it will be used, and *who* will use it. The focus on digitalization in practice is important to avoid simplified conceptualizations. As such, a focus on digitalization *in practice* is central to this book and has influenced the choice of both theoretical tools and empirical cases.

1.6 A Critical Sociotechnical Perspective

When we decided to write a book about *critical perspectives* on digital technology, it was not because we believe digitalization is "bad." Quite the opposite. We have chosen to become experts in digital technology precisely because we see the potential. Furthermore, our interest in digital technologies is not just a scholarly pursuit. Both authors of this book are highly frequent internet users (or, phrased in the internet's vocabulary, "extremely online"), active gamers, fans with many nerdy projects, and always eager to test out new platforms and electronic gadgets. Being critical is not about being negative or surly. Rather, it is about having a nuanced perspective about technology's potential and limitations—positive *and* negative.

Such a nuanced and critical perspective on the interaction between people and technologies is found in *sociotechnical* perspectives and theories developed by the STS field. The perspective directs attention to digitalization as a process of change, with attention to what changes, who effects change, what remains the same—as well as the unforeseen changes that take place.

Later in this book, you will learn what a sociotechnical perspective entails, and through this perspective, you will develop the skills needed for you to critically assess the digitalization processes you encounter. The aim is that you will be able to

- identify what digital technology does and doesn't do in society by understanding which practices are continued, created, and changed
- open digitalization processes to glean insights about where and how you can push processes in a desired direction
- be open to multiple interpretations of what a technology is, has been, and should be—as well as being able to explain why some interpretations have succeeded over others
- analyze digitalization processes from a user perspective and be able to evaluate the consequences of technology for different users
- understand the interaction between what a technology *can* do and what it *actually* does by examining which responsibilities and tasks are delegated between people and technology
- critically assess the premises for digitalization and not accept simple technological solutions as an answer to complex societal problems

1.7 The Structure of This Book

In this introduction, we have argued that you should enter the digital jungle and embark on the rewarding, yet challenging endeavor of exploring the unknown. This book aims to give you tools to navigate the (metaphorical) digital forest so that you may better understand what lives there—for even though it is messy and unclear, it isn't all unmapped terrain. Familiarizing yourself with research on digital technology will help you see patterns and trends in the unfamiliar and hint at how digitalization may develop in future.

Part 1 of this book, "A Critical Perspective On Digitalization" (Chapters 1 and 2), is about gaining an overview of this complex landscape. Chapter 2 introduces the term "digitalization" and provides insight into its (multiple) meanings by examining it from different angles.

Part 2 of this book, "Analytical Tools" (Chapters 3–7), dives into theoretical concepts that will help you see, understand, and analyze the interplay between digital technology and social change. In Chapter 3, we present sociotechnical theories that will strengthen your critical thinking about digital technology and social change, particularly through the concepts of *delegation*, *actor-network*, and *interpretive flexibility*. In the next two theoretical chapters, we continue to present theoretical tools you can apply in your own life. Chapter 4 on *domestication* and Chapter 5 on *script* show you how to understand technology use and design, respectively. Chapter 6 invites you to think about digital technology as "normality machines" and, consequently, how digital technology can have inclusive and exclusive effects. Chapter 7 rounds off the theoretical overview by presenting some historical and contemporary perspectives on digital technology.

Part 3 of this book, "Empirical Cases" (Chapters 8–12), will give insight into five empirical areas that show digitalization as a diverse phenomenon with many and complex consequences. Chapter 8 discusses the digitalization of health; Chapter 9 explores the digitalization of work; and Chapter 10 considers technologies of control and surveillance. In Chapter 11, we examine how digital technology forms cultural expression and shapes communities, while in Chapter 12, you will learn about technology and the self. Each of these chapters is built around three empirical examples (that is, factual, concrete situations) and research (not thought experiments or theories), and each discusses what these examples can teach us about digitalization. The theoretical perspectives introduced in Part 2 are applied in Part 3, and as such, Part 3 is also a demonstration of how these theories can be used in practice as well as how analyses of digitalization processes can be articulated.

Finally, Part 4 of this book, "Conclusions and Handouts" (Chapters 13–15), summarizes this book and tools for future use. It begins with Chapter 13, a summary of this book's main features, with emphasis on what the empirical analyses have taught us about digitalization processes regarding this book's main themes: social change, user perspectives, and critical thinking. There are two cheat sheets: one for

Pinch, T. J., & Bijker, W. E. (1984). The social construction of facts and artefacts: Or how the sociology of science and the sociology of technology might benefit each other. *Social Studies of Science, 14*(3), 399–441. https://doi.org/10.1177/030631284014003004.

Rosenberg, N., & Nathan, R. (1994). *Exploring the black box: Technology, economics, and history.* Cambridge University Press.

Sismondo, S. (2010). *An introduction to science and technology studies* (2nd ed.). Wiley-Blackwell.

Star, S. L. (1988). Introduction: The sociology of science and technology. *Social Problems, 35*(3), 197–205. https://doi.org/10.2307/800618.

Syvertsen, T., & Enli, G. (2020). Digital detox: Media resistance and the promise of authenticity. *Convergence, 26*(5–6), 1269–1283. https://doi.org/10.1177/1354856519847325

TechAltar. (2017, March 21). Why have modular smartphones failed? [Video]. *YouTube.* https://www.youtube.com/watch?v=CcQxd-jHlKO4&feature=youtu.be.

CHAPTER 2

What Is "Digitalization," Exactly?

We are often told that digitalization will lead to more effective, better, and simpler ways of doing things. Whether it concerns monitoring animals in the wild (see Chapter 10), making health care more efficient (see Chapter 7), or the introduction of self-driving cars (Stilgoe, 2019), digitalization is presented as a future oriented solution. Digitalization projects frequently promise to save us time and money, are framed as safer and more environmentally friendly than non-digital alternatives, and are in themselves seen as a sign of technological and/or societal development. In this sense, digitalization is often presented to us as a "technological miracle cure" that will solve any and all problems we might have. From science and technology studies, we know it is especially important to stay alert when new technologies are suggested as solutions to complex societal problems. In this chapter, you will learn more about why this is through the

DOI: 10.1201/9781003289555-3

concept of "technological fix" and be encouraged to think of digitalization as a social process that emphasizes certain values, functions, and users at the expense of others. We will also present various definitions of digitalization to show how the concept can be interpreted in different ways in different cultures and sectors, as well as give some starting samples of what a sociotechnical perspective on digitalization entails.

2.1 Digitalization as a Technological Fix

Attempting to answer big, complex societal problems with new technology is not unique to digitalization enthusiasts, nor is it a new endeavor. The belief in technological solutions as the cure for all of our woes has existed for a long time and is referred to as the *technological fix* (Weinberg, 1967; Rosner, 2004). The term comes from Weinberg, a physicist who, during the Cold War, began to wonder if there are problems that cannot—or should not—be solved by technology. Instead of presuming that technological progress automatically leads to societal progress, he asked what happens when technological solutions displace other (social and political) solutions and considered how new technology may also cause new problems.

Some examples of technological fixes are atomic weapons, invented to "fix war"; gene-modified food, invented to "fix hunger"; carbon capture, invented to "fix climate change"; or psychotropic drugs, used to "fix the problem of children not sitting still in class." Technological fix has a lot in common with the term *solutionism* discussed in Chapter 1, where there is a growing expectation that technology can solve all our problems (Morozov, 2013). Both technological fix and solutionism emphasize the risk of negative consequences when technology is offered as the *only* solution. Both concepts criticize how complex concerns are simplified, pulverize political responsibility, displace political solutions (such as reforms or other changes to resource allocation, research, legislation, or institutions), and individualize problems. In summary, the terms' critical potential lies in:

- rejecting the idea that societal problems can be solved by technology alone
- acknowledging that the implementation of new technologies often leads to new problems

That technology designed to fix a problem may actually prevent the issue from being resolved is not exactly intuitive reasoning. To show how it happens, we give some examples of how technological fixes and solutionism can displace more comprehensive political solutions (Box 2A).

The technologies mentioned in the below examples are relevant tools for the job at hand that may be quite useful. Those who plan to lose weight may find it helpful to have an overview of their calorie intake (which can be quite time-consuming to do manually with pen and paper), student

---

Box 2A. Examples: Technological Fix and Solutionism

Problem	Technological Fix	Examples of Displaces Policies
Obesity epidemic	Apps for calorie counting and weight monitoring	Regulation of food production; taxation of unhealthy foods. Access to outdoor spaces and affordable training within cities.
Lack of student-active teaching	Student response systems	Financing of teaching, particularly teacher density. Training teachers in student-active learning.
Mental health difficulties	Psychology apps based on artificial intelligence (AI)	Financing mental health services. More inclusive working life (being outside working life is an important factor for poor mental health).
Food waste	Apps that alert users when food will expire	Regulation of food waste and how (much) food is prepared. Changes to "best before" regulations.
People with dementia who wander at night	Apps that geolocate and provide alarms	More resources to nursing homes. Adapted housing and living spaces for those with dementia.

Box 2C.   Fact: Important Dimensions of Digitalization

	Information sharing	A social life organized around the handling, processing, and sharing of information, e.g., how common it is to be a knowledge worker.
	Media convergence	Convergence, or fusion, of various media types, infrastructures, devices, functions, and markets, e.g., how smart phones can be used to make calls, surf the net, edit films, and pay bills.
	Networked knowledge	Production of knowledge and culture happening in networks, usually outside of traditional channels and institutions, e.g., Wikipedia, which is a free, user-driven encyclopedia.
	Political instrument	Political participation and joint action organized outside established organizations and the emergence of new forms of activism, e.g., the use of social media for activism, as in the Arab Spring and #BlackLivesMatter.
	Globalization	Changes in social and global organization, through which the borders between nations take on different meanings, distances shrink, and power shifts, e.g., a conglomerate can operate globally with enormous power but will also face criticism from all over the world.

When looking at English dictionaries for the term digitalization, the results are quite disappointing. Whereas the Merriam-Webster dictionary only has a short entry where digitization and digitalization are treated as synonyms (Meriam Webster, 2023), dictionary.com only has a medical entry for "(in the treatment of heart disease) the administration of digitalis" and no mention of the digitalization process (dictionary.com, 2023). The Cambridge dictionary (2023) describes "to digitalize" as: (1) "to change something such as a document to a digital form (= a form that can be stored and read by computers)," which we have classified as "digitization" in the section above, and (2) "to start to use digital technology such as computers and the internet to do something." This second definition is surprisingly aged. In the 1990s, it might have been more apt, but as we have argued—digitalization encompasses almost all aspects of society—and we would argue that it's more about doing almost "everything" in our daily digital lives, rather than just "starting to use" the internet and computers (let alone all other digital devices and their connections) to do "something."

To contrast this aged perception, we also include a Norwegian source from *The Great Norwegian Encyclopedia*, where digitalization (translated from Norwegian) means "facilitating the generation of digital information as well as the handling and utilization of the information using information technology" (Dvergsdal, 2019). According to this source, digitalization has three consequences: increased power of expression (the same data set can be presented and formatted in various ways), less time and place constraints (data can more easily be saved over time and moved between places), and increased stability and predictability (data is standardized). In this definition, the conversion into numbers is central—that is, the translation of texts, pictures, and thoughts into zeros and ones, or what we have described as *digitization*. From this, we can argue that *The Great Norwegian Encyclopedia* presents digitalization as a largely technical process that has social consequences (as opposed to, e.g., a sociotechnical process where the social also shapes the technical). Social consequences are generalized and omit how the effects of digitalization depend heavily on context for use.

This technical focus is, however, still typical of older definitions of digitalization, and it is telling that the many social changes linked to digitalization in *The Great Norwegian Encyclopaedia* are summarized in a single sentence: "(…)'digitalization' is now also about using information technology to change the ways we do things and to create entirely new phenomena" (Dvergsdal, 2019). This claim, while correct, is a good example of how some approaches to digitalization are focused on the technical aspect, which often leads to reductive descriptions of the social consequences. It is worth noting that the Norwegian encyclopedia is edited by experts in the field (and thus depends on how they view the phenomena, their time commitment to edit entries, and many other factors), showing how definitions of concepts are also socially constructed by someone for someone.

The second definition of digitalization is from a blog post on the platform *Medium*. It was written by Colleen Chapco-Wade-Safina (2018), who works in digital marketing, and we chose this text to serve as an example of the industry discourse surrounding digitalization. Here, the social changes linked to digitalization are emphasized over the technical ones, but what is described as social is limited to organization of work and business models:

> Digitalization is a strategy or a process that goes beyond the implementation of technology and involves a deep change in the core of the entire business model and the development of the work […] Digital transformation requires a much broader adoption of digital technology and cultural change. Digital transformation is more about people than it is about digital technology. It requires organizational changes that are customer-centric, backed by leadership, driven by radical challenges to corporate culture, and the leveraging of technologies that empower and enable employees.

In Chapco-Wade-Safina's definition, we see the optimism that often characterizes debates about digitalization, where the changes resulting from digitalization are seen as both timesaving and cost-reducing—and above all, as a means to more profit. If digitalization actually improves profit, is impossible to say in advance (there are many factors that can affect both digitalization and profit margins), but there is no doubt that digitalization has had large consequences for how we work and how we buy, sell, and offer services. Several of the chapters in this book include examples from work life—for example, all of Chapter 9 discusses this theme. Chapco-Wade-Safina's definition also introduces the term *digital transformation* (see also Vial, 2019), which describes digitalization as a potentially radical process that changes the ways we work and earn money, with particular emphasis on the possibilities of new types of services and revenue streams. Especially in business contexts, digital transformation is often seen as the final third stage where digitization leads to digitalization, which leads to digital transformations (Prause, n.d.; Medium, 2018).

In a business context, the above definition makes sense. However, the world consists of far more than work and markets. Digitalization also has consequences for culture, for communities, for everyday life, and for self-understanding (to name some of the themes you will meet in this book). So even though Chapo-Wade-Sabina includes both technical and social elements in her definition, she has a rather narrow view of what the social entails.

Digitalization also has large consequences for politics, and is formed by politics, so the third and last example of how digitalization can be defined comes from politics—where digitalization, in some cases, is thematized at the highest level and even has its own ministerial posts. While the ways digital infrastructure and the ways digitalization impacts society vary considerably between countries (we recommend students and lecturers to get a good overview of how your national and regional context structures the governing of this), we provide an example from our situated context of writing, namely the cases of digitalization ministers in Norway.

In January 2019, Norway got its first Minister of Digitalization, Nikolai Astrup (Conservative Party of Norway), who wrote an op-ed in one of the national newspapers the same year stating, "we aim to offer the population seamless and proactive services across all levels of administration—so that you don't have to apply for services you are entitled to." (Astrup, 2019). The quote emphasizes an agile way of thinking about digital services: having digital technology work seamlessly behind the scenes to help people without them having to necessarily learn new digital skills to apply. In Norwegian society, this flow of digital information is in line with, for example, how a person's annual taxes are done automatically online and can be confirmed with the push of the enter key, and where health data is also centralized on one platform. The digitalization ministerial title was later passed on and widened to Minister of Regional Development and Digitalization. Since "regional development" was added to the area of responsibility, it was not surprising that digitalization was then linked to regional politics and the strengthening of industry in rural Norway.

We included this political example because it shows how flexible the term digitalization is and how it shifts in political use depending on context, knowledge, and goals. If the Minister of Digitalization post had been combined with, for example, education or culture, the minister's framing of what digitalization politics entails would likely have been different. Maybe digitalization would have been described as promoting knowledge or creativity rather than as ensuring a good life in the countryside. It is also worth noting that after the national election in 2021, the digital minister post was removed, only to be reintroduced again after the election in 2023 with the erection of a Ministry of Digitalisation and Government Administration, to be headed by Ms Karianne O. Tung (Labour party). We are not saying that there is one right or wrong way of conducting digitalization policies politically, but the many ways digitalization can be formatted politically is a reminder of how digitalization is interwoven into many different aspects of society.

Together, these three varied definitions, from dictionaries, industry, and policy, show that digitalization, as a concept, can accommodate a great many features: technical aspects that highlight handling information, changes in work and market conditions, and the political vision for Norway. The above definitions also demonstrate how visions are created through digitalization. *The Great Norwegian Encyclopedia* creates a vision of standardized and accessible data; Chapco-Wade-Safina a vision of new digital markets; and the digital ministers of Norway have a vision of digital technology working for people seamlessly. Therefore, we should pay attention to how digitalization is presented by those involved in the process, especially by those who initiate and drive change. Which premises are set for digitalization when it is presented as a solution? Which premises are set if it is presented as something good for the bottom line versus regional politics? Such questions are worth reflecting on since they make visible how digitalization processes are also about values. To be able to criticize digitalization processes, it is necessary to understand which values are linked to them.

So far in this chapter, we have explained digitalization through various definitions and overarching social, cultural, and technological trends. Another way to explore what digitalization includes is by describing changes as statistics about the prevalence of digital technology and its use. This will be presented in the next section.

2.4 A Digitalized World

Many countries have seen a rapid digitalization in the last few decades. We here use Norway as an example, as it is among the world's most digital countries (IMD World Competitiveness Center, 2019; Foley et al., 2018). The IMD World Competitiveness Center (2019) ranks and evaluates how companies, the public sector, and households relate themselves to digitalization, and this has changed rapidly during the twenty-first century. In 2000, only 52% of Norwegians were connected to the internet. By 2016, 97% were (Medianorge, n.d.). While only 47% of the global population has internet access, access varies widely: 74% of Americans have access to the internet, while 79% of Europeans do. The degree of digitalization in a country is linked to political decisions, market conditions, and individuals' choices regarding the use of digital tools. Norwegians, for example, have high purchasing power, driven by high wages and low poverty rates, and policies pushing for companies and individuals to digitize as much as possible. This makes Norwegians more likely to experience digitalization processes than Americans or EU citizens.

When it comes to smart phone ownership, Norway is also a global leader: 95% of Norwegians have a smart phone (Medienorge, 2020), compared with 67% of western Europeans and 69% of Americans. The same is true of social media: 85% of Norwegians have a Facebook profile, and of these, 82% use the platform daily, with 95% of users checking their profile at least once a week (Ipsos, 2020). If we look at the media habits of Norwegians, the use of digital devices has increased exponentially in the past 20 years, particularly among the young. However, we still find differences between age groups' use of media and devices. The young use digital devices and technology more and more often than their elders (Statistisk sentralbyrå,

2020), but there is little evidence to suggest that people stop using digital technology as they get older (even if their patterns of use may change). The data suggest that there will be increased usage of the internet and digital technologies across age groups in the future. Statistics on the use of digital technology suggest that Norway and its Scandinavian neighbors have a high proportion of services that are digital, have high access to digital technology, and have a strong digital infrastructure. These statistics reflect a national culture that both accepts and embraces digital technology, as well as political system that is proactive in digitalizing society (when compared with other countries). To think critically about digitalization requires that we also keep this in mind. We must remain aware that what is possible and what is desirable are not the same in every country. In addition, digitalization in Norway is influenced by several factors outside the country's borders.

It is an unavoidable fact that a handful of companies—Facebook, Apple, Amazon, Microsoft, and Google (often called the FAAMG companies)—dominate digitalization processes the world over. If they at one point appeared interested in creating a better world through technology, it is now clear that they are most interested in making money (Galloway, 2017; Foroohar, 2019; Zuboff, 2019). However, we can also observe that there is no "correct" or "perfect" way to digitalize—just look at how different countries chose to respond to the COVID-19 pandemic, with East Asian countries developing several digital tracking technologies, like in South Korea, where the number of masks in apothecaries was visible in pandemic apps.

In the public sector and at the state level, there are major powers at play that form the digital present and future. Consider how, for example, the EU's GDPR regulation, antipiracy laws, state incentives, educational goals, and political discourses will affect technological development. These frameworks shape how technology can be interpreted and used not only by individuals but also by nations, states, and organizations. At a macro level, digitalization is also affected by commercial developers such as the Irish Accenture, German SAP, Indian TCS and Infosys, French Capgemini, and Chinese Baidu, Alibaba, and Tencent (often called the BAT).

Despite the massive power that the FAAMG and BAT companies wield in particular, the stereotype of the IT developer as an underdog ready to break up the monopoly of the powerful and give "ordinary people" a voice has persisted. *The Social Network* (Fincher, 2010), a movie about the creation of Facebook, is a typical example of this stereotype, as Mark Zuckerberg was depicted as a bright but socially awkward young man who simply wanted to develop cool tech (Watercutter, 2019). After the Cambridge Analytica scandal, where Facebook allowed huge amounts of personal data to be gathered by third parties and used to affect political elections, it is difficult to see Facebook as an innocent or powerless actor—nor Zuckerberg as an underdog. If anything, it is clear that Meta (previously Facebook), like the other large companies, actively purchases competitors and develops its technologies in ways that prioritize profit. Neither revolution, community, nor justice are values that guide big tech's ever-expanding reach into our everyday lives and societies.

There are, in other words, many factors that affect digitalization, and many of them are outside of our personal reach—like national policy and big tech's innovation plans. Nonetheless, that we cannot affect these things directly, or easily, does not mean that they are beyond our control.

2.5 Digitalization as a Sociotechnical Process

Digitalization is one of the most important social changes we are facing—or, more accurately, the big social changes we see around us today and will face in the future are *also* digitalization processes. Whether we are faced with climate change, a migration crisis, or a global health calamity (as with the COVID-19 pandemic), digital technology and digitalization processes shape both what we consider problems and what solutions we think of as good. A central point in this book is that digitalization *is* social change, and to understand what digitalization does (and doesn't do), we must explore *both* technical and social changes to understand what it entails. This includes differentiating envisioned use from actual use, precision regarding what the digital tools do, and a broad view of what is actually being changed. To close this chapter, we offer four simple questions to help detangle the visions, practices, and technologies involved in digitalization processes:

1. **How is digitalization justified:** What does digitalization propose to achieve? Which promises are given? What problems will be solved? Who wants this digitalization? What is the envisioned goal?
2. **What is being digitized:** Which tasks, information, processes, etc. are rendered digital? Is it a work assignment? A service? Knowledge? What, specifically, is being translated into machine-readable zeros and ones?
3. **What is changed by digitalization:** Look for elements needed for digital technologies to work as intended. Is new knowledge required? New practices? New organization? New people? Other technologies?
4. **What remains the same despite digitalization:** Not everything changes through digitalization, so what is it that doesn't need reorganization, that manages with existing knowledge, technologies, or people?

Question 1 asks what visions and stories are created about the technology. Digitalization is often a rhetorical and political instrument to bring about social change through technological means. Visions, even when they are quite divorced from reality, are none the less interesting because they inform developmental trajectories. If the vision for a digitalization project is increased sustainability, it sets a different premise for the process than if the goal was, for example, increased accessibility or profit.

Question 2 is a reminder that the term digitalization is used to describe many different processes that, to varying degrees, are about digital solutions. Often, new digital systems must be integrated with existing analog, digital, and non-digital systems. For example, when new health care system implementation is described as elevating most of the hard work of nurses, in reality is information on paper that will be stored in databases instead.

Questions 3 and 4 are an invitation to be curious about what happens "on the factory floor" of the digitalization process, that is, how the actual users interpret, negotiate, and implement the technology. Too often, the voices of leaders and producers are the only ones to be heard, even if they are not the ones using the technology. To be able to get the most accurate picture of what the digitalization process entails, it is important to consider both what has changed and what has remained the same. We should not presume total transformation but pay particular attention to how old and new technologies work together.

These four questions are purposefully simplistic, and you don't need a degree or specialized education to answer them. They will help you determine *what* happens in a digitalization process, while at the same time ensuring a critical perspective that rejects technological fix mindsets and encourages sociotechnical considerations. We will use these questions when we analyze selected empirical cases in Part 3 of this book. If you wish to understand *how* and *why* a digitalization process turned out the way it did, which factors were affected, what worked or didn't work, and what could have been different, the above questions are insufficient. To make fuller and more complex arguments about digitalization, more fine-grained theoretical tools are needed. For this reason, the next chapters present theories and perspectives that will reveal complex and nuanced understandings of how technology and society affect each other.

2.6 Conclusion

Visions for digitalization tend to be overly optimistic and predict that digital technology will be a full-fledged solution to complex and compound problems. Even if digitalization can help solve important societal challenges, there is good reason to engage critically if the technological solution is presented as the total solution. We need to remember that new technologies can just as easily create new problems as solve old ones. Our roles, backgrounds, and goals shape how we define digitalization, and the existence of multiple definitions is a reminder of the many things that can be included in a digitalization process. We define digitalization as a sociotechnical transformation and emphasize the need to study both the technological and social aspects of digitalization. This sociotechnical perspective is the theme of the next chapter.

References

Astrup, N. (2019, October 4). Vi må digitalisere på en smartere måte. *Aftenposten*. https://www.aftenposten.no/meninger/debatt/i/rA3l9l/vi-maa-digitalisere-paa-en-smartere-maate-nikolai-astrup

Brennen, J. S., & Kreiss, D. (2016). Digitalization. In K. B. Jensen, E. W. Rothenbuhler, J. D. Pooley, & R. T. Craig (Eds.), *The international encyclopedia of communication theory and philosophy* (pp. 556–566). Wiley-Blackwell. https://doi.org/10.1002/9781118766804.wbiect111.

Cambridge Dictionary. (2023). *Digitalize*. https://dictionary.cambridge.org/dictionary/english/digitalize?q=digitalization

Chapco-Wade-Safina, C. (2018, 21 October). Digitization, digitalization, and digital transformation: What's the difference? *Medium*. https://medium.com/@colleenchapco/digitization-digitalization-and-digital-transformation-whats-the-difference-eff1d002fbdf

dictionary.com (2023). *Digitalization*. https://www.dictionary.com/browse/digitalization

Dvergsdal, H. (2019, 28 October). Digitalisering. *Store norske leksikon* [Great Norwegia Encyclopedia]. https://snl.no/digitalisering

Fincher, D. (2010). *The social network*. Columbia Pictures.

Foley, P., Sutton, D., Wiseman, I., Green, L., & Moore, J. (2018). International digital economy and society index 2018. *European Commission, Directorate-General of Communications Networks, Content and Technology*. https://doi.org/10.2759/745483.

Foroohar, R. (2019). *Don't be evil: The case against big tech*. Penguin.

Galloway, S. (2017). *The four: The hidden DNA of Amazon, Apple, Facebook and Google*. Random House.

IMD World Competitiveness Center. (2019). *IMD world digital competitiveness ranking 2019*. https://www.imd.org/wcc/world-competitiveness-center-rankings/world-digital-competitiveness-rankings-2019/

Ipsos. (2020). Sosiale medier tracker Q3'20. Juli-September 2020. *Ipsos*. https://www.ipsos.com/nb-no/ipsos-some-tracker-q320

Medienorge. (2020). Andel med tilgang til internett. *Medienorge*. https://www.medienorge.uib.no/statistikk/medium/ikt/388

Medium. (2018). *What is digital transformation, digitalization, and digitization: How API relateds to digital transformation*. https://medium.com/api-product-management/what-is-digital-transformation-digitalization-and-digitization-c76277ffbdd6

Meriam Webster. (2023). *digitalization*. https://www.merriam-webster.com/dictionary/digitalization

Morozov, E. (2013). *To save everything, click here*: *The folly of technological solutionism*. Public Affairs.

Prause, J. (n.d.). *Digitization vs digitalization | SAP Insights*. https://www.sap.com/products/erp/digitization-vs-digitalization.html

Rosner, L. (2004). *The technological fix*: *How people use technology to create and solve problems*. Routledge.

Ryeng, K. (2022, December 19). Trenger vi egentlig en digitaliseringsminister? *Digi.no*. https://www.digi.no/artikler/debatt-trenger-vi-egentlig-en-digitaliseringsminister/524459

Statistisk sentralbyrå. (2020, 19 May). *Andel som har tilgang til ulike elektroniske tilbud, personer 9-79 år*. https://www.ssb.no/teknologi-og-innovasjon/faktaside/internett-og-mobil

Stilgoe, J. (2019). Self-driving cars will take a while to get right. *Nature Machine Intelligence, 1*(5), 202–203.

Tenner, E. (1997). *Why things bite back*: *Technology and the revenge of unintended consequences*. Vintage.

Vial, G. (2019). Understanding digital transformation: A review and a research agenda. *The Journal of Strategic Information Systems, 28*(2), 118–144. https://doi.org/10.1016/j.jsis.2019.01.003.

Watercutter, A. (2019, 2 May). The social network was righter than anyone realized. *Wired*. https://www.wired.com/story/social-network-right-all-along/

Weinberg, A. M. (1967). *Reflections on big science*. MIT Press.

Zuboff, S. (2019). *The age of surveillance capitalism*: *The fight for a human future at the new frontier of power*: *Barack Obama's books of 2019*. Profile books.

PART 2
Analytical Tools

PART 2
Analytical Tools

CHAPTER 3

A Sociotechnical Perspective on Digitalization

So far in this book, we have encouraged you to engage critically with digitalization; to not be easily swayed by grand visions, and to be extra alert when digitalization is presented as a solve-all or fix-all solution. However, critical engagement with technology involves more than the ability to spot overly optimistic rhetoric and political spin; it requires a nuanced understanding how technology and society are related. Specifically, we need a way of approaching digital technology that captures both technological and social factors involved. In this chapter, we will introduce a *sociotechnical* perspective on digitalization and examine problems that arise from analyzing technology and society separately. This chapter will emphasize three key concepts within the sociotechnical perspective: *interpretative flexibility*, *delegation*, and *actor networks*, as potent analytical

DOI: 10.1201/9781003289555-5

approaches to the study of digitalization. These three concepts, together with script (Chapter 4) and domestication (Chapter 5), make up the five theoretical concepts of this book.

3.1 What Is a Sociotechnical Perspective on Digitalization?

Sociotechnical is a mashup of the words social and technical, and it can best be understood as an umbrella term for a set of approaches that explore the mutually shaping relationship between technology and society.[1] The perspective presumes that both technical and social factors work together, and influence each other, in the making of society. To understand how a sociotechnical perspective can be applied to digitalization, we highlight three useful concepts (see Boxes 3A–3C).

From the sociotechnical perspective, we learn that digitalization is a *process* where both technology and users can both shape and influence one another. With a processual

Box 3A.   Theory: Interpretative Flexibility

How a technology is used is not decided by the technology's technical functions alone. Use is also defined by how the technology is interpreted (Bijker et al., 1987; Doherty et al., 2006). A technology can be interpreted and used in various ways and can fulfill various functions. There is no one predetermined correct way to use a technology. Rather, what we understand as the correct use (and consequently, what we understand as its usefulness and value) of a technology is a result of a negotiation between the technology and its users. To see technology as interpretatively flexible goes hand in hand with "it could be otherwise," which highlights that established interpretations of the technology are not the only ones possible.

Example: Mobile phone users who look at mobiles as natural extensions of themselves will use mobiles in different ways than those who experience mobiles as a technological invasion of their everyday lives—even if the technology is the same and both groups have overlapping areas of use.

Box 3B.   Theory: Delegation

The relationship between technology and people can be understood as a set of delegations during which responsibilities and tasks are transferred, shifted, and distributed (Latour, 1992). When we implement new technology in our everyday lives and in society in general, it usually involves a shift in responsibilities or tasks. In some instances, new responsibilities or tasks are created, while in other instances, they disappear. In other words, it is not just humans who affect technology through design, interpretation, and use; technologies also shape us and require that we act and behave in certain ways to be able to function together with them.

Example: If you use a digital calendar, you have delegated "remember this date and remind me of it" to the technology. In return, the technology delegates responsibility to you, the user, to enter appointments in a format the technology understands.

Box 3C. Theory: Actor Network

Technology use involves more than "an object" and "a user" (Latour, 1999). Through its use, technology becomes part of a network that consists of many actors. The network is the result of negotiations between a technology's design and its users, other technologies, and other users—as well as political policies, public and local discourses, the economy, institutions, knowledge, gender roles, and much more. The use of technology is, in other words, a process that includes numerous actors at various levels working together in a network. This does not mean that the technology "is online," but rather that technologies function as they do because they are a part of a network made up of people, other technologies, knowledge, and phenomena. To think of technology as a network is a key principle of actor-network theory, also known as ANT (Latour, 1987, 2005; Callon, 1984; Law, 2008), but in this book, we refer to it as actor network to simplify the analysis and make the theory more accessible.

Example: When determining how much screen time a child should have, parents must navigate an actor network that includes the demands of the child, restraints in the technology's design, public debates about how much screen time is acceptable, opinions from other parents, and their own need to have time to do chores or time for themselves. User practices are thus formed by many other factors in a network than the actual design of the technology and personal preferences (Moltubakk & Ask, 2019).

approach, we open ourselves up to the idea that It Could Be Otherwise (ICBO), because explanatory power is given to the process instead of ascribing change to some quality inherent in the technology. Last but not least, a sociotechnical perspective acknowledges that digitalization processes are affected by many and varied factors, both social and technical. See more in Box 3D.

Box 3D. Summary: What a Sociotechnical Perspective Emphasizes in a Digitalization Process

Digitalization processes are not just technical processes; they are also meaning-making processes, and the meanings digital technologies hold determine how they work.

Digitalization processes involve negotiations about the technology—what it will be used for, its value, how it will be integrated, and who will use it.

The context of digitalization and the actor network it is a part of are crucial in determining what the effects of a given digitalization will be. A digitalization that works well for one group can have other effects for other groups (or other communities, nations, etc.).

Digitalization processes are composed both of humans and of nonhumans in actor networks. These actor networks can perpetuate existing practices and knowledge—or change them. Technology use can be analyzed both at the level of society and at the level of the individual. Because use is decisive, focusing on the user is important.

In a sociotechnical perspective, technology is understood as something that must be *interpreted* (by the user) to be usable, and that the technology can be interpreted (and consequently, used) in different ways by different users. (This applies regardless of whether "the user" is a private person, an organization, or a nation.) Following the principles of sociotechnical research means approaching digital technology as something *more* than just a set of functions and as something *more* than just a tool. Purely functional explanations about what a technology does or how it solves a task are insufficient; we must also consider technologies as symbolic—something that is given, holds, and conveys meaning. Or, put simply, we must recognize that technology communicates values and meanings in addition to performing tasks. In this perspective, technology use (and non-use) is about far more than whether technology does what it is asked to do; technology use is also about identity, belonging, creativity, politics, and more.

3.2 What Do We Mean by "Technology"?

In this book, we use the term *digital technology*, or just *technology*, to describe various services, apps, gadgets, and programs. In doing so, we risk treating different technologies as if they were similar and may inadvertently omit important variations and dissimilarities. However, the choice of words is deliberate. By framing digitalization as a study of technology (and its use), we are drawing on more general theories about technology and society, and the usefulness of a critical perspective on technology goes beyond the specific apps and systems we discuss in this book. Consequently, the sociotechnical perspectives introduced in this book will also be useful when new solutions, platforms, services, or software are developed. Given that digitalization is a process characterized by rapid change and sweeping trends, there is a particular need for perspectives and analytical tools that last longer than the next hype.

Since technology is a key concept for this book and central to its theoretical framework, let us take a closer look at what the term actually entails.

In daily conversation, we tend to use the word technology as a synonym for tool. We talk about technology as an object (or as a system of various things) that is used to achieve something: to do a job, solve a problem, or simplify a task. Because of this, it is easy to think that technology is first and foremost something functional, something that serves a distinct purpose and answers specific needs. While we should not dismiss how technology also gains value through its utility and its ability to help us do things, assuming that technology is made as solutions to human problems overestimates humanity's rationality and underestimates technology's potential for different interpretations—and for creating new needs and new areas of use.

Going far, far back in early human history, it is a well-known fact that technology gave the physically weak *Homo sapiens* a solid advantage in evolution: with the help of technology, we could tame animals, make fire, create tools, build houses, and kill both prey and enemies (Nye, 2007). However, rather than explaining technological development as a response to basic needs, like the need for food and shelter (things prehistoric humans acquired fairly well), we should instead consider how technological development also happened because our ancestors wanted to explore, tinker, create and broaden our existence without necessarily having a purpose or utility in mind. Instead of presuming that technology must be the result of a human need, we should consider how technology can shape our outlook and thus inspire new needs.

Nye (2007) explains that when we humans have tools, we tend to look for and find ways to use them. As such, the tool often exists *before* the problem, but through use, it is linked to a specific area or task and established as a "solution" to it (even if achieving that task wasn't considered a problem before). At the time of writing, we are seeing these phenomena play out in real time as generative AI systems like chatGPT are tested in different settings to find out what purpose they should have and who their users should be—outside tech enthusiasts. We may understand technology to have a built-in potential to transform (society), precisely because we will try to find ways to use it. In this way, humanity's and society's development has always been shaped by the technologies we have and the possibilities we see for them.

Obviously, technologies are often appreciated because they can simplify work or expand our abilities, be it a machine that cleans our clothes (saving hours of hard labor) or a device that alerts us to smoke (giving us surveillance capabilities in our sleep). However, a critical approach to technology requires us to go beyond a single-sided focus on utility, purpose, or need. We humans are not—and have never been—completely rational beings who only think about the end result or live life according to some cost-benefit analysis. The imagery of *Homo economicus* that lives in accordance with a cost-benefit analysis is both an inaccurate and silly description of humans. Yet, this fictional hyper-rational being is often presumed in the development and implementation of new technology. For example, when digital smart meters were installed in Norwegian households to enable end users to save energy. The idea was that end users would be motivated to use electricity during off-hours and reduce their power consumption by having access to live feeds detailing consumption and cost. In reality, other, rather mundane concerns, like not wanting to do washing in the middle of the night and enjoying a shower before work, took precedence (see Skjølsvold & Ryghaug, 2015; Winther & Bell, 2018).

From Stonehenge to Spotify, technologies are always inextricably linked to the meanings we give them, meanings that go beyond what problems they can solve or what tasks they can simplify. Furthermore, given that technologies do not have predetermined meanings (that would be technological determinism, which is described below), they also always have the potential for new and different uses and applications than those they were designed for.

If we look at the history of the term *technology*, it becomes clear that what we think of as technology is specific to our time and culture. Even though humans have a long history of making tools and artifacts, conceptualizing them under the heading "technology" is a rather new invention. The word technology has its roots in the Greek word *techne*, which means "skills in art." Consequently, it did not refer to objects at all but to a type of expertise. In Plato's hierarchy of knowledge, which placed science at the top and crafts at the bottom, *techne* held a middle position. The first examples of the use of the word technology were used to refer to systematic studies of artisanship in the form of books like "glassblowing technology" in the Renaissance, still emphasizing skills and knowledge rather than things. This definition held through the Industrial Revolution, and it was not until after the First World War that technology began to refer specifically to mechanical skills and mechanical objects more widely.

Since the 1930s, the word technology has been used to describe the many systems and machines society is built upon. The word is, however, difficult to define, as technology has also become a synonym for anything that uses electricity or can be connected to the internet. To complicate matters further, technology is often used to describe *new* solutions, regardless of their material features. This means that we often associate technology with "new" and "electric," and might forget how the alphabet or the wheel, at some point, were considered new. Today, when technology is associated with something mechanical and/or digital, the association reveals what contemporary society values as "new and exciting." Still, we must remember that almost everything was seen as "new technology" at some point, and in the future, we will likely develop new definitions of the term as new or different technologies emerge. Maybe the mobile phone will be just as unnatural to describe as technology in 100 years as "knives and forks" are today? Equally important, we must keep in mind that how technologies are used may differ across cultures, leading to vastly different developmental trajectories (fax machines are still clinging on in Japan, for example, and bicycle usage differs extremely just between neighboring countries based on infrastructure, policies, and personal preferences).

According to Bijker (2006), we can understand technology as comprising three components: (1) physical objects, (2) activities linked to the production and use of these, and (3) knowledge linked to their production and use. In this definition, technology is described as something more than an object; it also includes the actions, meanings, and knowledge linked to the object. Bijker's definition has a sociotechnical perspective where technology is understood as interpretatively flexible (i.e., it can be interpreted in many different ways) and as a part of an actor network where its meaning and use are shaped not just by its features but also by the other technologies and users it is linked to. The physical technology, the activities associated with it, and the knowledge linked to its use are all important components of understanding digitalization processes in society. In the study of digitalization processes, such a broad yet nuanced conceptualization of technology is valuable, as it opens for investigations of how material features (like functionality and design) are related to social conditions (like meaning, knowledge, and practice). In Box 3E's activity, you can reflect yourself on this.

Box 3E.   Activity: How Is Technology Defined?

Do a search for "technology"+"definition" in the languages you know to see how technology is described in various dictionaries and encyclopedias. What do these definitions emphasize? To what degree is technology described as something that is both material and social? Do you find definitions with a sociotechnical perspective (like Bijker's above), or do they describe technology as a purely material phenomenon? What impressions of technology do these definitions give, and to what degree do they agree with how we have presented the concept of technology in this book?

Reflect on which technologies are listed as examples and how this affects the definition of technology. Are the technologies linked to large technological systems (like broadband, the road network, or the power grid)—or does the definition also include everyday technologies like smart watches, mobile cameras, or social media? What about technologies that we now experience as "untechnical," like the aforementioned alphabet, wheel, and knife?

3.3 Technologies and Their Agency

When we move beyond simplistic ideas of technology as "tools" or "a response to human needs" and recognize how (a) a technology's utility is determined by its interpretation and use and (b) that technology can shape our perceptions of what constitutes utility, we open up a space to think of technologies as *actors*. When it was first proposed in the late 1980s, it was a rather radical idea to expand actor agency beyond humans.

The actor category has traditionally been reserved for humans. An *actor* is "someone who acts," implying that an actor has desires, intensions, and the means to act on them (aka agency). In sociotechnical approaches, however, humans and nonhumans are treated according to a principle of *symmetry*, where any member of an actor network can have actor status, including technologies and other nonhumans (Pinch & Bijker, 1987; Latour, 1987; Bloor, 1984). This is not to say that technologies have "desires, intentions, and means to act on them" due to self-awareness or consciousness, but rather that technologies are imbued with power to affect others when embedded into an actor network, and this power needs to be recognized if we are to have a clear and correct understanding of how technology and society influence each other. Neither is it a symmetry of importance, proclaiming that everything must be treated with equal importance during analysis. Since the focus of this book is digitalization, most nonhuman actors discussed will be various digital technologies (from apps to photo filters), but the term *nonhuman actors* cover everything that is not human, from cars to bacteria, dogs, visions, timetables, and policies.

It might seem strange at first to give actor status to nonhumans. It is certainly not as though computers dream about what they want to do when they grow up, nor can a selfie cast its vote in an election. On the other hand, there is no doubt that technologies have effects on us as individuals and on society as a whole, sometimes beyond what we humans intended them to have. If we only consider humans to have agency, excluding nonhumans like technologies, we risk omitting actors who play central roles in society and exert considerable influence on how society is configured. As an example of how something we consider deeply human and personal can be understood as an actor network of people and things where omitting nonhuman actors would give an inaccurate understanding, let us look at romantic love and relationships. We tend to consider "being in love" as a description of a relationship between two (or more) people. However, when we look closer with an attentive eye for nonhumans, we may see that love is also built and shared through technologies like SMS, social media, and dating apps and is cemented (or threatened) by joint ownership of items like washing machines, houses, and cars. Moreover, the presence (or absence) of condoms, wedding rings, roses, and dishes is difficult to detach from the rest of the relationship. How love can be expressed is not only a question of human feelings toward each other but also how technologies are included (or not included) in the relationship's actor network (Sørensen, 2004).

The problem with thinking of technologies as actors is, of course, that, as opposed to people, technologies aren't conscious. However, even if technologies cannot think, they can both communicate with others and act in ways that affect society (even if the actions they take are not based in some innate desire or intention but rather the result of programming and design). Technology will, through its features and design, tell stories about the world—about what is normal or abnormal and what is desired and undesired. Technology will also allow, limit, and prevent human action by supporting or stopping certain ways of doing things. Acknowledging that technology can hold such power is essential to maintaining a sociotechnical perspective. However, it is a difficult balancing exercise to recognize the power technology has without becoming deterministic. As such, in the next section, we explain what a determinist perspective on technology is and why it is problematic.

3.4 Why Technological Determinism Is a Dead End

A sociotechnical perspective criticizes and opposes deterministic explanations, including the variant related to technology, which is known as *technological determinism*. Technological determinism is the belief that technology's development is predetermined, that technology's role and function are given based on its design alone, and, consequently, that technology's effects are inevitable. In stark contrast to ICBO, which encourages us to see how things could be otherwise (and thereby increases the space of possibility), or interpretative flexibility, which presumes that any technology has multiple possible interpretations, a technologically determinist perspective would stress that technological development and social change can be explained by qualities, characteristics, or features of the technology. Technological determinism will also omit how technology is formed by the actor networks it is a part of, dismiss factors like politics, culture, or the economy, and preclude the possibility that a technology can have different consequences for different users. Not least, a technologically determinist perspective refutes the idea that technology can have unforeseen consequences.

Assertions like "Twitter caused the Arab Spring" (uprisings across the Arab world in 2010) are deterministic because they ignore the political and religious conditions that motivated the protests, how social media functioned together with traditional media like television, and the strong feelings that drove people out into the streets (Tufekci & Wilson, 2012). Instead of thinking of Twitter as part of an actor network in which various technologies, users, politics, and discourses work together, the above statement shows how technology is made the sole reason for social change and thus becomes deterministic. Other examples of deterministic statements are "AI will change the world," "Smart houses make everyday life simpler," and "Social media is here to stay." These statements may prove to be correct: it may be that AI will change society, that smart systems for buildings will simplify home management, and that social media will endure. However, we cannot know this in advance, and if they do, it will be due to reasons beyond the technology itself. Both creating "one-factor explanations" for historical changes (where technology is the only explanation) and extrapolating the future based on current technology are examples of deterministic explanations.

Technological determinism is often expressed either as technological optimism or as technological pessimism, where technology is either framed as the cure or the cause of our problems. Fascinatingly enough (but in line with technology being *interpretively flexible*), it is not uncommon for a given technology to be interpreted as both a solution and a problem. Healthcare technology (of which "welfare technology" is one example, see Chapter 8) can, for example, be interpreted both as the solution to loneliness in older adults, as they can stay in touch with their family and friends via digital surfaces, and as contributing to increased isolation because healthcare workers are given less time with each care receiver due to technological optimization. Similarly, some blame video games for making students tired and unmotivated at school, while others believe that the same games can improve students learning and motivation. The point is that no matter whether you focus on the positive or negative consequences, if the technology's effects are taken for granted or presented as inevitable, the perspective is deterministic (and we should critique it).

In the examples of healthcare technology and digital games, it is quite possible that the contradictory effects listed above are all true. That healthcare technology is both helping older users connect with family and friends while also reducing time spent with careworkers. That gaming is keeping students up at night while also helping them learn in class.

These technologies can have contradictory effects because of different contexts, not to mention how one technology can have different effects at different times. A deterministic worldview doesn't allow for such variation in interpretation and use, and a good reason to reject determinism is how easily observable the different effects of technology are.

In many ways, it is obvious that technology, in and of itself, cannot explain how society has changed or is changing—so why do we keep coming up with deterministic explanations? This has been criticized by scholars for decades (Chandler, 2012) (see Box 3F).

Box 3F. Fact: Why Technological Determinism Persist Despite Critique

Macro perspective

We usually discuss technological development at the macro level, focusing on the changes that happen at the level of society, and this simplification obfuscates a technology's many and varied interpretations and areas of use, making it seem like the technology is used uniformly and has the same consequences everywhere (technological determinism).

Technology as a finished product

We see the technology as a finished product, so we don't see the many negotiations, choices, and coincidences that shaped the design process. In other words, the cultural formation of technology is invisible to us.

Trapped in the "large technological systems"

"Large technological systems" (Hughes, 1987) shape society to a great degree, but because they become so big and affect so many aspects of our lives, we may experience them as forced upon us and outside of our control—as just one cog in a large system.

Controlled technology development

There are many actors who have a vested interest in convincing us that technologies have enormous influence. It is advantageous for politicians, developers, and leaders if we as citizens, users, clients, or employees accept the premise that technologies will have the promised positive effects because if they don't, politicians, developers, and leaders may be held responsible.

Fulfillment of expectations

Our goals and expectations in life are affected by the technologies we have and what they can do. If everyone has a mobile phone, you will expect to have one too, and you will be expected to use it in certain ways and to achieve certain tasks. This is called reverse adaptation, but it can also be summed up by the phrase "when all you have is a hammer, everything looks like a nail."

3.5 Technological Reductionism

With a deterministic perspective, all explanatory power is given to the technology. It is particularly common to find examples of determinism when technological success is explained as a natural consequence of the technology's quality through phrases like "ingeniously made" or "technologically superior." Within a technologically deterministic explanatory model, the demand for the latest iPhone or Samsung is explained by pointing to greater processing power, a better camera, or longer battery life. Other factors that affect mobile phone purchases, such as personal finances, advertisements, identity, accessibility, group pressure, environmentalism, or one of the many other explanations for our habits of consumption, are ignored. While it is certainly possible that the latest iPhone model has better processing power, cameras, and battery life than its competitors, that we consider these qualities to be important at all is a product of culture. It reflects a mobile phone practice that includes gaming and film editing (which require processing power), that smart phones have to a large degree replaced other cameras (which requires that mobile phones have good-quality camera lenses), and that we use mobile phones throughout the day (which requires good battery life). As such, what is considered to be valuable features, or just "good functionality," is also a question of culture and practice.

It is tempting to explain technological successes—and failures—as being caused by brilliant or terrible design. But if we reduce complex phenomena (as, for example, which smart phone model will become a success) to functionality and design, we take a reductionist approach. *Technological reductionism* involves reducing complex phenomena to a simple question of a technology's excellence (or lack of it). Technological solutionism and fixism (see Chapters 1 and 2), in which complex problems are expected to be solved by technology alone ("if we only used self-driving cars, nobody would die in traffic"), are examples of technological reductionism. Technological reductionism is a consequence of technological determinism, as technology is given all the agency to cause change. Reductionism is common when it is used to explain why something takes off (or doesn't) and in the marketing of digital solutions or products.

Where deterministic explanations emphasize design at the cost of use, empirical studies show that a technology's meanings and functions are in no way given. Users negotiate with technologies, show resistance, discover other areas of use, and find meanings beyond what the developers intended—both in accordance with and against what the design encourages. Bubble wrap was, for example, first thought of as a form of wallpaper before someone realized that it functioned exceptionally well as packaging; Viagra started out as a heart medicine before it gained its now well-known use (and it was discovered that heart problems were a side effect!); and Coca-Cola was invented to relieve morphine addiction. YouTube started as a dating website, Instagram as an app for location sharing, and Pinterest as a shopping website, but all three have now changed focus— and their focus may change again in their lifetimes.

Throughout history, we have seen many technologies change their meanings and areas of use without significant changes to their functions or properties. Technologies with the same properties gain different meanings in different places and at different times. Consequently, the success of any given technology cannot be explained by its design alone. Some technologies that were originally developed for use in outer space have now become everyday technologies for use here on earth, such as wireless headphones, LED lights, freeze-dried foods, memory foam mattresses, glasses with scratch protection, and insulin. But how can such changes occur? The answer lies in the interpretative flexibility of the technologies.

3.6 How Social Determinism Is Equally Problematic

We have so far argued that we cannot understand social change if we focus solely on technology and that we cannot explain technological success or failure by design or functionality alone. However, when we direct our attention to the social processes and relationships surrounding technology, we must take care not to ignore the power and agency of technologies. If we, in our attempt to reject technological determinism, end up omitting the technology's design and functionality from our analysis of uses and effects, we end up with *social determinism*. Social determinism is the belief that only sociocultural systems drive and shape society—something that is at least as problematic as technological determinism.

Social determinism is in most cases a "simple" omission of the role of technology by investigating how people react to and engage with technology without addressing the technology in question and how it directs, shapes, encourages, and discourages users in different ways. In its most extreme form, social determinism doesn't differentiate between different designs and models and treats technology as purely symbolic, where the only thing that matters is its meaning. While meaning is certainly important, material features also matter. It makes a difference for you whether the document you are writing is saved locally or in the cloud, or whether a social media platform is based on live content or stored content. A sociotechnical perspective is, in other words, just as much a rejection of social explanations that ignore the power and agency of technology as it is a rejection of technological explanations that ignore social dimensions like context, values, and practice.

3.7 Conclusion

To be able to understand the effect technology has on society, we must consider how it is interpreted, which responsibilities and tasks are delegated to it, and which networks of people and other technologies it is a part of. In this chapter, we have seen how sociotechnical perspectives reject all forms of determinism and embrace social change (of which digitalization processes are examples) as an interplay between technology and society. The key to a critical perspective lies in finding a balanced view in which both technological and social factors are included and carefully considered. It also acknowledges that one and the same technology can be used in various ways and, hence that the consequences of a digitalization process are not known.

Note

1 Sociotechnical is one of several terms that try to capture this merger of the human and the material. Others include technosocial, sociomaterial, and technoculture.

References

Bijker, W. E. (2006). Why and how technology matters. In R. E. Goodin & C. Tilly (Eds.), *Oxford handbook of contextual political analysis* (pp. 681–706). Oxford University Press.

Bijker, W. E., Hughes, T. P., & Pinch, T. J. (Eds.). (1987). *The social construction of technological systems: New directions in the sociology and history of technology.* MIT Press.

Bijker, W. E., & Pinch, T. J. (1987). The Social Construction of Facts and Artifacts: Of How the Sociology of Science and the Sociology of Technology Might Benefit Each Other. In W.E. Bijker, T. P. Hughes, & T. Pinch (Ed..), *The Social construction of technological systems new directions in the sociology and history of technology.* MIT Press.

Bloor, D. (1984). The strengths of the strong programme. In J. R. Brown (Ed.), *Scientific rationality: The sociological turn* (pp. 75–94). Springer.

Callon, M. (1984). Some elements of a sociology of translation: Domestication of the scallops and the fishermen of St. Brieuc Bay. *The Sociological Review, 32*(1), 196–233. https://doi.org/10.1111/j.1467-954X.1984.tb00113.x.

Chandler, J. A. (2012). "Obligatory technologies": Explaining why people feel compelled to use certain technologies. *Bulletin of Science, Technology & Society, 32*(4), 255–264. https://doi.org/10.1177/0270467612459924.

Doherty, N. F., Coombs, C. R., & Loan-Clarke, J. (2006). A reconceptualization of the interpretive flexibility of information technologies: Redressing the balance between the social and the technical. *European Journal of Information Systems, 15*(6), 569–582. https://doi.org/10.1057/palgrave.ejis.3000653.

Hughes, E.C., & Thielens, W. (1959). The academic mind: Two views. *American Sociological Review, 24*(4), 570–573. https://doi.org/10.2307/2089545.

Hughes, T. P. (1987). The evolution of large technological systems. In W. E. Bijker, T. P. Hughes, & T. J. Pinch (Eds.), *The social construction of technological systems: New directions in the sociology and history of technology* (pp. 51–82). MIT press.

Latour, B. (1987). *Science in action: How to follow scientists and engineers through society.* Harvard University Press.

Latour, B. (1992). Where are the missing masses? The sociology of a few mundane artifacts. In W. E. Bijker & J. Law (Eds.), *Shaping technology/building society: Studies in sociotechnical change* (p. 10). MIT Press.

Latour, B. (1999). On recalling ANT. *The Sociological Review, 47*(suppl. 1), 15–25. https://doi.org/10.1111/j.1467-954X.1999.tb03480.x.

Latour, B. (2005). *Reassembling the social: An introduction to social life.* Oxford University Press.

Law, J. (2008). Actor-network theory and material semiotics. In B. S. Turner (Ed.), *The new Blackwell companion to social theory* (3rd ed., pp. 141–158). Blackwell.

Moltubakk, S. T. & Ask, K. (2019, May 21–23). *Control for the sake of freedom: Negotiating play in Norwegian gamer families* [Paper presentation]. NordMedia Conference, Malmö University, Malmö.

Nye, D. E. (2007). *Technology matters: Questions to live with.* MIT Press.

Skjølsvold, T. M., & Ryghaug, M. (2015). Embedding smart energy technology in built environments: A comparative study of four smart grid demonstration projects. *Indoor and Built Environment, 24*(7), 878–890.

Sørensen, K. H. (2004). Cultural politics of technology: combining critical and constructive interventions?. *Science, Technology, & Human Values*, *29*(2), 184–190.

Tufekci, Z., & Wilson, C. (2012). Social media and the decision to participate in political protest: Observations from Tahrir Square. *Journal of Communication*, *62*(2), 363–379.

Winther, T., & Bell, S. (2018). Domesticating in home displays in selected British and Norwegian households. *Science & Technology Studies*, *31*(2), 19–38.

CHAPTER 4

Domestication

User Perspectives on Technology

People use technology in diverse, varied, and even contradictory ways. Have you ever noticed that you use your mobile phone differently than younger or older relatives or that you have other rules for when, where, and how you use it? Have you ever disagreed with how friends or family members use social media? Or maybe you have experienced that someone came across as grumpy or cross because they didn't use emojis in their text messages—or, alternately, that someone appeared too informal because they used emojis in an email? If you recognize these everyday scenarios, you have experienced the *interpretative flexibility* of technology, i.e., that the same

DOI: 10.1201/9781003289555-6

technology can be interpreted and used in different ways. The implication of interpretative flexibility is that we cannot know how a technology will be used based on its design alone. Consequently, we need to study users if we are to understand what a technology means or does in society. Not least because users are heterogeneous, and unexpected forms of use are common. A focus on use and users is called a *user perspective*, and it is a potent entry point into studies of digitalization.

In the previous chapter, we presented the sociotechnical perspective as a way to critically engage with digitalization through the concepts of interpretative flexibility, delegation, and actor network. These concepts direct our attention to what a technology means, what a technology is tasked with, and how the process of digitalization is formed by the different actor networks a technology is a part of. Across concepts is an interest in how technology is used and how use is related to interpretation and context. In this chapter, we will present the theoretical term *domestication of technology*, which can help us study use and users in a way that is sensitive to the importance of meaning and context. We will give an introduction to the term's content, history, and applications and will discuss why digitalization studies with a basis in the user are both useful and necessary.

4.1 A User Perspective on Technology

A user perspective is, simply put, approaching technology from the user's standpoint. The user perspective presumes an "active user" approach where users co-create their own technological practices in negotiation with other humans, technologies, knowledge, and values. The user perspective emphasizes how technologies are subject to many different interpretations and that new and unexpected areas of utility and meaning can be constructed through use. Instead of thinking of users as passive consumers that are powerless against the whims of design, developers, politicians, and bosses, "the active user" recognizes the agency of users. By presuming that use matters for what a technology "is" and "does," a user perspective is also a rejection of technologically deterministic approaches, where the function, role, and meaning of technology are given and use is treated as an effect.

The user perspective supports a critical view of digitalization by drawing our attention to how technology is actually used instead of relying on the visions of leaders or developers regarding how a technology *could* or *should* be used. By taking users' experiences, thoughts, and actions seriously, we may gain a better understanding of how and why a digitalization process turned out as it did. A user perspective lets us explore what happens when a technology is placed in a specific context with specific users and render visible the many variances and differences in use that exist. A sociotechnical theory that deals explicitly with the user perspective and use as heterogeneous is *domestication theory*.

4.2 Domestication Theory

Domestication theory is an analytical tool for the study of technology use. The term *domestication* comes from the Latin word *domesticus*, meaning "belonging to the house." Colloquially, domestication refers to the process of taming wild plants or animals so they can be adapted for human use. Domestication theory builds on the idea that technology, like animals and plants, must go through a taming process to become useable and (metaphorically or sometimes literally speaking) become a member of the household. Through domestication theory, we can focus on how users make actor networks out of technologies, beliefs, and practices in their own lives through the taming process, particularly in their everyday lives at work and at home. For a technology to become "part of the household," and a natural part of everyday life, users must develop routines, norms, identities, discourses, institutions, infrastructures, regulations, acquire new technologies, and negotiate understandings surrounding the technology in question. Even in the study of a single technology, such as an app or a gadget, the domestication process is something that often happens simultaneously in many places and with many actors—that is, it is a multi-sited, multi-actor process (Sørensen, 2006). Domestication studies direct our attention to this myriad of related activities, ideas, and knowledges and emphasize how this context cannot be separated from neither use nor technology.

Domestication has a sociotechnical approach, as it proposes that technology's interpretation and use cannot be separated from its technical features. Furthermore, it centers use (and non-use) as the deciding factor in what a technology "is" and "does." The perspective is open to how technology might find new and unexpected areas of use but is primarily interested in how technology use becomes "normal," mundane, and routine (regardless of if the use was intended or not).

The theory is also linked to the idea of actor networks (see Chapter 3). As such, domestication considers how the introduction of a new technology causes existing actor networks to be destabilized and examines the work that must be done to establish and stabilize new actor networks (Sørensen et al., 2000; Sørensen, 2006; Ask, 2016). To carry out a domestication analysis is to understand how the various actors, both human and nonhuman, relate to each other and which knowledges, practices, and interpretations are necessary to make the technology a usable, natural part of everyday life.

4.3 The Dimensional Model of Domestication

In a domestication analysis, the aim is to understand what factors shape technology use. To analyze technology in a way that maintains interpretative flexibility and considers how technologies form actor networks, we need to explore how users negotiate with the technology's instructions and how their own habits and contexts influence this negotiation.

To do this, domestication theory has identified three dimensions as central to the domestication process: practical, cognitive, and symbolic. The three dimensions address critical aspects of the domestication process and have proven to have great explanatory power when attempting to make sense of how and why a technology is being used (or not used) (see Box 4A) (Figure 4.1).

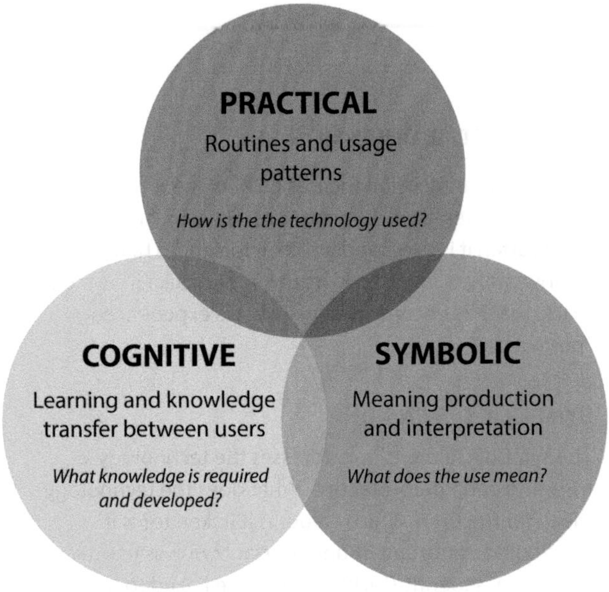

FIGURE 4.1 Dimensional Model of Domestication.

The three dimensions are connected and will usually blend into each other. How a technology is used (practice) is affected by how the technology is interpreted (symbolic), which, in turn, is shaped by the knowledge and skills the user has or develops (cognitive). Similarly, what knowledge and skills you have (cognitive) affect how you use the technology (practice), which, in turn, is shaped by how you interpret it (symbolic). A good domestication analysis is able to identify not only the different dimensions but also how they are related and together produce the user practice you are studying.

The most common mistake students make when doing domestication analysis is to make the research question a simple yes/no question: "Is the technology domesticated?" While this may be a relevant question in some instances, the real power of applying domestication theory comes from understanding *why* a technology is being used the way it is.

Box 4A.   Theory: Domestication of Technology—
The Three Dimensions in the Process

 PRACTICE DIMENSION

The practice dimension focuses on how the technology is used, who uses it, when and where it is used, how long/ much/often it is used, and which actors (both human and nonhuman) are involved in its use. A particular interest is in use that has become routine (what is experienced as "normal use").

SYMBOLIC DIMENSION

The symbolic dimension addresses the technology's meaning and interpretations. What does the technology mean for the user? Which values is it linked to? Is it considered important or unimportant? How is use related to the user's identity? Which norms are linked to using the technology?

COGNITIVE DIMENSION

The cognitive dimension concerns learning, both how the knowledge and expertise is required to use the technology, as well as how the user acquires them. Has the user taken a course? Read a manual? Guessed or used trial and error? Been taught by a partner or colleague? All technology requires knowledge to be used, but this requirement can be difficult to see if the technology is considered "intuitive to use" or if the associated knowledge is very common and thus taken for granted.

In a study of player communities in *World of Warcraft*, domestication theory was used to understand how three different groups of players appropriated the game in different ways. Even if there was a great deal of overlap in their playing practices (they were, after all, playing the same game), there were also key differences stemming from the different interpretations of the purpose of playing (symbolic), how they organized themselves (practice), and how they learned necessary game strategies (cognitive) (Ask & Sørensen, 2019). For an overview of how these differences developed, see Box 4B.

Box 4B.   Example: Three Different Domestications
of the *Game World of Warcraft*

Player Group	Symbolic Dimension	Practice Dimension	Cognitive Dimension
Hobby players	Playing is a social hobby	Playing with friends and friends' friends when they have time. Don't want participation to be mandatory.	Prefer to ask others to teach them things when needed.
Competitive players	Playing is about challenge and mastery	Only play with the best; must submit a written application to take part. Will play every evening (during certain periods) and will take days off from work to play.	Carry out their own tests and analyses to find optimal strategies. Write guides for players at lower levels.
"Softcore" players—both hobbyists and competitive	Playing is about being with friends and should also be challenging	Prefer to play with friends, but nonetheless submit an application. Are required to play two nights a week and keep attendance statistics.	Give "homework" and guidance to fellow players to ensure that they stay updated.

Of the three player groups, the first two, the hobby players
and the competitive players, were the most content. They
had a clear rationale (either to be social or to be "best") that
made them more likely to agree on shared interpretations
and practices, and the players felt that they got what
they wanted out of the game—even if they wanted
different things. The "softcore" players were the worst off.
They tried to be both hobbyists and competitive players
simultaneously and had to resort to extensive bureaucracy in
an attempt to balance the relaxing and competitive aspects
of playing. This led to exhausted officers (officers are players
responsible for organizing play sessions) and dejected

members. An important takeaway from this analysis is that domestication can be hard work. Even when it's a computer game that is being domesticated, some directed effort is always required from the users to establish a user practice.

Another domestication study of *World of Warcraft* focused on how the players needed to negotiate with non-users in the household, such as partners and parents, to gain the necessary space and time to play the game. While the first *World of Warcraft* study emphasized relationships between players as determining gaming practice, the second study is oriented toward the many seemingly small things in everyday life that affect gaming. Because the symbolic interpretation of the game differed between users and non-users—users saw *World of Warcraft* as meaningful and giving, and non-users saw the game as a waste of time that stood in the way of time together—gaming was a common source of conflict. Consequently, some users had to include "cleaning the kitchen countertops" and other strategies to stay on their parents' good side as part of their gaming practice, as without their parents' permission, there would be no gaming at all (Ask, 2011). In this way, the study showed that use is always anchored in everyday practices and is affected by many actors—not only other users. Ask and Sørensen (2019) conclude that domestication depends on either a unified moral community (with a high degree of agreement in the interpretation and rationale for use) or on leadership (to steer various rationales for use in the same direction).

Social interaction between users is also important for how technology is domesticated. To address this, Søraa et al. (2021) have suggested a fourth dimension to domestication, termed the social dimension, where the social interactions between various kinds of users of technology are considered particularly important for how the technology is domesticated and put into use. Here, concepts like primary, secondary, and non-users are seen as relevant, as they may all affect the network and the domestication of the technology. *Primary users* mean, in this context, those who are "end users" of the technology and are actively using it (e.g., older adults living at home with health care technologies for health monitoring), while *secondary users* are those who, through others' use, must relate (sometimes passively) to the technology (e.g., their family members or health care personnel who can look at the data). Or take, for example, how a grandfather (primary user) uses a mobile phone and depends on the grandchild's (secondary user) competence and help when something goes wrong. The point of this addition is thus to focus less on how users directly interact with technologies but rather on how social interactions between people create new ways of domesticating technologies that in a one-to-one setting between a user and the technology would look different.

Both Ask and Sørensen (2019) and Søraa et al. (2021) are studies that expand on the concept of domestication to capture how interactions between users, non-users, and user communities form domestication processes. As developments of the theory, these contributions are true to the roots of the concept of domestication in that they take users' roles seriously. Let us now consider how domestication theory came about.

4.4 The History of Domestication

The most cited source for domestication theory is Silverstone, Hirsch, and Strathern (1992). This pioneering study identified several key phases in the domestication of media technologies by households, including *appropriation* (acquisition of the product), *incorporation* (placement in the home), *objectification* (how use becomes a part of household routines), and *conversion* (how the technology also becomes a part of the household's self-perception and representation). This "phase model of domestication" understands domestication as a process that moves through four phases, from unknown to "fully tamed." However, the model does not make a normative claim about domestication having to go through all phases or even in that order, even if it is often used that way. In contrast, the dimensional model presented earlier was developed within Science and Technology Studies (STS) and emphasizes the *interaction* between different dimensions of the domestication process rather than seeing it as linear, as the phase model has traditionally done.

The phase model from media studies and the dimensional model from STS have much in common and can certainly be combined. In addition to the shared theoretical interest in context, everyday life, and meaning as determining factors of use, they also have a shared (early) interest in information and communication technologies' (ICT) uptake in the home. The early 1990s, when these theories were developed, was a period in which a series of new technologies, like computers and the internet, moved from offices and laboratories into people's homes. Understandably enough, many early domestication studies are analyses of how households acquired and established use of technologies like telephones (Frissen, 1994) and home computers (Aune, 1996).

While some studied domestication of a single technology, others chose to study selected groups of users' relationships with ICT based on demographics (Haddon & Silverstone, 1996) or interest/belonging (such as hackers in Håpnes, 1996). The concept of domestication has shown itself to be flexible and has gradually been applied to various phenomena at different levels. It started as an analytical tool to understand ICT, media, and how families brought new technology into their homes— in other words, as an interest in media technologies and in micro perspectives—but it has also been used on other technologies and macro perspectives, as in Østby's (2004) study of how cars are domesticated on a national level.

Even though Silverstone, Hirsch, and Strathern's (1992) study is the most commonly used reference for the term's origin, the theory did not develop in a vacuum, and domestication has many roots. From anthropology and consumer studies came an interest in how things and belongings become a part of our lives and which meanings they have (McCracken, 1986); from media studies, an interest in the contexts that form the uses of media technologies like television and computers (Lull, 1988; Morley, 1986); and last but not least, from STS, a connection to theories of technology as socially formed (Lie & Sørensen, 1996). While the phase model was developed in England, the dimensional model for domestication originated in Trondheim, at the Norwegian University of Science and Technology's (NTNU) Centre for Technology and Society. See Haddon (2007) and Hartmann (2020) for further information about the concept's history.

4.5 Strengths and Weaknesses of Domestication Theory

The strength of domestication theory is its emphasis on users in technological development and use, as well as how it captures how crucial interpretations and negotiations of meaning is for technology use. As such, the theory has an explicitly nondeterministic understanding of technology and instead is oriented toward the user's "doing" of the technology. Domestication is criticized, however, for being heavily based on qualitative studies, particularly case studies, which makes it difficult to generalize research findings. An overreliance on case studies puts one at risk of finding interesting individual stories about technology's domestication that provide limited information about the bigger picture (technology's use in society). The response to this critique is that domestication processes, even though they are diverse and varied, tend to follow patterns that are possible to identify across cases, as Haddon (2011, p. 313) points out: "Inevitably there are patterns, often a (limited) range of certain common experiences, albeit experienced in slightly different ways."

In this way, it is possible to identify more general features and trends by combining case studies—and not least, by combining methods. When one combines different methods, for example, qualitative interviews with survey data, this is called *triangulation of methods*, which may give even deeper insight into how things are connected. The critique of domestication theory could therefore be seen as part of a wider dismissal of qualitative social sciences and humanities research traditions, where qualitative studies are seen as "lesser than" because findings are neither generalizable nor presented as numbers, graphs, or predictions. Qualitative research cannot be generalized but helps us understand larger phenomena by explaining complexities, nuances, changes, and contradictions that can be difficult to measure. Such oppositions also do not consider the ways in which quantitative research is also shaped and determined by researchers' choices and perspectives, such as which questions they ask, what data they choose to collect, and from whom. For example, questionnaires requiring that participants identify as "male" or "female" are shaped by a focus on chromosomal sex rather than gender, and they do not take into account intersex individuals' existence. We have summarized the differences between qualitative and quantitative traditions/methods in Box 4C.

Box 4C.	Fact: Two Main Categories of Method	
	Qualitative Methods	**Quantitative Methods**
Focus	Qualitative (how/why)	Quantitative (how many/how much)
Method	Ethnography, in-depth interviews and observations, semi-structured and exploratory	Experiments/correlations like rigid questionnaires and numerical materials, not flexible to change underway
Data materials	Small, targeted data set	Large, randomized data set
Analyses	Inductive/abductive	Deductive
Findings	Contextual, holistic, and detailed	Generalizable, measured, overview

4.6 Re-domestication and Dis-domestication

Even if domestication has a possible endpoint (when the technology is a natural part of everyday life), it is also a process that must often be repeated, adjusted, or reevaluated. This is called *re-domestication*. If any actor in the network changes, be it a shift in everyday life, at work, how the technology is interpreted, the design, or a change in legislation (to mention some possibilities), the actor network can be destabilized, and the domestication must be repeated. As an example of this, consider a couple that has to establish new gaming practices (when, how, and with whom they play) after having a baby, or how new user patterns may emerge after a forced update of an operating system that changes functionality, icons, and their placement. It is normal to develop new needs and desires based on technology use, which may lead to re-domestications—or even domestications—of new technologies.

A telling example of technology-driven re-domestication that destabilizes the actor network is a study of smart home technology. Smart home technology is mainly made up of digital meters and controls that connect to standard household technologies such as lights, locks, heating, and household appliances. In one study, the introduction of smart home technology meant that users reevaluated the things they already owned and, when compared to the new "smart" technology, found faults and flaws with the older version. When they could suddenly control the hot water tank with a futuristic and sexy app, the old tank suddenly appeared both insufficient and outdated (Hargreaves & Wilson, 2017).

It is worth noting that not all changes will lead to a re-domestication where technology is reinterpreted and reestablished in everyday practices. In some cases, a change in the actor network will lead to *dis-domestication*, that is, no longer using the technology. The reasons for dis-domestication are many and easily recognizable: technologies can be destroyed or replaced by other technologies, fall out of fashion, or in other ways no longer fit into our everyday lives (or the current situation) (Sørensen, 1994). This is an example of how users can also become non-users, a type of user who surprisingly has a lot to teach us about what use is.

4.7 What Non-Users Can Teach Us about the Use of Technology

Non-use is a collective term for technology practices characterized by not being a user of said technology. Non-use is often explained as a lack of access or skills and paints a picture of non-users as deficient or lacking. Implicitly, such an interpretation reduces technology use to physical access and technical competence and thereby ignores the many and complex reasons that can prevent or limit use—especially the importance of attitudes toward the technology and motivation (or lack of motivation) for use (Wyatt, 2003). If we instead understand non-use as a part of a spectrum of use, we open ourselves up to the possibility that non-use can just as easily be an expression of resistance, something grounded in skepticism, or the result of a political choice. In an early study of the internet, researchers found four types of non-users (see Box 4D).

Box 4D.   Fact: Types of Non-Users

Resisters	Have not used the internet because they don't want to
Excluded	Do not have access to the internet, either due to technical restrictions (e.g., lack of infrastructure) or social restrictions (e.g., gendered expectations of use or discrimination)
Rejectors	Have voluntarily stopped using the internet because they believe it is, e.g., boring, too expensive, or unnecessary
Expelled	Have involuntarily stopped using the internet because they cannot afford it or have lost institutional access

That non-use can be made into four categories shows that non-use, like use, is both varied and complex. The categories are also a useful starting point for understanding non-use as an expression for different forms of motivation, understandings of technology, and accessibility. Later studies, carried out after the internet had become relatively affordable and accessible, have further emphasized motivation and technological understanding as deciding factors in non-use. A newer study of British and Swedish middle-aged non-users showed precisely that they have complex explanations for being non-users (Reisdorf & Groselj, 2017) (see Box 4E).

Box 4E.   Fact: Explanations of Non-use

No interest or need	Being online was not necessary at work and had no value for hobbies
Discomfort linked to technologies	Worried about data going astray or concerned with not "wasting" time in front of a screen, and for British users, age was also a factor
Complexity and complications	An impression of digital technology as complicated and difficult to learn
Physiological obstacles	Bad sight makes it difficult to navigate on a screen
Refusal	An active choice to cut digital technology out of one's own everyday life

Some non-users were very happy with their choice and did not miss it, while others felt that they were lagging behind and regretted not having learned how to use the internet earlier. Interestingly, most of the informants had friends or family who used the internet for them, so even though they were non-users, they were not entirely cut off from the internet (Reisdorf & Groselj, 2017). As such, their non-use was dependent on others' use. Considering how many day-to-day services have been moved online and how a life completely cut off from digital technology seems less and less tenable, the reliance on other users makes sense. In summary, non-use should be considered as a form of user practice, whether it is self-chosen, imposed, or more coincidental. In a user perspective, non-use must therefore be included as a possible form of use, and studies of non-users can give important insight into a technology's design and interpretations.

So far in this chapter, we have highlighted the active user and how users may oppose, reject, and negotiate with the technology. However, just because domestication has an explicit focus on use, users, and meaning as formative for technology's development, it is not an invitation to analyze technologies in ways that conclude that "the users decide everything." In the final section of this chapter, we will therefore emphasize morality as a way variation in use and patterns of use are reduced.

4.8 Normativity and Use

Stories about technology that gains radical new meanings and areas of use are charming (and important). And we appear to like such stories, given the popularity of so-called "life hacks," where everyday objects gain drastically new functions, like when a clean diaper is used to hide valuables at the beach or when the small plastic clips on bread bags are given new life as labels that clean up cable chaos (LaConte, 2020). From digitalization's history, we also have several examples of radical and innovative domestications that show the creativity and ability of users to find other areas of use than those defined by the producers. However, just because use is not predetermined does not mean that domestication is a boundless process that can have any outcome. If that were the case, the variation and diversity in use would be far greater and it would not be so easy to identify patterns of use and trends. There will always be elements in a domestication process that steer the outcome in given directions. To identify these factors, we need to do empirical studies and examine what elements are shaping individual domestication processes. There is nonetheless one aspect that consistently appears to shape domestication processes and that many domestication studies notice: *morality*.

By morality, we mean norms, rules, and moral evaluations that are made in connection to use, that is, what we consider to be "right" and "wrong" use. Some of these norms are based on laws (e.g., it is not legal to use a mobile phone while driving a car), others are prescribed (e.g., a reminder to turn off your mobile phone before a film starts), and others are less formal. It is, for example, not socially acceptable to spend a funeral surfing the internet on your phone, but this is neither written in any law nor something the priest asks of you. The situations mentioned in the introduction are examples of when norms for the use of social media, mobile phones, and emojis have been broken. As such, norms form how we develop our patterns of use and, thus, how technology is domesticated.

An interesting point here is that technology and norms mutually influence each other. Berker and Levold (2007) use the term *moral practices* to point out how patterns of use and norms are interwoven during domestication. In their study of heavy internet use, they show how evaluation of one's own use and interpretation of technology are two sides of the same coin. The informants who were always logged on understood technology as fascinating, while the informants who regulated their own use were concerned with ICT not taking up too much space because they saw technology either as a waste of time or as boring. Consequently, norms and patterns of use were created in relation to each other. Since both norms and technology are changeable, we can use domestication analyses to examine how morality and use affect each other, what effects domestication has on them, and why.

Another aspect that consistently shapes the outcome of domestication is *materiality*. That is, the directions for use that are included in the design—such as what the design encourages, precludes, or instructs. These preferences in the design are the theme of the next chapter.

4.9 Conclusion

In this chapter, we have considered user perspectives on technology and how domestication is a potent analytical tool for understanding how technology is formed through use. Domestication is, metaphorically speaking, the taming of technology and refers to the process through which technology moves from being unknown to become a part of everyday life. We have presented domestication's three dimensions: *practice*, how technology is used; *symbolic*, what use means for the users; and *cognitive*, how the user learns from and with the technology and how knowledge is transferred. The user perspective encompasses many technological practices, including re-domestication, when the technology must be tamed again; dis-domestication, when the technology is abandoned; and non-use, a user practice that is both nuanced and complex. In conclusion, we emphasized the importance of morality in the domestication process and how our understanding of "the right way to use a technology" is decisive for how we end up using it, as well as how use also shapes what we think of as "the right way." In the next chapter, we will introduce script theory, which is another concept with a clear user perspective. Where domestication is based in the user's everyday life, a script is useful for examining how design creates directions for use and prescribes ideal users.

References

Ask, K. (2011). Spiller du riktig? Tid, moral og materialitet i domestiseringen av et online dataspill [Playing the right way? Time, morality and materiality in the domestication of an online video game]. *Norsk medietidsskrift, 18*(2), 140–157.

Ask, K. (2016). *Ludic Work: The Assemblages, Domestications and Co-productions of Play*. [Doctoral dissertation]. Norwegian University of Science and Technology. https://ntnuopen.ntnu.no/ntnu-xmlui/handle/11250/2418295

Ask, K., & Sørensen, K. H. (2019). Domesticating technology for shared success: Collective enactments of World of Warcraft. *Information, Communication & Society, 22*(1), 73–88. https://doi.org/10.1080/13691 18X.2017.1355008.

Aune, M. (1996). The computer in everyday life: Patterns of domestication of a new technology. In M. Lie & K. H. Sørensen (Eds.), *Making technology our own* (pp. 92–118). Scandinavian University Press.

Berker, T., & Levold, N. (2007). Moralske praksiser i forbindelse med tung internettbruk [Moral practices in relation to heavy internet use]. In N. Levold & H. S. Spilker (Eds.), *Kommunikasjonssamfunnet: Moral, praksis og digital teknologi* [Communication society: Moral, practice and digital technology] (pp. 35–49). Universitetsforlaget.

Blizzard Entertainment. (2004, 23 November). *World of Warcraft* [video game].

Frissen, V. (1994). The domestication of the telephone. In A. J. Berg & M. Aune (Eds.), *Domestic technology and everyday life: Mutual shaping processes. COST Social Sciences vol. 1*. European Commission DGXIII Science Research and Development.

Haddon, L. (2007). Roger Silverstone's legacies: Domestication. *New Media & Society, 9*(1), 25–32. https://doi.org/10.1177/1461444807075201.

Haddon, M. (2011). *Modeling and quantitative methods in fisheries*. Chapman & Hall.

Haddon, L., & Silverstone, R. (1996). *Information and communication technologies and the young elderly*. University of Sussex. https://eprints.lse.ac.uk/62450/1/Information_and_communication.pdf

Hargreaves, T., & Wilson, C. (2017). *Smart homes and their users*. Springer International Publishing.

Hartmann, M. (2020). (The domestication of) Nordic domestication? *Nordic Journal of Media Studies, 2*(1), 47–57. https://content.sciendo.com/view/journals/njms/2/1/article-p47.xml.

Håpnes, T. (1996). Not in their machines: How hackers transform computers into subcultural artefacts. In M. Lie & K. Sørensen (Eds.), *Making technology our own? Domesticating technology into everyday life* (pp. 121–150). Scandinavian University Press.

LaConte, S. (2020, 18 June). 28 life hacks you won't believe nobody told you about until now. *Buzzfeed.* https://www.buzzfeed.com/stephenlaconte/life-hacks-simple-smart-organizing-cooking-cleaning.

Lie, M., & Sørensen, K. H. (Red.). (1996). *Making technology our own? Domesticating technology into everyday life*. Scandinavian University Press.

Lull, J. (1988). *World families watch television*. SAGE Publications.

McCracken, G. (1986). Culture and consumption: A theoretical account of the structure and movement of the cultural meaning of consumer goods. *Journal of Consumer Research, 13*(1), 71–84. https://doi.org/10.1086/209048.

Morley, D. (1986). *Family television: Cultural power and domestic leisure.* Comedia Pub. Group.

Østby, P. (2004). Educating the Norwegian nation: Traffic engineering and technological diffusion. *Comparative Technology Transfer and Society, 2*(3), 247–272. https://doi.org/10.1353/ctt.2005.0006.

Reisdorf, B. C., & Groselj, D. (2017). Internet (non-)use types and motivational access: Implications for digital inequalities research. *New Media & Society, 19*(8), 1157–1176. https://doi.org/10.1177/1461444815621539.

Silverstone, R., Hirsch, E., & Strathern, M. (1992). *Consuming technologies: Media and information in domestic spaces.* Routledge.

Søraa, R. A., Nyvoll, P. S., Tøndel, G., Fosch-Villaronga, E., & Serrano, A. S. (2021). *The social dimension of domesticating technology: Interactions between older adults, caregivers, and robots in the home.* Technological Forecast and Social Change.

Sørensen, K. H. (1994). *Technology in use: Two essays on the domestication of artifacts* (Vol. 2/94). Center for Technology and Society, University of Trondheim.

Sørensen, K. H. (2006). Domestication: The Enactment of Technology. In T. Berker (Ed.), *Domestication of media and technology* (pp. 40–61). Open University Press.

Sørensen, K. H., Aune, M., & Hatling, M. (2000). Against linearity: On the cultural appropriation of science and technology. In M. Dierkes & C. von Grote (Eds.), *Between understanding and trust. The public, science and technology* (pp. 237–257). Routledge.

Wyatt, S.M. (2003). Non-users also matter: The construction of users and non-users of the Internet. In N. Oudshoorn & T. Pinch (Eds.), *Now users matter: The co-construction of users and technology* (pp. 67–257). MIT Press.

CHAPTER 5

Script

Technology's Manuscript for Use

Have you ever tried an app or a gadget and thought, "What on earth did the designers think when they made this? Who is this for?" Then you have likely encountered a technology made with another user in mind, and the story embedded in the technology did not match up with you or your needs. Technologies are never a "catch all" as design deem some users more important (or potentially unwanted) than others. That technologies are more than a set of functions, and that design also promotes values and stories about the world,

DOI: 10.1201/9781003289555-7

becomes particularly clear when the values and stories don't match up with one's own. It is also apparent when the story that surrounds the technology is outdated, wrong, or based on harmful stereotypes.

When a workout app presents yoga exercises to women and weightlifting to men, the app is not only a workout tool; it is also a statement about gender. Though it may be well-meaning, and even reflect actual gendered differences in exercise practices, the technology is telling a story about what kind of exercise is appropriate based on gender and encourage its users to behave accordingly. Being able to read the stories that are made with technology is crucial to your ability to critically analyze them. In this chapter, you will therefore learn about *script theory*, which will allow you to explore how values are materialized and how values are conveyed through design. As such, script is suitable for understanding how technologies communicate preferences and worldviews through functionality and aesthetics.

5.1 Script as Technology's Manual

A sociotechnical approach requires that both human and nonhuman actors (like technologies) are included in the analysis. However, it can be challenging to identify and include the agency of technologies, as they (at least for now) cannot state their own desires, nor can we rely on the visions (or, rather, the sales pitches) made by the producers. To understand what technologies allow, disallow, encourage, and discourage, we must make strategic interpretations and translations of their functionality, design, and related symbols and stories. This is called a script analysis.

Technologies have preferences for how they should be used and by whom. Together, these preferences make up a script for use that implies different "scenes" that the users can perform. In the same way that a film script includes descriptions of various actors, what they should do, and how they should relate to one another, in the design of a technology, one can find instructions on who the user is, what the technology should be used for, and how it should be used.

Script theory is built on the assumption that the world view of developers will be materialized in the design. How a developer understands a problem and which qualities they attribute to their future users will characterize the final product. This includes which values the user should have, which tasks the user must complete, and which skills the user must have to understand the design. Technologies will communicate values, delegate tasks, and encourage (or discourage) certain actions, and script theory is an analytical tool you can use to identify what use and which users the technology envisions and which problems it is meant to solve (Akrich, 1992).

Script has been used to study different technologies, from apps to infrastructure, to show how technology shapes both use and users. Latour (1992) exemplifies how script encourages "correct use" (here defined as intended use by the producer or owner) of hotel keys by making them so big and clunky that one cannot forget to return them to reception before leaving. (Today, this script has largely been digitalized in the form of notifications on our mobiles that remind us to check out and follow the hotel's rules.) Similarly, Ingram, Shove, and Watson (2007) describe how toilets on the British train often have the "flush" button on the back of the lid, so that the script forces the user to shut the lid before they flush the toilet after using it. Other script studies are more concerned with which qualities in the users are required and which uses the technology facilitates, such as how the streaming platform Twitch.tv scripts its audience as gaming socialites with a willingness to pay for content (Ask et al., 2019) or how Disney scripts tweens as individualized future consumers (Sørenssen, 2018).

Central to script studies is the relationship between envisioned and actual use. In these studies, script is used to understand the tensions between the visions of the developers and the reality of use, and to highlight how users' values differ from the developers and lead to oppositional use. For example, studies that show how users of so-called "smart homes" opposed manufacturers' scripts to gain more control over their own everyday lives (Hansen & Hauge, 2017) or how health care workers felt it necessary to find ways of

Box 5A.   Theory: What We Can Learn about the Design through Script Analysis

Use	What the technology will be used for, how it should be used, and in which contexts it will be used
User	Who will use the technology and which attributes the user has (values, knowledge, motivations, political standpoint, etc.)
World	What problems the technology aims to "solve" also says something about how the developers understand the problems and, consequently, how they understand society

circumventing the script in the digital daily planner to get enough time to do their jobs responsibly (Bergschöld, 2016).

Circumventing scripts does not necessarily have to be about opposition. Players of a sandbox game (a game in which you can build your own things and levels) actively tested the borders of what they could and couldn't do within the game's frameworks as part of their creative exploration (Abend & Beli, 2016). While addressing different technologies and users, these studies share an interest in the negotiations between design and user, how design is embedded with certain values and norms, and how the script can be read in other ways than intended. Script theory has also been particularly useful for understanding how technology forms gender, ethnicity, sexuality, and (dis)ability—which you can read more about in the next chapter.

Script is a useful tool to make sense of digitalization processes (see Box 5A). Through script analysis, we can give the technology "a voice" in the analysis—so that when we attempt to understand the relationship between humans and technologies, the "perspective" of the technology is also accounted for. This may be useful when attempting to understand what values and practices are encouraged (and discouraged) by technology and how technology exerts power in society. In addition, a nuanced understanding of the user context is a good starting point for design, and a script analysis can assist us in assessing if the design is aligned with the problem it tries to solve and the needs of the user.

In summary, script theory builds on three central assumptions:

- The developers' understanding of society and visions of use/users are materialized in the technologies they make.
- Technologies communicate values in addition to doing a job.
- Envisioned and actual use needn't be the same.

5.2 The Historical and Theoretical Position of Script Theory

Akrich (1992) developed the concept of *script* to better understand how technology facilitates, encourages, or prevents something from happening. Script theory builds on the idea that technology can be thought of as a text, a concept originally suggested by Woolgar (1990). The approach considers design as "writing," technology as "the text," and use as "reading." As such, we can understand script theory as a part of the semiotic turn in STS, that is, a theoretical shift in focus toward signs and symbols and how these are used in communication.

The term script was first used in the text "The De-Scription of Technical Objects" (Akrich, 1992). Here, Akrich demonstrates that the gap between envisioned and actual use is a potent entry point for analysis. The technology Akrich analyzed was photoelectronic lighting kits, or more precisely, a set of solar panels, batteries, and lamps that could be assembled and function as a mobile energy source used for lighting. The kit was developed in Paris, but it was not until Akrich observed its use in a rural town in Senegal that she realized how many assumptions about society, the users, and use were written into the technology. In the design process, it had been an explicit goal of the developers to make an autonomous technology that worked "no matter what." It was the reason that they chose, for example, non-standardized parts that were more robust. However, this script fits poorly with the users' everyday lives in Senegal.

The problems began during installation, where, among other things, the non-standardized parts made it difficult to adapt the kit for rooms of varying sizes, and repairs were made more difficult because new parts were only available in large cities. To complicate things further, only pre-approved technicians were allowed to carry out repairs because the developers thought local electricians would not have enough/the right expertise. The developers wanted to make a technology that was safe and reliable, so they designed it to be robust and difficult to tinker with. Despite good intentions, the design ended up alienating and disenfranchising users who were accustomed to repairing and modifying technologies based on their own needs. That developers prioritized robustness over flexibility resulted in a technology that fit poorly into users' everyday lives. Akrich's study shows how important an accurate and nuanced understanding of the actual user is for good design, and the case of photoelectronic lighting kits illustrates how producers' worldviews and values become materialized in the design. Had the designers envisioned their users as technically competent and their use as varied and changeable, they would likely have made other priorities when making the kit.

The photoelectronic lightening kit example also shows that what may be considered good functionality is not universal. Instead, "good functionality" is decided by the context in which the technology is to be used. In this case, robustness, which is generally seen as a good thing in design, was shown to hinder use rather than support it. Finally, the case is another example of how important knowledge about the users' lives and needs is when designing a technology and reminds us of the value of a strong user perspective in technology development.

5.3 How Do You Do a Script Analysis?

The most important aspect of a script analysis is identifying which uses and users are envisioned in the design. This can be done by either (1) analyzing the process of making the technology, (2) studying users and how they engage with the script, or (3) "reading" the design (and supplementing sources) using script theory. In this chapter, we will focus on the latter to emphasize how script can be used to understand the stories technologies tell and investigate how technologies gain and exert agency.

A script analysis combines interpretation of design (functionality, aesthetics, and settings) with a critical reading of supplementing sources. The script analysis can inform you not only about what use is envisioned but also who the envisioned user is. What values, skills, attitudes, affiliations, actions, and more characterizes the user? In turn, these insights can be used to raise critique regarding who technology is made for (and who is excluded), improve our understanding of how technology shapes our lives, and inform design processes.

Supplementing sources are relevant because script theory presumes that technologies are part of an actor network (that is, that they are a part of a network with other actors, not that they are "online"). Consequently, script analysis involves studying not just the chosen artifact but also other related sources such as promotional material, product descriptions, and instruction manuals.

Identifying and describing functionality, aesthetics, and settings is a good way to map out and understand the design, but it is not in itself a script analysis. For the script to be identified, we must translate these descriptions into stories about envisioned use, users, and the world. Let's say you are doing a script analysis of a workout app, and you have identified "step counter" as the most important function. To translate that functionality into a script, the next (and very important) step is to consider what it tells us about the envisioned user. In this case, the envisioned user is someone who exercises by walking or jogging, as the technology measures steps in a workout context. That it only counts steps means that users who prefer to bike or use a wheelchair are not part of the script.

Stating that a workout app with a step counter is scripted for users who walk or jog may seem redundant. It is rather obvious, so why do a script analysis? Because the value of a script analysis comes from addressing what *several* (if not all) functions, as well as aesthetics and settings, say *together* about envisioned use and users. If the hypothetical workout app has a pink color scheme decorated with flowers and butterflies, you can assume that the envisioned walking/jogging user is a woman (and you may also note that it communicates this to its users in highly stereotypical ways). If the app converts "number of steps" to "calories burned," it also says that the envisioned user is walking/jogging to lose weight (as opposed to, for example, enjoying nature or discovering local cultural sites). If it is connected to social media so that users may post their daily workout sessions, the scripted user is envisioned as being socially oriented and motivated by sharing success. As you go through the list of features and design choices and translate them into stories about use and users, you end up with a far more complex image of the envisioned user than "likes to walk/jog" and the value-laden story about use and users starts to emerge.

To be explicit and clear about what you should look for in a script analysis, we have summarized questions you can ask of your data to examine a technology's functionality, aesthetics, and setting in Box 5B—and further, what these questions can tell you about the design's envisioned use, users, and assumptions about society.

Script may be used in conjunction with domestication theory (see Chapter 4) to get a nuanced and complex understanding of how technology design and use are related.

Script theory has a series of sub-concepts that, when applied, help nuance relationships between the producers, designer, and user (see Box 5C). Some key terms that are useful for explaining how users both follow and oppose the script are in-scription (when the script is made), de-scription (when the script is read), sub-scription (when the script is

Box 5B.   Questions for the Data: Script Analysis

	Functionality	Which functions does the technology have? What can it do? How are the functions arranged (see, e.g., positioning that is prominent or hidden to separate between main and supportive functions)?
	Aesthetics	What is the aesthetic and appearance of the design? Which symbols are used (choice of color, logo, style choices)? Which users are visible (see, e.g., pictures and illustrations showing the technology in use)?
	Customization	What are the standard settings? Which choices are offered in settings (look for, e.g., which genders you can choose in the registration process or modify later)? Are there any functions one cannot choose in the free vs. the paid version?
	Envisioned use	What is preferred use? What is undesired use? When, where, and how should the technology be used?
	Envisioned user	Who is the imagined user? Which attributes does the imagined user have (values, interest, gender, age, sexuality, nationality, etc.)? Are there any undesired users?
	Envisioned society	What assumptions about the world is the technology built on? What is considered valuable/worthless, wanted/unwanted? What societal development/future is implied in the design?

Box 5C.   Theory: The Script's Vocabulary

Script	Perceptions about use, users, and the world that are written into technology
In-scription	Process of developing, or "writing," the script, i.e., the design process
De-scription	The process during which users interpret, or "read," the script
Sub-scription	When the user follows the scripts, and the intended and actual use are the same
De-inscription	When users resist the script and try to negotiate with it
Anti-program	When the preferred use is set aside, the user's wishes/interpretations take over, and the use becomes radically different than the scripted use
Pre-inscription	What a technology allows or forbids its users to do
Re-inscription	When the technology gets a new script through use, modification, or redesign
User-script	The scripts (the notions of use, users, and the place of technology in the world) made by the users themselves (Gjøen & Hård, 2002)
Co-script	Script that is created in partnership by the producer and the user, particularly in connection to digital platforms where users are responsible for producing content (Ask et al., 2019)

followed), and anti-program (when the script is rejected). They are mainly from Akrich and Latour (1992) and reflect the underlying framework where making and using are conceptualized as a type of writing–reading process.

5.4 Making Scripts through Technology Development

So far, this chapter has focused on how you can read a technology's script to understand which preferences, values, and encouragements/discouragements are included in its design. Another way of doing a script analysis is to study how the technology was made. Instead of focusing on the "reading" of the script, you may focus on the "writing" of the script by studying producers/developers. By investigating how producers/developers work to delineate a problem or need (which the technology will solve), how they conceptualize

we may learn what uses and users are scripted. Script analysis can be used to address the biases of developers and designers, which in turn can be used to lift important critiques and make fairer and better technologies. Overall, script is a way to address how no technology is neutral but is instead imbued with ideas, values, and prescriptions regarding use, users, and society.

References

Abend, P., & Beil, B. (2016). Editors of play: The scripts and practices of co-creativity in Minecraft and LittleBigPlanet. *Transactions of the Digital Games Research Association*, *2*(3), 5–30. https://doi.org/10.26503/todigra.v2i3.51.

Akrich, M. (1992). The de-scription of technical objects. In W. E. Bjiker & J. Law (Eds.), *Shaping technology/building society*: *Studies in Sociotechnical change* (pp. 205–224). MIT Press.

Akrich, M., & Latour, B. (1992). A summary of a convenient vocabulary for the semiotics of human and nonhuman assemblies. In W. E. Bjiker & J. Law (Eds.), *Shaping technology/building society*: *Studies in sociotechnical change* (pp. 259–264). MIT Press.

Ask, K., Spilker, H. S., & Hansen, M. (2019). The politics of user-platform relationships: Co-scripting live-streaming on Twitch.tv. *First Monday*, *24*(7). https://doi.org/10.5210/fm.v24i7.9648.

Bergschöld, J. M. (2016). Domesticating homecare services: Vehicle route problem solver displaced. *Nordic Journal of Science and Technology Studies*, *4*(2), 41–53. https://doi.org/10.5324/njsts.v4i2.2184.

Gjøen, H., & Hård, M. (2002). Cultural politics in action: Developing user scripts in relation to the electric vehicle. *Science, Technology, & Human Values*, *27*(2), 262–281. https://doi.org/10.1177/016224390202700204.

Hansen, M., & Hauge, B. (2017). Scripting, control, and privacy in domestic smart grid technologies: Insights from a Danish pilot study. *Energy Research & Social Science*, *25*, 112–123. https://doi.org/10.1016/j.erss.2017.01.005.

Ingram, J., Shove, E., & Watson, M. (2007). Products and practices: Selected concepts from science and technology studies and from social theories of consumption and practice. *Design Issues*, *23*(2), 3–16. https://doi.org/10.1162/desi.2007.23.2.3.

Latour, B. (1992). Where are the missing masses? The sociology of a few mundane artifacts. In W. E. Bijker & J. Law (Eds.), *Shaping technology/building society: Studies in socio- technical change* (pp. 151–180). MIT Press.

Søraa, R. A. (2014). *Konnichiwa robot, sayonara humans? - Construction and domestication of robots in Japan* [Master's theses]. Norwegian University of Science and Technology, Trondheim. https://hdl.handle.net/11250/279794.

Sørenssen, I. K. (2018). Disney's *High School Musical* and the construction of the tween audience. *Global Studies of Childhood, 8*(3), 213–224. https://doi.org/10.1177/2043610618796722.

Wachter-Boettcher, S. (2017). *Technically wrong: Sexist apps, biased algorithms, and other threats of toxic tech.* W. W. Norton & Company.

Woolgar, S. (1990). Configuring the user: The case of usability trials. *The Sociological Review, 38*(Suppl. 1), 58–99. https://doi.org/10.1111/j.1467-954X.1990.tb03349.x.

CHAPTER 6

Technologies as Normality Machines

Technologies will, in addition to being useful, also promote values and ideas about the world and its users. Through their design, technologies tell stories about the world that needs to be critically examined. Technologies shape what we understand to be "normal" and, as such, what we think of as right, correct, expected, and/or desired. In this sense, we may understand technologies as machines that produce "normality." *Normality* is a potent construction of values that delineates what we see as "acceptable" (and "unacceptable") that shape how we relate to each other and to technology. So, which normality (or rather normalities) are created through digitalization?

In assessing what qualifies as a "successful digitalization," we need to go beyond whether "it works or not."

DOI: 10.1201/9781003289555-8

We must also consider how digitalization is shaping society, what normality is created, and who stands to benefit or be harmed by it. In this chapter, we turn our attention to how digitalization can cause exclusion of vulnerable groups and have discriminatory effects. We invite you to reflect on the effects (digital) technologies have on society and how the development and implementation of digital technology have the potential to strengthen or subvert injustice and inequality. Finally, we also invite you to reflect on the ethical responsibility that developers, users, and students of technology have in ensuring digitalization has just and fair outcomes. To start this reflection, we begin with a thought experiment about a student app before we go on to discuss "the digital divide" and technology as discriminatory.

6.1 A Thought Experiment about a Student App

Imagine that you are a new employee at a tech company, and you are tasked with designing a new student app. You and your team have just received the assignment and are about to start brainstorming ideas for the design. Think about how you would design an app for students. Which functions should be included? Which problems should it solve? How should it look? Should it cost anything? Use a couple of minutes to come up with ideas for what the app could do and look like. Make simple notes, sketch out a design, and make a list of functions you would like to have.

The next step is for you to take a mental step back and look at the design ideas you have noted down. Without evaluating whether your ideas are good or bad, reflect on *which users* they address. When you sketched out some ideas for the design, you have (knowingly or unknowingly) had an envisioned student in mind—but which student is it?

- Is it a new student fresh out of high school, a student who is nearly finished with their degree, or maybe an older student who is taking further education after several decades of working life?

- Is it a student who can afford a few impulse purchases a month, or is it someone who is living on a strict diet of carefully portioned servings of noodles?
- Is the student social and involved in several student clubs, or are they more reserved without a large social network?
- Is the student you imagine a man, a woman, or maybe nonbinary? What sexual orientation do they have?
- Which ethnicity does the student have? What skin color?
- Does the student like technology and new gadgets, or are they more interested in limiting technology's influence on their everyday lives?

The answers you give in this exercise are not important. The point is to make it clear:

a. that it is not possible to imagine a technology without simultaneously imagining a form of use—and consequently, a user.
b. that no design is neutral, and our understanding of the world is materialized as bias in design.

Even if you have not created an actual app, the act of thinking up a design means you have started the creation of a script. If your design agrees with students' own understandings of themselves and their needs, there is a good chance that the app will be considered "useful" or "suitable" (here in quotes, because what is considered "useful" or "suitable" is highly subjective). The design will feel natural, as if it were "made for me as a user." At the same time, if students do not recognize themselves in the premises of the design, the app will be considered "useless" and "unsuitable" (again, the use of quotation marks indicates that such evaluations are subjective). Either way, your app will contribute to our collective understanding of what students are about and what problems they face (and are considered worth addressing).

Students who download this hypothetical app will not only get a piece of software but will also be presented with a story about what a student "should be" through various functions, default settings, aesthetic expressions, price points, and other features of the app. In this way, the technology becomes *normative*: it says something about what is right and wrong, wanted and unwanted, normal and abnormal. Latour (1992) argues that the ability to be moral actors, that is, actors that affect and uphold norms, is central to understanding the role technology has in society. By materializing norms into technologies they become more robust and harder to change than if they existed simply as ideas, discourses, or behaviors. Consider, for example, how a shift from car-centric life to a more environmentally friendly alternative, such as cycling, is hindered by an infrastructure that favors cars in the United States. The omnipresence of car infrastructure, like highways, gas stations, and parking lots, makes the transition to car alternatives more difficult. Not only does their sheer presence support the normalcy of cars, but they are also costly to rebuild.

Maybe you imagined an app that would function partially as a social platform where you could contact fellow students to get discounts at local shops or do assignments together. If so, you took for granted that the envisioned user has a strong social network to leverage. If the app were given to one of the many students who experience their time at university as lonely—which is true for nearly one-third of students according to the student health and wellbeing survey (2018)—such a design could seem alienating, as if it was not made "for me." Equally important, it promotes a story about student life where being lonely is "not normal," even if it is statistically likely.

6.2 Technology as Inclusion or Exclusion?

Through technology, we are encouraged to do things in a certain way and think about society in certain terms. In this way, we can consider technology (and its use) as a way to establish and spread *norms*. Some technologies, like safety technology, give us explicit orders about how to behave; for example, a loud and unpleasant alarm rings if you start your car without fastening your seatbelt (Latour, 1992). Other times, the technology will give mild encouragement, like when you are prompted by social media to share a picture with your post to get more likes or how Netflix asks if you want to take a pause when you are "binge watching" for multiple hours. Other examples of how technology contributes to the making and policing of norms are more indirect. For example, beauty filters that make your face smaller and whiter in the profile picture, as many beauty filters do, imply that if you are not thin and white, you are not beautiful (Rettberg, 2014). Or how a workout app that cannot be adapted to account for chronic illness or other disabilities contributes to normalizing good health as something exclusive to able-bodied people.

A critical perspective on technology allows for identification of the values that are being spread through technologies' designs and functionalities and extrapolation of how such values create limitations about *who* can participate in a technological society and on whose premises the participation is based.

To understand how technologies act as moral actors, let us take a closer look at *default settings*. A potent attribute of digital technology is customizability, which means that you, as a user, can choose between different settings to customize the technology according to your needs and preferences. Think of how you can choose the difficulty of a computer game or adjust the types of alerts you receive in an email app. On the one hand, the possibility to customize a technology is a way to allow diversity in use because it takes into account that different users will have different needs and use the technology in various ways. On the other hand, the way in which settings are designed with certain choices set as defaults is also a way to enforce norms because the default settings *produce* normality. The default settings affect how we perceive our preferences as well as the choices we make.

As mentioned in the previous chapter about scripts, default settings tell us a lot about how developers envision their use. Default settings are also a good example of how design advocates something as "normal," and, consequently, something else as "abnormal." As an example, when electronic payment was introduced in New York cabs, the standard settings in the payment software were 20%, 25%, or 30% tips. Overnight, the average tip went up from around 10% to 22% because a full 70% of customers preferred to choose between the standard alternatives instead of calculating and entering a tip themselves. In summary, we can think of technologies as normality machines: they shape what we consider to be normal.

Since technology conveys values and can exercise power, it has the potential to be discriminatory. A critical perspective on digitalization must therefore also include awareness of whom the technology includes and excludes.

If the hypothetical student app required that you register your gender in the profile but only had "man" and "women" as alternatives, it could potentially alienate trans and nonbinary users. Or maybe the app does not apply universal design (see Box 6A) and is inaccessible to, for example, the visually impaired. In these cases, the technology is not only normative by telling a story about who is "normal" or "wanted" (and thus implicitly who is "abnormal" and "unwanted"); the technology's design perpetuates and strengthens discriminatory structures in which the technology is only accessible to specific groups. If these preferences were varied and diverse, it wouldn't be a problem, but it is neither random nor coincidental who falls outside the "normal" when new technology is made. The script concept can help us understand how this happens.

Box 6A.   Fact: Checklists for Universal Design Cover

Universal design is about planning and designing technology (as well as environments, products, and services) so that they can be used equally by as many people as possible. The main aim of universal design is to curb discrimination due to (dis)ability and thus give everyone equal opportunity for participation in society. The Norwegian Digitalization Agency's checklist for universal design covers, among other things, navigating websites by keyboard, making text larger, making text machine-readable, using contrasting colors, including alternative text explanations for pictures, and so forth. Universal design is included in many laws around the world to ensure equal access to buildings, services, and education, as well as to prevent discrimination.

6.3 Scripting Use and Users to Create Differences

Technological scripts don't just inform us of envisioned uses and users, they also say something about society and power relationships within society. Just like in a movie script, technological scripts have main characters that are given importance, agency, and space (often at the cost of others). And just like actors take on roles that give unflattering, limited, or discriminatory portrayals, we as users will also be presented with technological scripts that position us in undesired ways. One example of this is how ideas about gender are inscribed into everyday technology.

To show how stereotypical understandings of gender are materialized and perpetuated, Lie (2010) compares two everyday tools: the electric hand mixer and the drill. Both are tools where you select appendages depending on the task at hand (either the whisks or the drill bits), and the machinery makes those parts spin quickly (to whip or to drill). While mechanically rather similar, these two technologies are radically different when it comes to the envisioned technical competence and interests of their users. While the drill appears technical, with visible mechanical elements and screws to allow the user to disassemble and potentially fix/examine the drill, the hand mixer hides all mechanical features and cannot be taken apart. The hand mixer script therefore assumes that the user has no interest in understanding how the hand mixer works. While the envisioned user of the hand mixer is a woman who is assumed to be disinterested in technology, the envisioned user of the drill is a man who is assumed to be both technologically interested and competent. The example shows how ideas about gender (that men like technology and women do not) are materialized. We find similar patterns in other technologies like clocks and razors (Oudshoorn et al., 2002), where models made for men play up the technological components and models for women hide or downplay the technology involved, perpetuating the (wrongful) idea that technology is a male-only domain. Here we see how designs based on stereotypes or prejudices about various groups can contribute to social inequality.

Even new technology that actively aims to counteract bias can be discriminatory. One example is Amazon's attempt to use machine learning in its hiring processes. In 2014, Amazon attempted to automate hiring processes by deploying AI in its search for the best candidates. The experimental tool was supposed to evaluate applicants and rate them, and by doing so, minimize the work of finding good candidates—a job that is both time-consuming and risky (Dastin, 2018). The idea was to avoid the influence of human prejudices by letting a computer (perceived as a neutral agent) rank applicants. However, the algorithm did not work as planned, and it undervalued female applicants to the benefit of male applicants. This was not because women applicants had weaker grades or less experience, but simply because they were women, and the algorithm considered this a drawback.

The reason why women applicants were downranked was not some nefarious plot to keep women out of Amazon. However, it is a feature of how machine learning works. The algorithm used to rank applicants was trained on a dataset consisting of applications and information about hiring at Amazon in the past 10 years. In these 10 years, Amazon, like most other tech companies, hired far more men than women (Wachter-Boettcher, 2017). Consequently, the algorithm learned that the word "woman" was negative because applications with the word "woman" in them had not been evaluated as "best" in the historical dataset. So, when an applicant described, for example, that she was the "leader of the women's chess club," the application was given a lower score even if her leadership experience should have given a positive result (Dastin, 2018).

Using script to study inequality is not limited to addressing exclusion; it may also be used to understand how technology becomes inclusive and how design is appropriated by excluded groups. For example, the sign-up process on Pinterest directs the user toward collective and collaborative actions (as opposed to competition and ranking as found on sites like Reddit), and through this script, women users feel more at home on the platform (Friz & Gehl, 2016). Or how Inuit youth negotiate with Facebook's script to make space for their own identity and community by making space for various groups, discussing sociocultural questions, and renewing and remembering cultural traditions (Castleton, 2018). Play around with scripts in the Box 6B exercise.

We need critical understandings of design to address the inequalities and assumed qualities of different groups. Both to address direct harm from exclusionary design and to identify how technology reinforces and/or rejects biased perceptions of groups of people, particularly minorities.

Box 6B.   Exercise: Script Genderflip

That design conveys both preferences and values, become particularly visible when we look at gender. Designs aimed at women will typically include elements of pink, flowers, and curves, while designs aimed at men are usually blue and have more squares and straight lines (The Checkout, 2014). That this way of gendering technology can be incredibly foolish becomes very visible when you turn the issue on its head, something the witty Twitter account @manwhohasitall likes to do: "My friend is designing a laptop for men. It will be like a normal laptop, but specially adapted. What features should it have?" (manwhohasitall, 2019).

In this exercise, you will start with a clearly gendered technology, i.e., a technology that you feel has clearly been designed with either women or men in mind. Attempt to turn the script on its head: If the technology was aimed at women, what must you change to aim the script at men? Or the opposite: if the technology was aimed at men, what must you do to change the script so that it is aimed at women? Not least, what must you do for the script to be gender neutral—that it does not include any gendered preferences or maybe follows a nonbinary script? Think about what changes you would make to the aesthetics, functions, and settings to change the gendering of the design.

6.4 The Digital Divide

The term *the digital divide* (sometimes also called *the digital gap* or *digital exclusion*) refers to how people have different access to and opportunities to use digital technology. Research has found digital gaps due to, among other things, gender (Sørensen et al., 2011), age (Neves et al., 2018), and ethnicity (Fairlie, 2017). The digital divide has also been thematized as a divide between "north and south" (Luyt, 2004), urban and rural (Labrianidis & Kalogeressis, 2006), and rich and poor (class) (Lindblom & Räsänen, 2017). Strategies for reducing the digital divide are a political goal for both the OECD (n.d.) and the UN (2015). The reasons for differences will vary from divide to divide; what is worth noting is how the digital divide follows established power structures, and groups who are already considered privileged in society (white, upper-class men in large cities in Europe/the USA) have far better chances of being able to take advantage of the benefits of digital technology than others.

Let us take a closer look at the digital divide as it pertains to gender to gain a better understanding of what it entails. A salient point from this brief topical exploration is how seemingly personal choices are structurally shaped and that because digital divides are structural, they are complex and may be difficult to change.

The digital divide has been studied for many decades, and a number of mechanisms of exclusion that produce inequality have been identified. Exclusion based on gender in the ICT sector is due to educational politics, how educational institutions are organized, and a lack of female role models and mentors. Tech culture tends to value stereotypically masculine behavior and attributes, and boys are more likely to be socialized in communities and practices linked to ICT. In addition, personal experiences with digital technology and interests are also crucial, as young girls have fewer socially legitimate ways of engaging with technology than boys. A key takeaway from this research is that exclusions take place on many levels simultaneously (individual, institutional, and societal levels), and to be able to understand how men choose data technology studies, careers, and hobbies while women are less likely to do so, we must examine how the different levels work together (Sørensen et al., 2011).

To understand the digital divide, we must also consider how digital technology is made and the process of inscribing technology with values and preferences. In technology development, "I-methodology" is widespread. In "I-methodology" developers use their own experiences, preferences, and needs as a starting point and aim to make technologies that they themselves would like to use.

The approach has some merits, perhaps particularly for motivation, but tends to result in technology with scripts that give preferential treatment to users who are similar to developers (Oudshoorn et al., 2004). Now, if technology developers were a diverse group with representation from all walks of life, the I-method might not be a problem, but that is definitely not the case. The tech industry is dominated by the worldview of "straight, white men," whose thoughts on users are seen as neutral, objective, or "entirely natural," while in reality being one perspective and experience among many.

The problem is not primarily that designers make technology based on their own experiences or cater to their own desires, but rather that the (digital) world ends up being built in a way that gives preference to users who are similar to the developers (in effect giving priority or privilege to straight, white, male users). The sector must therefore take steps to increase diversity among developers and/or include work processes that nuance the picture of who users can be (Sørensen et al., 2011; Wachter-Boettcher, 2017).

It is important here to point out that the biases in design or discriminatory effects of technology needn't be conscious or intended. In fact, much of the problem lies in how developers themselves are unaware that "useful" or "good" design is not a universal standard but rather a valuation based on their own position in society. Examples of design choices that perpetuate inequality and discrimination (from Wachter-Boettcher, 2017) are presented in Box 6C.

Box 6C.   Examples: Toxic Digitalization

Sexist chatbots	Apple's digital assistant, Siri, answered with jokes if you said, "I have been raped," or, "My husband hit me."
Minority discrimination	Facebook didn't approve Indigenous names and flagged them as breaches of name regulations.

Heteronormativity	Etsy sent an alert on Valentine's Day to buy gifts "for him," assuming that all women have a male partner (and that all users are female).
Gender capitalism	Games often have male avatars as the standard and may require payment to unlock female avatars.
Racist algorithms	Google Images automatically tagged selfies of two black individuals as "gorillas."

Individually, the presence or absence of certain features in a given app or service is not necessarily a serious issue of justice. We have all experienced installing a program and then thinking, "No, this is not for me," deleting it, and moving on with our lives. The problem is that it happens again and again in patterns that closely mirror existing structural inequalities. Meaning, if you are *not* a straight, white, able-bodied cis man, you are far more likely to encounter technology that is not suited to your needs than if you are. If we do not look at technology critically by evaluating which values it conveys, what it defines as normal, and who it includes or excludes, we can end up increasing inequalities in society through technology. To ensure that digitalization will not become a process through which those who have power gain more while those who are marginalized are further excluded, the design and implementation of digital technology must be conscious of whom the technology takes into account and whom it excludes.

It is also important to emphasize that a focusing on social justice is not just a question of ethics; it is also a point of entry into understanding why digitalization processes succeed or fail. If a technology is designed based on a small (and unrealistic) idea of who the user is, the chance that the technology will not be used increases, as does the chance that it will be used in other ways than intended. If we instead develop technology based on the idea that variation is and that users are not the same—that they have different assumptions, interests, skills, and aims—the chance that the technology will work as desired will increase.

If we let technology become "normality machines" without consideration of which normality they create and for whom, we risk producing normalities that only benefit a few at the cost of others. By being aware of both *explicit* and *implicit* design choices for technologies, we will create normalities that capture the breadth of human experience and are more inclusive.

6.5 Conclusion

In this chapter, we have shown how technologies, through their scripts and through the actor networks they are part of, are normality machines. We have shown that technology is not simply experienced as normal or not, but plays a part in forming what society considers *to be* normal. If we are not aware of which normality a technology advocates or how technologies end up having and conveying values, we are in danger of digitalizing a world with a normal that is both limiting and ostracizing—and which perpetuates and strengthens existing structures of power. Given that digital technology, so far, has been developed by a relatively small and homogenous group of people, we must be particularly careful when implementing and evaluating digital technologies to ensure we are aware of the normalities we are introducing into our lives.

References

Castleton, A. (2018). Technology and Inuit identity: Facebook use by Inuit youth. *Alter-Native: An International Journal of Indigenous Peoples*, *14*(3), 228–236.

Checkout, The. (2014, 17 April). Gendered Marketing [Video]. *YouTube*. https://www.youtube.com/watch?v=3JDmb_f3E2c

Dastin, J. (2018, 11 October). Amazon scraps secret AI recruiting tool that showed bias against women. *Reuters*. https://www.reuters.com/article/us-amazon-com-jobs-automation-insight-idUSKCN1MK08G

Fairlie, R. W. (2017). Have we finally bridged the digital divide? Smart phone and Internet use patterns by race and ethnicity. *First Monday*, *22*(9). https://doi.org/10.5210/fm.v22i9.7919.

Friz, A., & Gehl, R. W. (2016). Pinning the feminine user: Gender scripts in Pinterest's sign-up interface. *Media, Culture & Society, 38*(5), 686–703. https://doi. org/10.1177/0163443715620925.

UN. (2015, 25 October). *Closing digital divide critical to social, economic development, delegates say at second committee debate on information and communications technologies*. https://www.un.org/press/en/2015/ gaef3432.doc.htm

Labrianidis, L., & Kalogeressis, T. (2006). The digital divide in Europe's rural enterprises. *European Planning Studies, 14*(1), 23–39. https://doi. org/10.1080/09654310500339109.

Latour, B. (1992). Where are the missing masses? The sociology of a few mundane artifacts. In W. E. Bijker & J. Law (Eds.), *Shaping technology/building society*: *Studies in sociotechnical* change (pp. 225–258). MIT Press.

Lie, M. (2010): Tingenes kjønn: En utstilling om gjenstander og teknologi [The gender of things: An exhibition about artefacts and technology]. In B. Rogan & A. Bugge Amundsen (Eds.), *Samling og museum*: *Kapitler av museenes historie, praksis og ideologi* [Collection and museum: Chapters of museum history, practice and ideology] (pp. 151–163). Novus forlag.

Lindblom, T., & Räsänen, P. (2017). Between class and status? Examining the digital divide in Finland, the United Kingdom, and Greece. *The Information Society, 33*(3), 147–158. https://doi.org/10.1080/01972243.2017.129 4124.

Luyt, B. (2004). Who benefits from the digital divide? *First Monday, 9*(8). https://doi.org/10.5210/fm.v9i8.1166.

manwhohasitall. [@manwhohasitall]. (2019, 13 August). My friend is designing a laptop for men. It will be like a normal laptop, but specially adapted. What features should it have? [Tweet]. *Twitter*. https://twitter.com/ manwhohasitall/status/1161246036360335361?s=20.

Neves, B. B., Waycott, J., & Malta, S. (2018). Old and afraid of new communication technologies? Reconceptualising and contesting the "age-based digital divide." *Journal of Sociology, 54*(2), 236–248. https://doi. org/10.1177/1440783318766119.

OECD. (n.d.). *Bridging the digital divide*. https://www.oecd. org/site/schoolingfortomorrowknowledgebase/ themes/ict/bridgingthedigitaldivide.htm

Oudshoorn, N., Rommes, E., & Stienstra, M. (2004). Configuring the user as everybody: Gender and design cultures in information and communication technologies. *Science, Technology, & Human Values*, *29*(1), 30–63. https://doi.org/10.1177/0162243903259190.

Oudshoorn, N., Saetnan, A. R., & Lie, M. (2002). On gender and things: Reflections on an exhibition on gendered artifacts. *Women's Studies International Forum*, *25*(4), 471–483. https://doi.org/10.1016/S0277-5395(02)00284-4.

Rettberg, J. W. (2014). *Seeing ourselves through technology: How we use selfies, blogs and wearable devices to see and shape ourselves*. Palgrave Macmillan. https://doi.org/10.1057/9781137476661.

Sørensen, K., Faulkner, W., & Rommes, E. (2011). *Technologies of inclusion: Gender in the information society*. Tapir Academic Press.

Wachter-Boettcher, S. (2017). *Technically wrong: Sexist apps, biased algorithms, and other threats of toxic tech*. W. W. Norton & Company.

CHAPTER 7

Digital Technologies in the Past and Present

"Governments of the Industrial World, you weary giants of flesh and steel, I come from Cyberspace, the new home of Mind. On behalf of the future, I ask you of the past to leave us alone. You are not welcome among us. You have no sovereignty where we gather. […] We are creating a world that all may enter without privilege or prejudice accorded by race, economic power, military force, or station of birth. […] We will create a civilization of the Mind in Cyberspace. May it be more humane and fair than the world your governments have made before."

A Declaration of Independence of Cyberspace—Barlow, J. P. (1996)

DOI: 10.1201/9781003289555-9

Few texts exemplify excessive belief in the internet's transformative power quite like Barlow's *A Declaration of Independence of Cyberspace* from 1996—also known as "The Internet Manifesto." In pompous, yet powerful, prose, the internet is described as a technology of revolution that is going to free us from authoritarian structures, stop injustice, elevate knowledge and debate, and create a new society where you are judged on your words and actions—not your background or social status.

In hindsight, the text appears quite naïve. While the internet has undoubtedly affected society, it never became a template for a new social order dedicated to elevated debate and unbiased discussion (and it never was; see Phillips, 2015, 2019). We should, however, be careful about judging past imaginaries about the internet. The "internet manifesto" is worth revisiting because it reflects how computing technology and the internet were interpreted and understood at that point in time.

It is a reminder that the grand stories we tell about digitalization are also subject to change, and by addressing historical narratives about digital technology, we can render visible how our own, current, interpretations of digital technology are not objective, neutral, or more "correct" than those that came before. In this sense, the historical perspective allows us to challenge our experience of normality and our own taken-for-granted perceptions of digitalization. It directs our attention to how we collectively, as a society, make stories about technologies in our lives that shape how we use them. Try this for yourself in the Box 7A exercise about the telephone.

In this chapter, we draw on both historical and contemporary accounts of digitalization to address grand narratives about digital technology and its role in society and, once again, show the relationship between how we interpret technology and how technology is used.

Box 7A.   Exercise: Historical Interpretations of
Contemporary Technology—The Telephone

Examine how the telephone has changed, in terms
of both functionality and meaning, throughout its
history. To get the perspective of someone who used
the technology when it was new, have an informal chat
with some older users (such as an older relative) about
how the telephone has been used in different ways
throughout their lives. How did they use the telephone
several decades ago? Who called whom, and what
did they talk about? Which rules did their family have
regarding phone use?

In addition, you can search old newspaper articles (or
historical documents) to see how the telephone was
portrayed at different times. For example, when landline
telephones became common, when the mobile phone
was introduced, or when smart phones arrived. Reflect
on the various interpretations of the technology—both
how the users relate to the technology's functionality
and how functionality and interpretations reflect a
specific era.

7.1 Becoming a Communication Society

Barlow's internet manifesto is symptomatic of how tech
enthusiasts thought about the internet in the 1990s. It was a
period when home computers were becoming increasingly
common and the internet was made accessible to the public,
hailing the advent of personal computing. At the time, it
was seen as a radical shift in how computers should be used
and by whom. To understand why it was seen as strange
to put computers in the homes of regular people, we must
look back in time and make sense of earlier narratives about
computing technology and its visions for use.

The word *computer* was first used in 1613, but with a
somewhat different meaning. In the book *The Yong Mans
Gleanings* by Richard Brathwait, *computer* was used to
describe a person who carried out calculations and referred
to the process of breaking down complex calculations into

simpler, solvable ones (Oxford University Press, n.d.). The first *mechanical* computer is attributed to Charles Babbage, who in 1882 invented the difference engine, a tool we would call a calculator today. In 1843, Ada Lovelace wrote what would become known as the first algorithm (Lovelace, 1843)[1] and, as such, was a pioneer who saw potential beyond calculations (more historical figures in Box 7B). Nearly a century later, in Germany in 1938, Konrad Zuse created a machine called Z1 in his parents' living room. It was the first programmable electric computer—and it weighed almost a ton!

Box 7B.   History: Computer Technology Was Not (Just) Developed by Straight White Men

Computer technology is often highlighted as a field of study and employment sector with very little diversity—in short, as a an arena overpopulated by straight white men—with the explanation that "it's always been that way." But is that really the case? Both in the early phases of computer technology's history and in the years that followed, computer technology has been developed by a diverse set of people who have rarely been named in the history books. Far too often, computer technology's history is twisted into a story of straight white men's brilliance—men who, in their garages or boys' bedrooms, built the world's best, most wonderful things based on their ingenuity alone. But the reality is that women, people of color, and LGBTQ+ individuals, as well as other marginalized groups, have always been central to the development of digital technology.

In the 1950s, programming was actually understood as an activity most appropriate for women because it required painstakingly puzzling together line after line of code, which fit with the contemporary understanding that women loved puzzles (Light, 1999; Thompson, 2019). It was not until programming became high-status work that women and other minorities were pushed out and made invisible—which often happens when occupations are positioned as particularly "masculine." This, we would argue, can negatively affect the great potential digital technology has as a tool for diversification. To highlight some contributors who are rarely named (in addition to Ada Lovelace), we can name Alan Turing and Gerald "Jerry" Lawson. Turing worked for the Allies, cracking the Nazi Enigma encryptions with the help of his self-built computer, Colossus. He was later better known for creating the Turing test.[2] Turing was also gay—for which he was sentenced to chemical castration—and eventually died from cyanide poisoning. Lawson was a Black American man who, in 1976, developed the first gaming console with swappable game cartridges (Kohler, 2011). There are many more examples (see, e.g., Gaule, 2016; Streeter, 2017), but the point is that marginalized groups are often underrepresented in the stories we tell about technological progress, even though they have always been present.

The size, cost, and complexity of early computers should not be underestimated. By the 1950s, computers were in use, but only by powerful organizations with close ties to the state, primarily the military and academia, in rich nations. The machines were big enough to fill an average living room, they cost a (small) fortune, and they required extremely specialized professional knowledge to use. The computer was seen as a large calculator for complicated calculations that humans were unable to do or could do a lot easier. Like contemporary narratives about the effects of computing on work life, early computing was perceived as a tool for *control* and automation. The fear then, like now, was that computing technology would automate away important jobs and/or deteriorate workers' rights as they would have to collaborate or compete with machines that never got tired.

It is also worth noting that even if computers were usually understood as calculators, this interpretation was not universal. In 1961, the first computer game, *Spacewar!*, was developed by researchers at the Massachusetts Institute of Technology (MIT) (Juul, 1999). The interpretative flexibility of technology meant that some users interpreted the room-sized machine of resistors and cables not as a calculator but as a toy and remade computing technology to also allow for play and fun (Ask, 2023).

In the 1980s, computers became increasingly common features of office work and were used to organize, store, retrieve, and search through information. In this period, called the *information society*, users fed machines information and received desired calculations, with many similarities to how office workers today feed into and receive information from databases and spreadsheets. The conceptualization of information technology (IT) was still characterized by instrumentality, meaning a means-to-end understanding in which computers were seen as tools that could simplify the workday. However, one important change from the earlier control narrative was an increased optimism regarding the effects computing would have on society. Because computers were associated with knowledge work, the related changes were understood as an intellectualization of society. IT was seen, not just as a tool for office work but as a technology that would create new jobs and services as part of social progress from an industry society to an information society.

By the mid-1990s, computers were becoming increasingly mainstream as they moved from offices to homes and were used for both work and leisure. They were generally interpreted as a technology for "anyone and everyone" (anyone who could afford it, that is), as opposed to only professionals, and were seen as a toy as much as a tool. The acronym IT was expanded to ICT (information and communication technology), and the introduction of the C (communication) demonstrates a shift in the use and interpretations of computing toward interaction and socializing. This period is described by Levold and Spilker (2007) as the *communication society*. The communication society is characterized by increased mediated communication and the interweaving of the digital and non-digital. The period is also marked by a shift toward interaction between users (rather than solitary data processing, which were emphasized in the information society) and away from the instrumental view of computers as large calculators (as in the control society).

The communication society does not primarily denote a society where we "communicate more." Rather, it represented a shift to a society increasingly organized around technologies that made communication and interactions across various groups and borders possible. The period was also characterized by the blurring of boundaries between work and leisure, as well as between the public and private. There were no longer specific times and places for the use of digital technology—it was being used everywhere, all the time. In this sense, we may understand the communication society as the beginning of a cyborgification where humans and machines are inextricably woven together.

7.2 What Comes after the Communication Society?

On the path from a control society to a communication society, computers have gone from being state-owned machines for specialists, via office tools, to everyday technology with a long list of uses (summary in Box 7C). That the interpretations of computer technology changed so much over a few decades is partly material: computers are vastly more powerful now than before and have far more capabilities than in the 1950s. The sheer computing power and range of functionalities of a mobile phone are staggering compared to early machines. However, we should not reduce the history of computing to a series of technological innovations and developments; it is just as much about how our interpretations of these functions have changed and how new functions have spurred on new interpretations.

Levold and Spilker's work on the communication society was published in 2007, and much has changed since then. For instance, we do not call digital technology ICT anymore. When we nevertheless choose to highlight the communication society, it is both as a contrast to earlier technological discourses and because it still accurately describes the technology-society relationship we have today. Firstly, how central communication and interaction are for today's uses of digital technology (just think of how important email and social media are). Secondly, our relationship to technology is one of fusion, where the lines between humans and technology are blurred through our expansive use of digital services, tools, and infrastructure. This ubiquity affects our relationship to digital technology, and we may rightly consider ourselves to be "cyborgs" (see Box 7D).

The *communication society* is one of many possible ways of describing a digitalized society. We can understand the term

Box 7C.   Fact: The Emergence of a Communication Society

	Control Society	Information Society	Communication Society
Period	1950–1980	1980–1990	Ca. 1995–
Acronym	EDP (electronic data processing)	IT (information technology)	ICT (information and communication technology)
Keywords	Control and automation	Ordering and streamlining	Communication and interaction
View of computers	Large calculators	Text and number processing	Interactive multimedia toy
Arenas	Military/public regulation	Work/service provision	Leisure time/home
People's relationship to machines	Machine supervisors	Machine caretakers	Cyborgs (fusion of machines and humans)

Box 7D.   Theory: Cyborg Theory

Cyborg theory is a feminist theory that comes from Donna Haraway's (1987) somewhat philosophical approach to understanding how humans and technology exist together. The theory has long been popular in fields ranging from critical feminist studies to human-computer studies. A *cyborg* is a cybernetic organism, a fusion of organism and technology, of human and machine, but also of fiction and fact, myth and material reality (Moser, 1998, p. 39). Haraway's theory, or thought experiment, suggests that we can use future human-machine coexistence as a catalyst for discussing ethics, power structures, and identities. At the same time, it is difficult to avoid identity markers such as gender when, for example, developers knowingly reproduce gendered identities for robots—the more human a robot becomes, the more gendered humans make it (Søraa, 2017). Cyborg theory need not necessarily be used on physical machines; it can also be used to understand digital technologies. Our understanding in this book is that the cyborg represents hybrid couplings between human and machine; a fusion of human and technology, nature and

> culture. Haraway's philosophical—semiotic-material—
> approach was originally a thought experiment seeking to
> explain how humans transcended technology, but we see
> now that the prediction has come true—we are now all
> cyborgs in some sense (Case, 2010).

as a diagnosis of our times, that is, a description of society
that seeks to capture large and important trends across
sectors and levels (Hammershøj, 2015). Like other diagnoses
of the times, communication society is an imprecise
description, as you will always find many counterexamples.
There are, for example, non-users of the internet who do
not wish to be cyborgs and who find non-digital ways to go
about their everyday lives. The point of a diagnosis of the
times is, as such, not to provide a description that covers
everything and everyone but rather to articulate some traits
that characterize change in the present and that can help us
to understand the larger shifts society is going through.

To consider what changes to contemporary society you find
important, take a moment to reflect on how you relate to
the present and which overall narrative you would use to
describe how society has changed with digitalization. To
what degree do you think communication society is a good
description of the present? Which aspects are recognizable,
and which seem strange or irrelevant? If you were to set up
an era *after* the communication society, what would be the
starting point? And what would you call it? What do you
believe characterize our view of digital technology, where is
it used, and what affects our relationship with technology?

Later in this chapter, we will present some possible
diagnoses of the times and concepts that identify trends in
digitalization. We again emphasize that none of these terms
are entirely comprehensive—they necessarily focus on
some elements of the digital present and omit others—but
they can be useful for capturing changes in society linked
to digitalization and can thus help you turn your attention
toward some critical aspects of digitalization processes.

As you read, we ask you to reflect on how they match
with your own perceptions and your own diagnosis of the
times: are they complementary or conflicting? Why do they
highlight the same or different aspects? What can you learn

from other descriptions to improve your own diagnosis of the times?

7.3 Digitalization and Some Sample Diagnoses of the Times

- *Network society*: A network is, simply put, a way of organizing actors so that everyone can have direct contact with each other and doesn't have to, for example, go through a middle manager or representative. A family is an example of a network because all actors can talk directly to each other. Humans are network-building creatures, and networks have always existed, even long before the internet. With the internet, we have created new and increasingly complex and large networks for organizing society. The term *network society* describes a "society where the key social structures and activities are organized around electronically processed information networks" (Castells, 2004, p. 3). It is not just that we are building social networks or that we have the internet, but that we are also configuring society around them. Castells attributed the transition to a networked society to the restructuring of industry as a market, the civil rights movement, and a revolution in information and communications technology.
- *Platform society*: The platform society focuses on digital platforms and how they shape and affect the ways in which we communicate, work, shop, participate in democratic processes, and organize ourselves (Van Dijck et al., 2018). "Platformization" is characterized by "datafication" (through which more and more aspects of our lives are quantified), "commodification" (through which objects, activities, feelings, and ideas are transformed into commodities), and "selection" (through which algorithms steer users toward specific, tailored content). The term is also associated with criticism of platforms, specifically a lack of regulation, and how we need governmental control of the technologies (and data) that are vital to our private lives, businesses, and public lives.
- *Acceleration society*: Acceleration society refers to how society is changing at an increasing speed. Acceleration is described by sociologist Hartmut Rosa (2013) as a

characteristic of modernity—and consequently, of today's society. Even if digitalization promised more (free) time from more efficient and automated solutions, it has instead created a social world in constant flux where we experience less and less time as simply "the present." Simultaneously, theoreticians like Wajcman (2018) emphasize that it is not a given that the feeling of "lack of time" should be a consequence of digital technology. Our interpretations, institutions, and practices do not necessarily have to follow the logic of immediacy, in which, for example, emails should be answered immediately or we should be available 24/7. Wajcman's critique highlights how various groups in society experience acceleration in different ways, where highly educated professionals, in particular, tend to experience this acceleration.

In addition to diagnoses of the times, there are a number of concepts that have been developed in response to digitalization. Terms like *attention economy* (Simon, 1971; Terranova, 2012) which refer to a shift from information scarcity to information excess in society, meaning the challenge is no longer accessing information; the challenge is to capture the public's and users' attention. The *gig-economy* (Wood et al., 2018; Friedman, 2014) describes a job market characterized by contract work often accessed via digital platforms (e.g., Uber, Airbnb). Finally, the *internet of things* (Atzori et al., 2010) is a term used to describe how everyday technologies are connected to the internet and made "smart." For example, an alarm clock that does not only to wake you up but also tells you the weather, turns on the news, and tells your smart coffee maker to start brewing a cup.

New phenomena require new words, so it is not surprising that many of the changes we see in the wake of digitalization also have resulted in the creation of new terms. Maybe you have your own terms that help you explain society and make sense of it. Based both on history and several diagnoses of the present, it is time for you to try to define some trends in contemporary society. What is *your* diagnosis for the present? (see Box 7E).

Atzori, L., Iera, A., & Morabito, G. (2010). The internet of things: A survey. *Computer Networks, 54*(15), 2787–2805. https://doi.org/10.1016/j.comnet.2010.05.010.

Barlow, J. P. (1996, 8 February). *A declaration of the independence of cyberspace.* https://www.eff.org/cyberspace-independence

Case, A. (2010). We are all cyborgs now [video]. *TED.* https://www.ted.com/talks/amber_case_we_are_all_cyborgs_now?language=en

Castells, M. (2004). *The network society: A cross-cultural perspective.* Edward Elgar.

Essinger, J. (2014). *Ada's algorithm: How Lord Byron's daughter Ada Lovelace launched the digital age.* Melville House.

Friedman, G. C. (2014). Workers without employers: Shadow corporations and the rise of the gig economy. *Review of Keynesian Economics, 2*(2), 171–188. https://doi.org/10.4337/roke.2014.02.03.

Gaule, D. (2016, 23 June). Programming pride: 10 LGBT pioneers of computer science. *New Relic.* https://blog.newrelic.com/culture/10-lgbt-computer-science-pioneers/

Hammershøj, L. G. (2015). Diagnosis of the times vs description of society. *Current Sociology, 63*(2), 140–154. https://doi.org/10.1177/0011392114556577

Haraway, D. (1987). A manifesto for cyborgs: Science, technology, and socialist feminism in the 1980s. *Australian Feminist Studies, 2*(4), 1–42. https://doi.org/10.1080/08164649.1987.9961538.

Juul, J. (1999). *A clash between game and narrative: A thesis on computer games and interactive fiction.* University of Copenhagen.

Kohler, H. (2011, 11 April). Jerry Lawson, inventor of modern game console, dies at 70. *Wired.* https://www.wired.com/2011/04/jerry-lawson-dies/

Levold, N., & Spilker, H. S. (Eds.). (2007). *Kommunikasjonssamfunnet: Moral, praksis og digital teknologi* [Communication society: Moral, practice and digital technology]. Universitetsforlaget.

Light, J. S. (1999). When computers were women. *Technology and culture, 40*(3), 455–483. https://www.jstor.org/stable/25147356.

Lovelace, A. A. (1843). Notes by A. A. L. [August Ada Lovelace]. *Taylor's Scientific Memoirs, 3,* 666–731. https://www.fourmilab.ch/babbage/ sketch.html.

Moser, I. (1998). Kyborgens rehabilitering [Rehabilitating the cyborg]. In K. Asdal, A. J. Berg, B. Brenna, I. Moser, & L. M. Rustad (Eds.), *Betatt av viten, bruksanvisninger til Donna Haraway* [Taken by science, a guide to Donna Haraway] (pp. 39–74). Spartacus Forlag.

Oxford University Press. (n.d.). Computer. *Oxford English Dictionary*. https://www.oed.com/view/Entry/37975.

Phillips, W. (2015). *This is why we can't have nice things: Mapping the relationship between online trolling and mainstream culture*. MIT Press.

Phillips, W. (2019). It wasn't just the trolls: Early internet culture, "fun," and the fires of exclusionary laughter. *Social Media + Society, 5*(3). https://doi.org/10.1177/2056305119849493.

Rosa, H. (2013). *Social acceleration: A new theory of modernity*. Columbia University Press.

Simon, H. A. (1971). Designing organizations for an information-rich world. In M. Greenberger (Ed.), *Computers, communications, and the public interest* (pp. 40–41). The Johns Hopkins Press.

Streeter, J. (2017, 1 February). 7 Black pioneers in computer science. *New Relic*. https://blog.newrelic.com/culture/black-history-month-computer-science-infographic/

Søraa, R. A. (2017). Mechanical genders: how do humans gender robots? *Gender, Technology and Development, 21*(1–2), 99–115.

Terranova, T. (2012). Attention, economy and the brain. *Culture Machine*, 13. https://culturemachine.net/wp-content/uploads/2019/01/465-973-1-PB.pdf

Thompson, C. (2019, 13 February). The secret history of women in coding. *The New York Times*. https://www.nytimes.com/2019/02/13/magazine/women-coding-computer-programming.html

Van Dijck, J., Poell, T., & De Waal, M. (2018). *The platform society: Public values in a connective world*. Oxford University Press.

Wajcman, J. (2018). Digital technology, work extension and the acceleration society. *German Journal of Human Resource Management, 32*(3–4), 168–176. https://doi.org/10.1177/2397002218775930.

Wood, A. J., Graham, M., Lehdonvirta, V., & Hjorth, I. (2018). Good gig, bad gig: Autonomy and algorithmic control in the global gig economy. *Work, Employment and Society, 33*(1), 56–75. https://doi.org/10.1177/0950017018785616.

PART 3
Empirical Cases

CHAPTER 8

Digitalization of Health

Networks of Care and Technology

DOI: 10.1201/9781003289555-11

Maintaining good enough physical and mental health to manage everyday life is important for most people. To this effect, many digital technologies are developed, tested, and used so that people can live healthier lives and to relieve suffering and illness. But what does the digitalization of health entail on a user level? What assumptions about health are materialized in the technology that is being developed? In this chapter, we will look at the link between health and digitalization, specifically how our conceptualization of "good health" is shaped by technology. We explore how digital technologies construct understandings of health through the examples of social robots, games for exercise, and online support groups. This chapter addresses physical, mental, and social health and explores the consequences of simplifying, streamlining, and optimizing health care through digitalization processes.

8.1 In Search of Good Health: Robots to the Rescue?

Health, both physical, mental, and social, is a recurring topic in films about technology's possibilities and limitations. In the Disney film *Big Hero 6* (Hall & Williams, 2014), mental and social health are central to the story of two brothers who are ingenious robot inventors. The movie follows 14-year-old

Hiro after he loses his big brother in a tragic fire and his relationship with Baymax, a social robot left behind by his brother whose purpose is to help and care for him. Baymax is a large, puffy creation with a good-natured and cuddly appearance who is liberal with hugs. The protagonist is able to face dangers and challenges with the help of the social robot, with whom he develops an increasingly emotional bond. In the movie, the relationship between Baymax and Hiro is portrayed as central to healing Hiro's mental health. However, the movie also depicts how the robot becomes an (almost) fully-fledged being that through brotherly comradery becomes a social replacement, as well as saving him from physical danger.

The movie *Robot and Frank* (Schreier, 2012) is also about robot relationships but is focused on how technologies can enable older adults to live in their own homes as long as possible. In the film, a retired diamond thief, Frank, has early onset of dementia and is given a choice by his children: to get a social robot or be sent to a retirement home. Frank reluctantly chooses the robot and is soon put on a strict health care regime by his robot companion. The robot frames care as a holistic web of physical activities leading to mental wellbeing, and replaces unhealthy fast food with fruit and vegetables, and encourages exercising and gardening as hobbies. The film portrays the tensions that can exist around care, specifically intergenerational care, and how technology affects this relationship. It shows how technology can perform many types of care tasks, which can also include performing care tasks that some wish were reserved for humans (Søraa et al., 2020b). For example, Frank's grown daughter moves back home to her father because she feels guilty about having a robot take care of him, yet she quickly discovers that the robot does many things she finds neither engaging nor interesting, like making breakfast and dusting. The film emphasizes questions of what care entails, who should provide it, in what form, as well as how humans experience being controlled and forced to conform to technological regimes. In the end, however, the film portrays the social care of humans as superior to that of robots because they cannot understand human relationships.

The two movies both depict close relationships between humans and robots. In both movies, the robots are engaged in improving the main character's health. However, where *Big Hero 6*'s conclusion is that good health (and happiness) is achieved by accepting the care of the robot, *Robot and Frank* is a story about how important human relationships are to us and that good health is (also) reliant on connection with other humans. Both fictional examples address tension related to how robots—which are digital technologies with a physical form—can help humans achieve better health, and how health is affected by which technologies an individual can access.

To account for the role of technologies in health, a sociotechnical perspective can be used to address health as something constructed of a complex actor network of different people, technologies, institutions, and knowledges. Health should not be reduced to something purely physical or individual. Rather, what we consider "good health" is the result of how technologies and society (among other factors) are organized.

8.2 Digital Technology for Better Health?

The World Health Organization defines health as "a state of complete physical, mental, and social well-being and not merely the absence of disease or infirmity" (WHO, n.d.-a). This definition grew out of a critique of earlier understandings of health that were either about "not being sick" or entirely focused only on physical health—which is why mental and social health were added. How we understand health has changed over time, and the fact that we still discuss what we should be able to expect health-wise from both ourselves and society illustrates that health is not a given. Rather, health is an expression of how contemporary society thinks about wellbeing and illness, and the concept is subject to change and influence, including from digitalization and user practices of healthcare technologies.

For a more inclusive approach to health, Fugelli and Ingstad (2001, p. 3601) define health based on three concepts— wholeness, pragmatism, and individualism:

- *Wholeness*: Health is a holistic phenomenon. Health is interwoven in all aspects of life and society.
- *Pragmatism*: Health is a relative phenomenon. Health is experienced and evaluated based on what people find reasonable to expect given their age, illness or injury, and social situation.
- *Individualism*: Health is a personal phenomenon. Humans are different; therefore, health as a goal and the path to health varies from individual to individual.

We should approach health as a holistic and relative phenomenon that includes both body and mind and encompasses intricate social networks with other people. The sociotechnical perspective adds to this by making visible how health is networked with institutions and technologies, in which medicine, pill dispensers, robots, crutches, and walkers make up decisive parts (what we describe in Chapter 3 as an *actor network*).

To understand how technology shapes our understanding of health, consider how disability is decided, in large part, by what our technological infrastructures, health services, and social norms define as "normal" (Hamraie & Fritsch [2019]; for further readings on care and disability, see Piepzna-Samarasinha [2018]). Take architecture as an example: if every building in a city is universally designed (designed to be used by everyone) with ramps, elevators, and wide, flat streets, moving around that city using a wheelchair would be rather hassle-free. In comparison, a city with cobblestone streets and flights of stairs at every entrance (not universally designed) would be practically unusable for someone using a wheelchair. The person using a wheelchair is the same, but the severity of their mobility disability increases or decreases depending on what the architecture lets them access.

Just as architecture plays a role in defining mobility, so too does digital technology play a role in forming what counts as good or bad health, including what we understand as disability and illness.

Technologies made for caring purposes—whether they are classified for welfare, wellbeing, older adults, or assisted living—have for long been a focus for science and technology studies and related disciplines in many countries outside Scandinavia. Take, for example, the English healthcare system that aimed to "create a digital health learning ecosystem across a national health service" (Cresswell et al., 2021, p. 1), Japan and their focus on robots to mitigate aging population issues (Robertson, 2019; Wright, 2023), and the complex US systems of care provision (Knopes, 2019; Burstin et al., 2016)—all of which show that care, especially in a digital form, are complex sociotechnical choices with no "one-size fits all." Test a digital tool for health yourself in Box 8A. Different regions and communities prioritize differently based on demographics, resources (both human and financial), and many, many other factors.

Box 8A.   Exercise: Meet Your New (Robot) Psychologist

Mental illness affects a large number of people and is exacerbated by the lack of funding for mental health. In this exercise, you are going to try out a robot alternative to a psychologist, a so-called *robot psychologist*, which is a chatbot designed to support those with mental illnesses. Robot psychologists are designed to give users advice and provide social contact. The programs appear autonomous in that they are programmed to appear to have a personality and "being." In this exercise, you will have a chat with just such a program.

Choose one of the popular chatbots from the App Store or online, for example, Replica, and use 15 minutes to chat with the chatbot. Reflect as you do so: How does the conversation flow? What can the chatbot answer? What can't it answer? How does it speak to you, and what does it seem to learn about you during the discussion? Does it feel like you are talking to someone? Why or why not? For a more advanced exercise, take a look at the chatbot's script. Who made it and why, and who are the intended users? The goal is to explore how chatbots mimic human interaction. Do not take it's "advice" seriously.

There are several ways digital technology relates to health. One example is *e-health*, which has been described as "an emerging field in the intersection of medical informatics, public health, and business, referring to health services and information delivered or enhanced through the Internet and related technologies" (Eysenbach, 2001). It draws on the concept of "telemedicine" from the 1980s and includes, for example, digital medical records which collect and systematize health information about individuals and make it available to patients and/or healthcare providers. This comes with its own problems, like vulnerability to cyberattacks and the requirement of digital literacy. As such, some countries use only physical records, which, although more cumbersome, are safe(r) from digital sabotage. More recently, *m-health*—that is, mobile health—has also become an important term. M-health refers to technologies individuals carry on their bodies daily, like mobile phones. Step counters are a good example of m-health technology.

Both e-health and m-health are of interest to many governments. In the Norwegian national e-health portfolio, digitalization of the healthcare sector is expected to be a driving factor for better and more efficient health care services. Digitalization of work processes, better coherence in patient processing, better use of health data, and a shared foundation for digital services are emphasized as important areas. The goals outlined in the e-health portfolio are comprehensive and challenging. One example is how the aim of implementing health technologies universally across various municipalities will have challenges due to the different size and composition of populations, geographies, and resources (Kleiven-Jørgensen, 2020).

8.3 Welfare Technology: A Nordic Approach?

The world's population is rapidly aging. According to the WHO (n.d.-a), "Between 2015 and 2050, the proportion of the world's population over 60 years will nearly double from 12% to 22%." In the face of an aging population, known as "the silver tsunami," different strategies have been developed to meet the upcoming challenges.

Norway has invested heavily in technologies that can help older adults live at home as long as possible. In 2018, 12% of Norwegians were over 70. By 2060, this group will make up 19% of the population, so nearly one in every five people will be over 70. While today there are 4.5 workers for every older adult, there will only be 2.5 by 2060. In addition, there is a critical shortage of healthcare workers in Norway, and more and more research suggests workers have too little time to carry out the tasks required by their professions (Billeter-Koponen & Fredén, 2005). In Norway, politicians argue for innovation, and especially technological innovation, as the solution to these problems (see "Technological Solutionism" from Chapter 1 (Section 1.4) and "Technological fix" from Chapter 2 (Section 2.1)).

In the Nordic countries, another key term related to digitalization and health is *welfare technology*. Welfare technology refers to technology used to make life better and easier for people by improving safety, proficiency, and wellbeing. It also involves changing the way services are designed to provide care. Since our understandings of the world, including values, shape technological design (see Chapter 5 on *Script*), welfare technology may be understood as a technological expression of how Nordic countries think about health.

Welfare technology is a Nordic term that does not easily translate outside the region.[1] The term was first coined in Denmark in 2007 and was further defined in the Norwegian context as "technological assistance that contributes to increased safety, security, social participation, mobility, and physical and cultural activity, and strengthens the individual's ability to cope with everyday life despite illness and social, mental, or physical disability" (NOU, 2011, p. 99). The definition further emphasizes that welfare technology should make care work easier for relatives and reduce the need for institutional care. The concept has similarities with other terms but is different in key ways: *care technology* (focusing on caring features of technologies), *gerontechnology* (care for older adults specifically), or *assistive technologies* (which are seen more as specific tools and less as holistic care networks), to name a few. While welfare technology is a direct and literal translation of the

Scandinavian term (no. velferdsteknologi), the term welfare has specific and local meanings. Due to this, we recommend non-Nordic readers think of "welfare technology" more as "wellbeing technology"—focused on all citizens living good lives—rather than economic welfare programs that specifically target poor or vulnerable groups.

Welfare technology is, in other words, an umbrella term accommodating a number of different technologies, political visions for health and the healthcare sector, as well as many different types of users, patient groups, and healthcare workers. While older users are emphasized in welfare technology discourse, they are not the only users, and young people can also benefit from these technologies. For example, in their research on disabled children and youth, Trondsen and Knarvik (2017, p. 3) have found that welfare technology provides "increased participation in and mastery of daily activities and chores."

We can sort key welfare technologies into four categories (Nakrem & Sigurjónsson, 2017): safety and security technologies, assistive and wellness technologies, social and communication technologies, and care and treatment technologies (Box 8B). These are not exclusive categories, and most welfare technologies will probably fit within several categories depending on their use. Zoom can, in one instance, be a communication platform at work while also becoming a technology for mitigating loneliness, showing how all technology is *interpretively flexible* and is defined through use.

Health technology does not have to be custom-made or acquired via one's family doctor or other care providers to be used for health purposes. "Welfare technology" and "e-health" are important concepts in discussions about health and technology, but there are multiple other technologies that also contribute to our health. Patients and users have an amazing ability to innovate and find ways to use technology to help themselves (Robinson et al., 2015; Frennert, 2016). In what remains of this chapter, we will present three different technologies that show how digitalizing health happens from multiple perspectives. The first example is about "Tessa," a robot flowerpot, and how this welfare technology reshapes the home.

Box 8B. Fact: Four Categories of Welfare Technology

Safety and security technologies help people before and after an injury occurs by alerting healthcare workers or other caregivers that they need assistance. Classic examples of such technologies include personal safety alarms (which allow people to live at home longer because they can press a button on a wristband if they fall), digital pill dispensers (which remind users of when they need to take their medications and dispense the correct doses), GPS tracking (which can be used to find, e.g., individuals with dementia who get lost), and medical sensors. The purpose of these types of welfare technologies is to prevent accidents. They often involve depriving the user of some freedoms in exchange for safety.

Assistive and wellness technologies include technologies that compensate for reduced senses or functions, such as hearing aids, glasses, heart rate monitors, crutches, and walkers. Many of these technologies are thought of as general-use technologies, and these technologies are suitable for directly remedying, replacing, or compensating for a loss of function.

Social and communication technologies help people who are lonely and lack social contact with others. Welfare technology that is used to improve social contact often includes standard communication technologies like video chats (e.g., Zoom, Skype, or MS Teams). However, there are also technologies specially made for those with low digital literacy, like the "KOMP" tablet, which has just one button to press when answering a call. A more advanced example is social robots, which offer services that link people together through teleoperation or which themselves talk to the user. Japan is a leader in the production and use of social robots, including the android Pepper and the robot seal Paro.

Care and treatment technologies can help patients who must undergo treatment programs to cure or treat illnesses. If the illness is persistent or chronic, the technology aims to help reduce its effects. An example of this is medical telemonitoring, which allows a patient who has been sent home to continue to receive care from healthcare professionals digitally, with the help of communication technologies.

8.3 Talking Flowerpots: Welfare Technology in the Home

Even if wellbeing is the goal of welfare technology, the motivation for heavy investment in the field is economic and should be seen in relation to the "silver tsunami." In short, it is far more expensive to house someone in a healthcare facility than to pay healthcare providers to make home visits. Consequently, solutions that allow people to live at home are a socioeconomic benefit (and perhaps a necessity), even if it is not without cost to retrofit homes for inhabitants in need of care. Add to this the fact that many older adults express a desire to live at home as long as possible, and the home emerges as an increasingly important site for care work and welfare technologies. As our first empirical example of health technology, we have therefore chosen "Tessa," which is a welfare technology made for home, based on a research project that examined how older adults with dementia can live at home for longer (Casaccia et al., 2019; Søraa et al., 2020a, 2021).

People with dementia often forget appointments, have difficulty following simple routines, and struggle to establish new habits. To address this, the research project eWare examined whether you could prolong participants' time living at home by using robot and sensor technologies to send reminders, as well as support users in maintaining habits and routines. The system tested by researchers had two components: (1) a sensor system that learned the habits of the older adult with dementia (primary user) and could be monitored by family members and healthcare workers like home nurses (secondary users); and (2) a robot flowerpot called "Tessa" (developed in the Netherlands) made to remember user habits and also tell through its loudspeaker messages and placed in the living room of the primary user (see Figure 8.1).

FIGURE 8.1 The social robot Tessa together with an ordinary flower pot.

One of the tasks delegated to the social robot Tessa was to remind the primary user to eat. To do this, the system first used several weeks to "learn" about the eating habits of the user by mapping when the refrigerator door was opened (via a sensor in the door). After a pattern had been established, the system would engage if the refrigerator door did not open in the regular time slot. So, if a user would usually have breakfast every day between 8 and 9, and the clock reached 10 without the user's opening the refrigerator door, the sensor system would alert Tessa the robot, who spoke out loud, to the user, saying, "It's ten o'clock! Would you like to eat breakfast?"

Tessa is designed to look like a flowerpot covered in wood and felt, which gives it a distinctly "non-technological" look. By hiding the technical components behind natural materials, it is scripted for users who are not technologically competent and/or who are not used to using digital technology. As such, the script matches stereotypes about older adults as digitally incompetent and disinterested in technology. However, studies assessing the digital competence of older adults differ, and Olson et al. (2011) warn against relying on such stereotypes because there is a great deal of variation in their abilities. This is supported by Quan-Haase et al. (2018), who encourage us to ignore notions that older adults "cannot use digital technology"— as such stereotyping of users risks making homogenous categories. The design of the robot as a flowerpot also clearly dictates that this is a technology for the home, where it will become a natural part of its surroundings. Researchers found that Tessa quickly became a natural part of everyday life for its users, and the analysis of the domestication process gives us insight into the challenges and possibilities surrounding welfare technology in the home while keeping in mind that design is often based on stereotypes. See also Zhang (2023).

Research on Tessa showed that to use the technology well, instruction was necessary. Instruction is often a necessary part of implementing new technology. Interestingly, with Tessa, the primary users (people with dementia) were not the only ones who needed to learn how to use the technology. Also, secondary users, like family members who had responsibility for overseeing the primary users' daily routines, had to become proficient users. This illustrates that even though welfare technology is intended to make our lives easier and safer and relieve the need for care, family members still have a great deal of responsibility for performing care and must acquire new skills when taking care of their parents. In the case of Tessa, we learn that this can include "taking care of their technology." Welfare technology is therefore a part of and creates an *actor network* with far more actors than just an older adult user and a flowerpot robot: relatives, sensors, fridges, policies, and municipal services are a few of the many actors (human and nonhuman) included in welfare technology networks, as the example of Tessa demonstrates.

The robot was a social component in an otherwise quiet, and potentially lonely, daily routine for the primary user (that is, the person with dementia). However, the study also discovered that the security features were seen as important for secondary users (family and friends). As long as both primary and secondary users have compatible interpretations, technologies like Tessa can ease care work and support both user groups. However, it is worth considering what would happen should a conflict emerge. Tessa supports the security and wellbeing of individuals with dementia but is also beneficial to the dementia patient's family, who feel more secure and involved due to the surveillance and communication the technology allows. We should not presume that primary and secondary users will always be in agreement and must be aware of whose needs matter most, or rather, who would be best equipped to argue their case should a conflict arise.

Policies, cost analyses, and research on older adults all suggest that allowing individuals to live in their own homes as long as possible is a good thing—if done responsibly. Technologies like Tessa are examples of how technology can make this possible by (1) helping older adult users in their everyday lives and (2) by giving relatives support and ways to intervene if necessary.

While welfare technology, like social robots, can be a source of wellbeing in users' lives, Sharkey and Sharkey (2012a, b) warn against an uncritical adoption of welfare technologies and social robots. They map out several possible negative effects: (1) a potential reduction in human contact, (2) increased feelings of objectification and a loss of control, (3) loss of privacy, (4) loss of personal freedom, (5) deception and infantilization, and (6) power, control, and whether it is ethically acceptable to use robots to monitor older people. It is, as always, important to think broadly and holistically about who is affected by technology, how, and why. Turkle (2012) asks, among other questions, whether we are becoming "alone together" when we increasingly live our lives with and through digital technology—and if technology that is designed to make us social can also have the opposite effect?

8.4 Exergames: Gamifying Health

Exergames (exercise games) are games that combine game design and technology with workout equipment or activities. The idea is to employ the motivating and engaging aspects of game design to make it easier to start and complete workouts. Can games be the solution to boring workouts and an increasingly sedentary and overweight population? Most exergames combine exercise, like an exercise bike or step machine, with game technologies so that the physical movements have consequences in the game. One example is Pedal Tanks, developed by the Norwegian University of Science and Technology (NTNU), where players steer tanks by stepping on the pedals of exercise bikes and pressing on specialized controllers. Players are split into two teams, each with two players, and the game involves taking the other team's flag while guarding your own (known as "capture the flag"). Being fit is an advantage, but so is having a tactical mind and good eye–hand coordination if you are going to take out your opponent (Hagen et al., 2015). There are also commercially developed exercise games, like Pokemon GO (Niantic Inc., 2016), where you walk around the neighborhood to capture and collect Pokemon and other resources. Other examples are gaming platforms like the Nintendo Switch, which let users connect movement sensors to a console so that input is controlled by moving the body rather than pressing on controllers.

Exergames are a form of *serious* game, meaning they are not only for entertainment but also have a "serious" purpose (Susi et al., 2007). The idea behind serious games, regardless of whether they are for working out, learning, or something else, is to take advantage of how the game format supports fun, interactivity, and engagement. Research on serious games has shown how common game design ideals also make them suited to motivate and engage users. For example, games are motivating because they are designed around progression, where one can clearly see one's own advances and is faced with new challenges as one's skills improve (Gee, 2007).

Exergames can be understood as an attempt to make a new *script* for exercise technology where values like playfulness and entertainment are highlighted. The envisioned users are people who want to exercise but do not have enough motivation or do not train because they find it boring. The underlying premise of exergames scripts is that the greatest obstacle to fitness is a lack of motivation and that exercise is boring, something the gamified design addresses. However, there are many other reasons why the general population is inactive, including sedentary working lives, injury or illness, poor finances, expensive gyms, and a general lack of time. In exergames' script, all these problems are reduced to a question of individual motivation for working out and if we can make exercising "fun enough." As such, we can also understand exergames as a technological fix, where a technology is presented as a simple solution to large and complex problems (linked to public health).

We are not arguing against exergames, as exercise can certainly be boring, and exergames can be beneficial for their users. Rather, what we are arguing is that the narrative surrounding such technology tends to displace other, more comprehensive political solutions, such as stricter requirements for food production, shorter working days, or better financing of gyms, sports clubs, and healthcare. From studies of health apps that also use gaming elements in their design, we have seen that exercise technologies that try to "fix" users' motivation can be problematic when they are institutionalized and made into the solution (with a capital S) for health problems by both employers (who want fitter, more productive workers) and health services (who want inexpensive solutions to problems) (Lupton, 2014).

In sum, we can say that workout games, through their design (including their functions, aesthetics, and settings), see exercise as an individual concern for which a lack of motivation and passion are the main problems and for which the solution is making exercise fun. On the one hand, exergames can be seen as an important service and as an innovative way to think about exercise because they acknowledge how important joy and desire are for sticking to exercise routines. On the other hand, such technology is in danger of individualizing exercise and health issues, making invisible other factors that affect health, such as healthcare services, disabilities, and social and working contexts.

8.5 Support Groups in Social Media: Communities for Mental Health

Our third and last example of health technology is social media. Specifically, how social media is used to promote better mental health through online support groups. Mental illnesses are widespread, with almost 1 billion people having a mental illness (WHO, n.d.-a), and an estimated 25% of all people will develop a mental illness during their lifetime, leading to 14.3% of all deaths worldwide (Global Mental Health Statistics, 2022). In Norway, the number of students who experience mental illness is even higher: four out of ten students report experiencing signs of mental illness, and the proportion of students with serious mental illness increased from one in six in 2010 to more than one in five in 2018. Female students are particularly subject to mental illness, reporting both higher levels and more serious effects than male students (Studentenes helse-og trivselsundersøkelse, 2018). There are complex reasons why students experience this, but recurring themes include increased pressure to succeed, body image, pressure to drink, and loneliness. Can support groups on social media help?

Support groups on the internet are not new. A study from 2002 on Norwegian forums to discuss mental health showed that users experienced the forums as valuable because they were a rich source of experience-based knowledge from others in the same situation and because they felt supported by other users. They felt it was easier to share their stories anonymously online and found a community around something in their life that usually made them lonely (Kummervold et al., 2002). More than 20 years later, the reasons that people use social media to discuss mental health are largely the same: community, acceptance, and knowledge. Since mental illness often leads to isolation due to feelings of shame but also due to the barriers the ailments create (e.g., social anxiety), online support groups with low thresholds for participation are particularly valuable. Through online support groups, users can gain access to information about their own mental illness, find support to fight stigmas, and receive encouragement to seek professional help. Even when communities are not clearly defined, as, for example, on TikTok, users engage with mental health content to learn more about their situation, get practical advice on how to manage everyday life, and feel "seen" (Milton et al., 2023)

The appeal of support groups on social media is in part due to the possibilities that technology offers and what possibilities it holds depends on the platform. On social media, users can choose to be anonymous, something that lowers the threshold for participation and sharing experiences that many fear will lead to social exclusion. In addition, communication is asynchronous (in contrast to face-to-face discussions, where questions are answered immediately), which means that users can take their time articulating themselves and reflecting on what they want to share, even returning to a post to read it again to clarify their understanding of it. The high degree of control over communication can increase users' self-confidence (Naslund et al., 2016).

There are also some risks linked to online support groups, namely that users can be given advice from unqualified people, that they can become increasingly disconnected from everyday life because they are focused on their online world, or that they can experience harassment (see Box 8C). Nonetheless, research shows that most users are critical of the information they get online; for some, socialization online is better than none at all; and there is little evidence suggesting that people suffering from mental illnesses are particularly prone to harassment online (although they are more likely to be exposed to discrimination in general) (Naslund et al., 2016). On platforms like TikTok, where content is algorithmically curated, users can find it challenging to control the algorithm and may experience it as a "runaway train" that pulls them toward content they are not interested in, or at least not all the time (for example, content dealing with trauma) (Milton et al., 2023).

Box 8C.   Advice: Seek Help Before It Gets Too Hard

We would like to point out that even if such support groups can fulfill important functions, in that they create acceptance and belonging as well as being a place to share experience-based knowledge, they should function as an addition to professional services—something they often do. If you feel that everyday life is gloomy, which statistics unfortunately suggest is likely to be the case given the prevalence of mental illness among students, we recommend that you contact your GP or student health services immediately. If you break a bone, you need help to heal. The same goes for mental health. Professional help helps!

As an example of health technology, social media is interesting because the technology was not originally designed to improve health, and as such, it shows how technology is *interpretively flexible* and that people can find other areas of use for it than the developers intended. As a result, we can understand the development of support groups in discussion forums as an example of technology's being *domesticated* to have another function than was originally intended: from a technology for sharing everyday stories and interesting links to a technology that is (also) for health. The example is also interesting because health technology is often top-down, as it is with both e-health and welfare technology, while support groups for mental health are bottom-up; that is, the users have defined what the technology means and how it should be used.

8.6 Digitalization Makes the Actor Network of Health Visible

Across the three examples, we see that "better health" is a major reason for developing and/or using technology, but also that health is configured in different ways. If we look at how these different technologies are *scripting* good health— that is, which values and conceptualizations of health are materialized in the design—we will find different messages. In Tessa's example, good health is being able to live at home, being independent enough to manage everyday life (even with cognitive declines), and having relatives on standby to help when necessary. For exergaming, good health is about being entertained while hitting your exercise goals. Social media is not aimed at health per se but is instead designed to foster social bonds and exchange knowledge, and as such, it indirectly suggests that good health relates to knowledge (of one's own illness or problems) and a sense of belonging.

To maintain a critical approach to digitalization processes, we must pay special attention to what is and is not being digitized. Digital solutions are often portrayed as revolutionary systems ready to upheave the status quo, while the reality is that digitalization more often involves making some elements digital while also enmeshing the digital with existing non-digital technologies and systems.

That is also the case with Tessa. Tessa is a welfare technology designed for safety and security as well as socialization and communication. However, if primary users have an unforeseen problem or simply wish to do something out of the ordinary, relatives and healthcare workers have to step in. Even if Tessa converts "having to keeping an eye on" to "automated surveillance with alerts," it is still humans that must intervene and act when an alert is given. Instead of thinking of welfare technology as something that replaces family, care workers, or care institutions, welfare technology is something that is included in and shapes how care is performed. Returning to the movie *Big Hero 6* from the intro, we see that Tessa has many similarities with the robot Baymax: it has a nontechnical appearance, is made of soft/fluffy materials, and aims to be a friendly supporter in everyday life. However, in contrast to *Big Hero 6*, Tessa does not replace the need for human care (even if some of the tasks are made easier or is fulfilled by the technology) and shows how complicated care work is and thus difficult to automate.

Exergaming, in turn, combines exercise technology with gaming technology to create a new hybrid technology. By adding playful elements and experiences, the goal is to make exercise more entertaining and, hopefully, lead to people exercising more often and for longer. Exergaming can change the experience of exercising by transforming the mindless pressing of pedals into an epic battle for your opponent's flag. However, it is worth noting that the technology does not exercise *for* you. Since exercise is dependent on the movement of one's body, exercise is something that cannot be *delegated* to technology (for now), and the changes invoked by exergaming are about meaning and experience, with the physical movements remaining the same.

Lastly, online support groups can offer acceptance, belonging, knowledge and opportunities for learning about professional help for people struggling with mental health issues. That the arena is digital makes it more accessible, and that the communication is asynchronous functions well for a user group that may struggle with social situations. However, the support groups' value does not come from the technology alone but rather from how it is used. The internet makes it easy to set up an interest group, such as a support group, but it is still each individual member's responsibility to give good advice, show empathy, and share knowledge.

8.7 Conclusion

Let us lastly reflect on what the digitalization of health can teach us about digitalization as a process. In the digitalization of health, new technology, especially digital technology, has been framed as the solution to a sector facing increasing challenges and workloads. It is therefore important to note in the above examples, particularly in the examples of the flowerpot robot and social media support groups, that the need for healthcare professionals and healthcare institutions remains. Care work may change as it is accompanied by digital technology, but the flexibility, adaptability, and expertise of humans are not easily replaced by technological systems. Robots like Tessa can help people with dementia live at home for longer, but they are still reliant on human caregivers (both professional and family) to make it work. If there is no one to respond to the alerts Tessa gives, the robot cannot provide safety for its users. The support group example also shows how technological innovation can be user-driven, and that innovative use of technology can be highly effective without having to be radical. However, in this example, the need for mental health care professionals remains and is even highlighted by the community itself. Overall, the examples show that digitalization is best understood as a changing actor network: it is not just about delegating specific tasks to a digital technology; rather, it is about how we re-organize our lives, health, and work around and with new technology.

In this chapter, we have seen how technology shapes how we understand and relate to health. Since technology is a materialization of values, norms, and policies, studies of health technology can give us insight into different ways we can think about health. In this chapter, we have presented three different examples of digital health technologies. First, we saw how welfare technology aimed at older adults can make it possible for them to live at home longer. Sensors and measurements can create safety, particularly for relatives and healthcare providers, but their use brings with

Knopes, J. (2019). Science, technology, and human health: The value of STS in medical and health humanities pedagogy. *Journal of Medical Humanities, 40*(4), 461–471.

Kummervold, P. E., Gammon, D., Bergvik, S., Johnsen, J.-A. K., Hasvold, T., & Rosenvinge, J. H. (2002). Social support in a wired world: Use of online mental health forums in Norway. *Nordic Journal of Psychiatry, 56*(1), 59–65. https://doi.org/10.1080/08039480252803945.

Lupton, D. (2014). Apps as artefacts: Towards a critical perspective on mobile health and medical apps. *Societies, 4*(4), 606–622. https://doi.org/10.3390/soc4040606.

Milton, A., Ajmani, L., DeVito, M. A., & Chancellor, S. (2023). "I see me here": mental health content, community, and algorithmic curation on TikTok. *Proceedings of the 2023 CHI Conference on Human Factors in Computing Systems* (pp. 1–17). https://doi.org/10.1145/3544548.3581489.

Nakrem, S., & Sigurjónsson, J. B. (2017). *Velferdsteknologi i praksis. Perspektiver på teknologi i kommunal helse- og omsorgstjeneste.* Cappelen Damm Akademisk.

Naslund, J. A., Aschbrenner, K. A., Marsch, L. A., & Bartels, S.J. (2016). The future of mental health care: Peer-to-peer support and social media. *Epidemiology and Psychiatric Sciences, 25*(2), 113–122. https://doi.org/10.1017/S2045796015001067.

Niantic Inc. (2016). *Pokemon GO* [Mobile app]. Apple App Store. https://itunes.apple.com/us/app/pokemon-go/id1094591345?mt=8.

NOU 2011: 11 (2011). *Innovasjon i omsorg*. Helse- og omsorgsdepartementet. https://www.regjeringen.no/no/dokumenter/nou-2011-11/id646812/

Olson, K. E., O'Brien, M. A., Rogers, W. A., & Charness, N. (2011). Diffusion of technology: Frequency of use for younger and older adults. *Ageing International, 36*(1), 123–145. https://doi.org/10.1007/s12126-010-9077-9.

Quan-Haase, A., Williams, C., Kicevski, M., Elueze, I., & Wellmann, B. (2018). Dividing the grey divide: Deconstructing myths about older adults' online activities, skills, and attitudes. *American Behavioral Scientist, 62*(9), 1207–1228. https://doi.org/10.1177/0002764218777572.

Robinson, H., Broadbent, E., & MacDonald, B. (2015). Group sessions with Paro in a nursing home: Structure, observations and interviews. *Australasian Journal on Ageing, 35*(2), 106–112. https://doi.org/10.1111/ajag.12199.

Robertson, J. (2019). *Robo sapiens japanicus: Robots, gender, family, and the Japanese nation.* University of California Press.

Schreier, J. (Director). (2012). *Robot & Frank* [Film]. Samuel Goldwyn Films.

Sharkey, N., & Sharkey, A. (2012a). Granny and the robots: Ethical issues in robot care for older adults. *Ethics and Information Technology, 14,* 27–40. https://doi.org/10.1007/s10676-010-9234-6.

Sharkey, N., & Sharkey, A. (2012b). The eldercare factory. *Gerontology, 58,* 282–288. https://doi.org/10.1159/000329483.

Søraa, R. A., Nyvoll, P. S., Grønvik, K. B., & Serrano, A. (2020a). Children's perceptions of social robots: A study of the robots Pepper, AV1 and Tessa at Norwegian research fairs. *AI & Society.* https://doi.org/10.1007/s00146-020-00998-w.

Søraa, R. A., Nyvoll, P. S., Tøndel, G., Fosch-Villaronga, E., & Serrano, A. (2021). Mitigating loneliness with robotic gerontechnology at home: The social dimension of domestication between older adults, informal and formal caregivers in a technological test setting. Technological Forecasting & Social Change.

Søraa, R. A., Sutcliffe, T. E., & Bruijning, N. (2020b, 19 March). Human-robot care relations: A reflection on the movie 'Robot and Frank'. *Cyborgology.* https://thesocietypages.org/cyborgology/2020/03/19/human-robot-care-relations-a-reflection-on-the-movie-robot-and-frank/.

Studentenes helse- og trivselsundersøkelse (2018). *Psykisk helse og trivsel* [Mental health and wellbeing]. https://www.studenthelse.no/tema/psykisk_helse_og_trivsel.

Susi, T., Johannesson, M., & Backlund, P. (2007). Serious games: An overview. *IKI Technical Reports, Vol. 1-HS-IKI-TR-07-001,* p. 28. Institutionen för kommunikation och information, Högskolan i Skövde, Skövde. https://urn.kb.se/resolve?urn=urn:nbn:se:his:diva-1279

Trondsen, M. V., & Knarvik, U. (2017). *Velferdsteknologi for barn og unge med funksjonsnedsettelser.* Nasjonalt senter for e-helseforskning.

Turkle, S. (2012). *Alone Together: Why we expect more from technology and less from each other.* Basic Books.

Wright, J. (2023). *Robots won't save Japan: An ethnography of eldercare automation.* Cornell University Press.

World Health Organization. (n.d.-a). Ageing and health. Retrieved from https://www.who.int/news-room/fact-sheets/detail/ageing-and-health

Zhang, M. (2023). Older people's attitudes towards emerging technologies: A systematic literature review. *Public Understanding of Science*, 09636625231171677. https://doi.org/10.1177/09636625231171677.

Digitalization of Work

*Automation, Responsibility,
and Reskilling*

DOI: 10.1201/9781003289555-12

What does the digitalizing of work entail? Digital technology is being introduced in most sectors, promising to simplify, streamline, and improve work by automating various tasks and jobs. But what type of work can be automated? Are some professions more exposed to automation than others, and how is work changing due to the introduction of digital technology? To explore these questions, we have chosen three different empirical examples of automation in the workplace: self-service checkouts, digital stopwatches, and the automation of craftspeople in the construction industry.

This chapter illuminates how digital technology creates new ways of working and ways for people and machines to cooperate. In particular, this chapter uses the concept of *delegation* to explain how digitalization transfers tasks and responsibilities from people to technologies and vice versa. To understand the changes that are happening at work today, we will begin by examining two fictional visions of the future.

9.1 Two Visions of Future Work

The consequences of digitalized work, and particularly automation, are frequently explored in science fiction, which provides us with different visions of how technology can change society and our relationship with work. Let's compare the TV series *Star Trek: The Next Generation* (Roddenberry, 1987) with the film *WALL-E* (Stanton, 2008) to see how these different visions are based on different understandings of the effects of technology (Wisecrack, 2019). In both examples, we meet humans who live on an advanced spaceship with technological systems that have removed the need for manual labor. The technologies in these stories are relatively similar, but the depicted consequences of them are completely at odds. Where *Star Trek* is optimistic and hopeful about the future ushered in by advanced technology, *WALL-E* is a warning about how overreliance on technological solutions leads to social decay.

In *WALL-E*, automation leads to human devolution. The film unfolds on board a luxury spaceship where all work, from food production to cleaning, is done by robots. Since all the work is automated and robotized, people have nothing to do other than laze about and be entertained. The humans we meet in *WALL-E* have had such a relaxed life, scooting about in lounge chairs, sipping slurpies, and watching TV, that they literally have trouble standing upright. After several generations have spent their days lounging around, humans have devolved into "couch potatoes," who can neither walk nor stand on their own. They are animated as obese and appear both dumb and self-absorbed—at least in the beginning. An important turning point in the story occurs when the captain overrides the autopilot system and, in the process, takes (back) control over his body, the ship, and his fate. It is by returning to his work as captain and taking away technology's control that the hero saves the day. In other words, the moral of *WALL-E* is that automation will make us lazy and self-absorbed, and that it is through work that we are able to fully realize what being human is about.

In *Star Trek*, automation is also crucial to how society is structured. But in the Star Trek's vision, automation leads to liberation. Thanks to automation, humans (and other races) can focus their attention on science, culture, and the exploration of space. In *Star Trek*'s utopian vision of the future, technological progress has created a wealth of resources and made possible a new social order without poverty, illness, or inequality. Money no longer exists, and people are not focused on material goods. Everything can be made with the help of replicators, and humanity is dedicated to intellectual and cultural pursuits (Geek's Guide to the Galaxy, 2016). The series' motto, "to explore strange new worlds, seek out new life and new civilizations, and boldly go where no one has gone before," summarizes a worldview in which humanity's curiosity and urge to explore are placed above all others. People in *Star Trek* still have jobs (you find many engineers, interpreters, cooks, etc.), but since it is not a necessity to put food on the table and a roof over their heads, work is about self-expression, contributing to the community, and learning for the sake of learning.

In both stories, automation is central to how people understand themselves and the role of work and has led to an upheaval in the organization of society. But where *WALL-E* sees automation as a potential danger, *Star Trek* presents automation as a way for us to escape *forced labor* and dedicate ourselves to *meaningful labor*. From a sociotechnical perspective, the contrast between these two visions of the future acts as a reminder that technology's effects are not given and that we must avoid deterministic thinking. That means avoiding technological determinism, which claims the consequences of automation are given (the examples above show that automation can have many and potentially conflicting effects), and social determinism, which claims that technological development doesn't actually play a role in social change (the examples above show that automation will affect how we understand and carry out work and cannot be dismissed out of hand).

In this chapter, we will explore different ways of thinking about the digitalization and automation of work, emphasizing how digitalization can have multiple and contradictory effects and shape work in different ways. However, before embarking on this, let us start with the foundational question: What is work?

9.2 From Animal Laborans to *Homo Faber*

Work is a term that describes many phenomena. Overall, the word work means to make a targeted, conscious effort or carry out an effortful, purposeful activity. The effort can be paid or unpaid, exciting or boring, complicated or simple, safe or risky. To get a better understanding of work as a phenomenon and especially how work is related to technology, we will look at some examples of how work has been a cornerstone that societies have been organized around.

In Ancient Rome, for example, one distinguished between work of the hand and work of the spirit, where the latter was preferable and philosophers enjoyed high status, while farmers and laborers had lower status. Because this was a slave-based society, most "work of the hand" was carried out by slaves, except for war, which was seen as important work. In medieval Europe, tradespeople had become an important social group, including high-status workers who were organized in guilds. Nonetheless, guilds exerted strict control over their members and their work, which feudal societies categorized hierarchically, continuing to define one's place in society. At the same time, the church strongly influenced how people should work according to laws and norms and what work should mean (Kildal, 2005). One should submit to nature as an *animal laborans*—a working animal—and find the treasures God has provided through hard work. One should not master nature or create something new. Later, *homo faber*—the creating human—became the central ideal. As Protestantism spread in Europe, humans became seen as the stewards of "creation" (Kildal, 2005), and to create something new with one's hand was increasingly valued (Sennett, 2008). The shift from *animal laborans* to *homo faber* involved not only a shift in the meaning of work but also a change in workers' relationship to technology: from being subjugated to nature to a creator of things and tools to make nature submit to it.

During the Industrial Revolution, which began in England in the 1700s, a new working class emerged, as did the separation between work and free time (Kildal, 2005, p. 6). The introduction of machines, which automated many tasks that previously required specialist knowledge and experience, was particularly important in the changes to working life at this time. The automated loom, for example, largely replaced weavers. Machines required mechanics rather than tradespeople, and shift work developed as employers sought to keep their machines running 24/7.

In the 1800s, right up until the Industrial Revolution, it wasn't unusual to work 10–16 hours per day in Europe, 6 days per week, with only Sunday free to go to church. Child labor was also common. In 1817, the English industrialist Robert Owen coined the slogan "Eight hours labor, eight hours recreation, eight hours rest"—but it would be a long time before this became the norm in Europe—and in many countries, this is still not the norm. In 1847, England, the working days of women and children were legally limited to a maximum of 10 hours, and in France the following year, thanks to the February Revolution, all French workers worked a maximum of 12 hours per day. It would, nonetheless, be over a century before Owen's vision of an 8-hour workday came into force. In most Western countries, 1919 was the first year in which the 8-hour day was imposed. A century later, we are talking about the possibility of a 6-hour day. We will return to these possible workday configurations later in this chapter, but first, we will take a look at what automation means for workers. It is, however, important to keep in mind that these are situated understandings of work written in the context of the authors (see details in Box 9A) and that many different work configurations exist—both historically and in contemporary societies around the globe.

From these brief glimpses into the history of work, we can see that work has always been about something more than "just getting a job done" or "having an income." Work has been central to how we organize society and how society conceptualizes work for the individual.

Box 9A.   Fact: The Nordic Working Life Model

The Nordic working life model, which partly makes Nordic welfare states possible, is one way to organize work. Compared to models in other countries, it is characterized by high wages, high taxes, and a high degree of both trust and leisure time. Among other measurements, Nordic countries score high on the Human Development Index, National Happiness Index, and BNP per capita. This is in large part due to the model of working life implemented in the Nordic region after striking workers fought for their rights in scuffles with the military and police. The Nordic model, which today seems very peaceful, was won by bloodshed. Because this model is so central to the good health and happiness enjoyed by Nordic citizens, the region has reason to be cautious of major changes that put the model at risk.

9.3 Automating Workers?

Most of us work to put food on our tables and roofs over our heads (or maintain a certain lifestyle) by trading our time for money. To have and keep a job, as well as how we organize our work, are pillars of human life and society. But work is changing, and relatively quickly (Ford, 2015; Susskind & Susskind, 2015; Brynjolfsson & McAfee, 2014). It is estimated that 33%–50% of all jobs will be affected by automation, digitalization, and robotization in the next 20 years (Pajarinen et al., 2015; Frey & Osborne, 2017). In the parliamentary report *Digital Agenda for Norway* (Meld. St. 27 (2015–2016)), we can read that we will soon be facing major changes in most sectors:

> We see increasing automation—not just in industry but also in e-processing, for example, in banks and insurance. When the content of work changes, the skills required also change. Routine and automatable jobs are disappearing and being replaced by more specialized and knowledge-intensive jobs in most industries. This creates a growing need for the adaptation of the workforce to new technologies— otherwise, we can develop a skills gap in both the private and the public sectors.

However, automation will not impact all workers or nations the same. Norway, as an example, is considered to be one of the industrialized countries least likely to be affected by automation in the future. This is because the Norwegian industry is extremely specialized and dependent on specialized skillsets. The main export (and related industry) is oil and fish, and because we do not have typical industries such as car or textile manufacturing, Norway's jobs are less vulnerable to automation. Only one out of the three jobs in Norway is considered vulnerable to automation. In Sweden, Germany, and the USA, however, automation will supposedly hit harder: half of workers are threatened by automation (Frey & Osborne, 2017). As such, a major upheaval in working life is predicted, and automation is becoming an increasingly important political issue. In later years, AI has also received particular attention from the wider public.

Even if there is political awareness about the major challenges posed by automation, it is difficult to predict how these changes will play out and shape the work life of individuals. And, importantly, the question of how we will meet these changes is as much political as it is technical. Some believe we require government support to soften the impact of digital transformations, while others argue that the market will regulate itself. Depending on what political approach we choose to respond with, the consequences of automation vary greatly. The point is that the consequences of a digital shift will depend just as much on *how* technologies are implemented as on what jobs technologies can do.

Robotization is often framed as something happening in the future, but is actually happening already. In Norway, 0.05% of industrial workers are robots; in the USA, 1.9%; in Sweden, 2.2%; and in Germany, 3.1%, but this is nothing compared to the almost 10% of robot workers in South Korea (Dhiraj, 2018). Research suggests that this proportion will increase. Very few professions will be unaffected by the digital shift or the increase in mechanical workers. Many service jobs— for example, cashiers, fast food workers, and cleaners— typically pay badly and have no education requirements, something that makes them easier to automate through the use of self-service checkouts and cleaning robots. As such, the robotization trend suggests that low-status jobs will be the first to be automated, and this illustrates how digitalization is a process that will have different outcomes for different groups of people—in which those with power, status, and privilege will (as always) come out better off than those without (see Box 9B). But, as we are seeing with the introduction of several AI technologies, other typical middle-class professions are also at risk.

Box 9B.   Fact: Undesirable Jobs—The "3D Jobs"

Jobs that people don't particularly want to do are often described as "dirty, dangerous, and demeaning/demanding," but somebody (or something!) has to do them. The phrase is borrowed from the Japanese *kitanai* 汚い (dirty), *kiken* 危険 (dangerous), and *kitsui* きつい (demanding).

It is worth pointing out that the fear of automation is not new. As early as 1964, USA's President Lyndon B. Johnson wrote, in reference to the mechanization of the industrial sector, that "The USA is on the on the brink of a social and economic crisis due to an increase in automation!" This "danger" is now linked to digitalization rather than mechanization. As machines become increasingly sophisticated, they will also perform manual jobs that do not include routines and enter sectors that were previously reserved for knowledge workers. Use the exercise in Box 9C to reflect on the future of your dream career. In medicine, for example, computers are used in diagnostics—IBM's Watson computer, for example, diagnoses chronic illnesses and suggests which cancer treatment will have the (statistically) highest chance of success. In recent years, chatbots and AI technology like ChatGPT have also started to shake things up by doing work humans previously had monopoly on doing, like journalism, travel planning, and content creation.

Once again, it is important to remember the human factor. In terms of medical technology, "success" does not necessarily mean the highest chance of surviving a treatment but can include a number of variables such as disease progression, possible complexities, possible loss of functions, and insurance coverage, to name a few. A banal and simplified example: you are near death, but you learn you can take Operation A, which will lengthen your life by 10 years but only has a 50% chance of success, or Operation B, which will only give you 5 years but has an 85% chance of success. Which would you choose? And would you leave that choice

---

Box 9C.   Exercise: Your Job in the Future

What is your dream job—and how will it look in the automated future? In this exercise, you will reflect on how professions change over time, particularly with the introduction and use of technology. Start by thinking about a profession that interests you. Consider how the job looks today and how it might look in the future. Start with today: How many people work in the profession? Does it pay well? Which tasks are typical of this profession? What is the demography (age, gender, ethnicity/race, class) of workers within the profession?

Then consider the future of the profession you dream about. Consider, for example, the likelihood that the job will be automated (cf. the list from Frey & Osborne, 2017), as well as how relevant unions and interest organizations see the future of the profession. See, for example, sites like willrobotstakemyjob.com. Use the questions above to address concrete trends in the job market. Finally, reflect on how you think work will look in 20 years and what your dream job will look like then. Once again, use the questions above to make your vision concrete. By now, you have moved into the realm of fiction, so use this exercise first and foremost to become aware of how you see the development of the job market.

to a computer? Such examples show the minefield of ethical and responsibly demands that AI will have to face. Or consider the ethical conundrum of whether experimental drugs with limited effects should be prioritized over other, more pressing matters.

In the following three examples, we examine the digitalization of working life in different ways. Self-service checkouts show how the digitalization of work can include a transfer of work from the cashier to both the machine and the customer. We will consider the digital stopwatch as a technology used by home nursing services and how a goal of increased efficiency can result in increased surveillance. Finally, in the third and last example, we will consider what it is like to work with robots on a construction project.

9.4 Who Operates Self-Service Checkouts?

Retail has been attempting to automate for many decades, through scanners one picks up in the store, through food delivered to your door, and through self-service checkouts. Retail is the biggest private work sector in Norway, employing over 13% of all workers in the country, but the proportion of workers in retail and the jobs they do are changing due to new technologies. Self-service checkouts have been used more and more frequently in Norway, particularly in the past few years—we now use them when we buy fast food at McDonald's, furniture at IKEA, and most often at grocery stores.

A self-service checkout is, as the name states, a checkout you use yourself. Instead of putting your purchases on a band for the cashier to scan, the customers themselves scan the barcodes. The introduction of self-service checkouts is often justified as a way to eliminate long queues, cut costs, increase efficiency, improve the customer experience and customer satisfaction, and increase productivity (Orel & Kara, 2014). This is a visible form of automation, where human employees are completely removed from the work of scanning goods—or more accurately, the function of the human employees has shifted as there is still at least one person who must be on stand-by, ready to aid customers, to check on and clean the machines, and to ensure bags are available. The other cashiers will not necessarily remain a part of the store's workforce. Who remains and works in the store? What happens to those who lose their jobs? Are there alternative jobs available?

Questions can be asked about how customers (who now scan the goods) have become unpaid employees and why jobs have been lost in the process. This form of work can be understood as a transfer of responsibility and work tasks, a *delegation*. Take a normal grocery store in the USA as an example. Here, there are often low-paid employees who pack your purchases in bags for you. In Norway, customers have bagged their own goods for a long time. Now, scanning is also the customer's responsibility rather than the store clerks, and this is also a transfer of responsibility and practices (Anitsal & Schumann, 2007). It is possible that, in the future, we will consider self-service checkouts completely normal.

In addition, one can ask who is being included in and who is being excluded from the "new normal" at the grocery store. For many elderly customers, for example, small talk with the cashier at the local grocery store is an important social arena and a chance for human contact. It is not as easy to talk to a self-service checkout, much less to operate one, if one does not have the necessary digital skills. Self-service checkouts therefore create waves in the *actor network* of shopping not only by being a new technical device but also by changing the interpersonal social experience of shopping by, for example, removing an opportunity for chitchat. It also makes visible a script in which the imagined customer is independent, technologically competent, and disinterested in chatting.

The *script* of self-service checkouts can have many shortcomings when it is implemented and meets actual customers. One example is visually impaired customers, who may have problems reading the screen. Another is the rather technical process associated with weighing, scanning, or pasting labels on fruits and vegetables—not to mention finding the right type of apple in the list, which can require both certain technical skills and knowledge of the specific store's systems. Users can also oppose the script, such as when children are reported to the police for choosing the wrong type of pastry on the machine—shown in the illustration at the start of this chapter. Olden (2018) therefore recommends that shops continue to have at least *some* human cashiers so that customers are not forced to use automated systems.

An increasingly digitized and automated workplace creates a need for workers with new attributes and skills. To work with five colleagues at a grocery store, where one rotates between sitting at the checkout to scan goods, sorting fruits and vegetables, filling freezers, and minimizing food waste, is a completely different than being one person watching over five automated checkouts where the customers themselves scan, weigh, and pay for goods. The employees shift from taking care of goods and serving customers to taking care of customers and "serving" machines, in that machines now require the employees help whenever something goes wrong. This still relates to taking care of goods in a specific manner so that they are correctly registered and thus properly paid for, but rather than needing to ensure that the goods are properly scanned, the worker needs to ensure that the customer is scanning the goods properly. As such, their role is more like that of an inspector. Digitalization thus leads to new forms of control and trust. For example, we might be increasingly asked to become "members" at stores to access certain benefits and discounts, but these memberships come at the cost of sharing our personal data, and they may influence what we buy and when, while self-checkouts check and measure what we do. In addition, the remaining "human guard," who checks that everything is done as it should be, is always there to keep an eye on things. In this way, the digitalization of grocery shopping leads to a greater degree of control and surveillance.

9.5 The Digital Stopwatch and the Attempt to Automate Care Work

Control is also a concern in the health sector, where attempts to automate are supposed to make care work more effective and less expensive. Norwegian elderly care has gone through major changes, mainly focused on shifting care from taking place in institutions to taking place at home. As a result, "there is no longer an 'elderly care service' but rather 'individualized care services'" (Tøndel, 2018, p. 288). One example of how healthcare workers digitalize their services to reach individuals in their own homes is the use of so-called digital stopwatches in home care services. Digital stopwatches give every task a standard length of time for completion. Having allotted time for different tasks is not in itself something new, but through digital technology, the functions of the stopwatch have been expanded: it has become a work list (providing an overview of the work tasks and the time allotted for each), a registration tool (confirming work has been performed), and a control tool (allowing bosses to see what has been done and when).

Home care services in Norway are administered at the municipal level and are provided for those who, due to reduced health or for other reasons, require assistance at home. Help offered by home care services includes but is not limited to treating sores, providing medicines, making and serving meals, undertaking medical observations, and helping with personal hygiene, laundry, and cleaning. Since this is a service that is performed in the home of the person being cared for, the working day comprises visiting the homes of various people to help them with different tasks.

In a study of home care services in Trondheim (Bergschöld, 2016, 2018), employees who were instructed to use a digital planning tool in their work—a Vehicle Route Problem Solver (VRP)—explained that the tool was both a hindrance and some help. The app has the home caregivers' daily calendars, including an overview of whom they need to visit, how much time is allowed per visit, and which tasks are expected to be carried out at each home, as well as a function that registers how much time they use at each home. When visits start, the watch is at 0:00; it counts until the allotted time is used and then warns that time is up by changing color from green to red. When the caregiver ends the visit, the watch stops automatically and sends its measurements to an external server, which administrators and managers can access. The idea behind introducing technologies like VRPs is to automate planning work (who should receive help and in what order) and recording work (previously carried out at the end of the day). The vision was to save time and make the day easier for home caregivers. How were these visions put into practice?

First, it turned out that the function for creating optimal routes was turned off because the municipality's allocated time for each visit did not include travel time, nor did the function satisfy political guidelines.[1] So every day, the list was filled with users, and a morning meeting continued to be used to set up routes, based on the expertise of the home caregivers, between residents based on their locations and needs (Bergschöld, 2016). When the home caregivers arrived, the automatic stopwatch started in the app, but it was determined that it should not be decisive for the care they provided (in a regime they described as cynical), so if they went beyond the allotted time, they simply went into the app and manually adjusted the time so that they registered the "correct" number of minutes for the visit. The possibility of having oversight over all necessary information as well as logging visits while they were occurring were functions the carers valued, and they thus experienced VRPs as useful. But the question is whether the registration requirements (which now include the number of minutes spent with each user) positively impact the care provided.

For those employed in home care services, "too little time" was already a major concern even before the introduction of

VRP. And with a technology that used time as an important measurement of performance, the work was more often described in terms of time: they "earned time" when a visit was shorter than planned, and they "stole time" if the visit went longer than planned. Assessing who needed extra help, who could wait, and who did not need acute help was also judged by whether it was a sensible or unsensible use of time. Bergschöld (2018) therefore argues that home care services' care work in large part focuses on organizing and administering time: to succeed as a home carer, it is not enough to be skilled at caring; one must also know how to "save time," know where one must use extra time, and be quick on one's feet, no matter what. An earlier focus on time thus became even stronger through the introduction of VRP.

The digital stopwatch did not create the problem of too little time, but it did materialize a policy that allowed for less flexibility in the workday. When Bergen introduced a similar regime in 2015, the response was overwhelmingly negative: 89% of the employees in home care who were required to shift to a more controlled workday felt that their workday was made worse by the stopwatch regime (Østby, 2017). As such, the digital stopwatch teaches us that digitalization may promise a better and simpler workday, but digital systems for registering and organizing work have the potential to be both surveilling and controlling—and can force ways of working in which resistance is the only ethical solution. We can therefore understand the home caregivers' "cheating" with numbers and times as an *antiprogram*, a radical reinterpretation of the script (imagined use) in which other values and practices than those that were imagined are applied.

9.6 Craftspeople at Construction Sites Working with Robots

In the third example of how digitalization affects work, we will take a look at craftsmanship at construction sites. In many ways, trades stand in contrast to the digital world because they are characterized by work carried out by hand. In recent years in Norway and other Nordic countries, a great deal of energy has been spent on increasing the number of young adults who choose to pursue vocational careers, including in trades such as carpentry and other craftsmanship. This is especially important for the construction sector, which is undergoing major changes due not only to automation and new construction methods but also to climate and energy requirements and operations. Can automation and robotization be a part of the solution to the challenges faced by the sector, and which work would be given to technology?

Building a house is a complex process. Nevertheless, traditionally, a small group of tradespeople could handle most of what was required from beginning to end. Now, however, we see trade work as an assembly line process, broken down into small, defined tasks that are carried out by people and machines that do not need to have a sense of the whole project. One consequence of this is construction defects—a growing problem and one that can have fatal consequences if defects remain unnoticed. A recurring concern among tradespeople whom Fyhn and Søraa (2017) spoke with in the construction sector in Norway was an avalanche of problems linked to building defects, and particularly moisture damages, which lie hidden within the buildings constructed over the last several decades. When tradespeople don't receive enough training, there is a great deal of room left for sloppy work, which negatively affects homeowners.

An increase in permanent positions within the sector could remedy construction defects by contributing to better organization of work. This would also provide better conditions for taking care of the communities of practice essential to developing and preserving quality craftsmanship. Permanent positions will presumably become increasingly important as buildings become increasingly complex and filled with technology. A mantra in the sector is "good work takes time." That there are many defects in construction is not necessarily the fault of individuals as much as it is a lack of a stable community in which to learn: it takes time to learn the trades—one learns from one's colleagues long after one's apprenticeship and qualification exams. Teaching and learning is a part of trades work, but such learning requires working together over decades in a community of practice. Construction firms with permanent employees can house such communities, but firms that base their practice on hiring temporary workers for each job cannot offer this at the same level. Some firms that Fyhn and Søraa (2017) researched based their practices not solely on casual labor but also on a small core group of permanent employees whose job it was to correct the errors that inevitably arise during construction. This job was described, somewhat unsurprisingly, as unsatisfactory and it is here that technology comes into play—for example, in training, VR is used as a way to try out one's skills before going "out into the field." Alternatively, technology acts as one's "colleague," as with the robot control system "Vision-Based Integrated Mobile Robotic System for Real-Time Applications" (Asadi et al., 2018).

Models and plans for buildings are not always updated with the actual status on the building site, and some building sites solve this with a "control robot," which links the digital model of the building site with the physical building. This robot drives around at night, when the human workers have gone home, to ensure that everything is as it should be. When it finds defects, it will mark them in the system so that people can correct the errors (Schia et al., 2019).

A two-part vision is created here. On the one hand, the robot is expected to function as a supplement; it is expected to provide a warning if something is incorrect and help minimize construction defects. On the other hand, we can ask whether the robot is replacing human labor, whether workers become apathetic when they are being controlled in this manner, or whether they feel as if they are being surveilled (see also Chapter 10 on control). What changes through digitalization is not just the process of searching for and notifying errors but also the systematic and holistic oversight of the building project and its processes. When one knows that a machine will check everything one does, new ways of working develop, and it becomes less clear who is responsible for preventing errors because the robot has been *delegated* the task of checking for errors.

The example of tradespeople and control robots shows us that automation is not always helpful, or rather, that it can help in the present but perhaps create more problems in the future. The problem for tradespeople is not actually technology or a lack of technology, but rather a lack of a solid professional community that makes it possible for them to develop the skills they need. What happens if the control robot takes over? Who will take care of the expertise the control robot is built around? When there are not enough workers able to carry on a profession, it dies out. We must therefore be critical of what is automated away if this depletes necessary expertise and communities of practice.

9.7 What Will We Do in the Future— And How Will We Do It?

When digital technology is implemented in a workplace, it is most often with the aim of increasing productivity. Digital technology is linked to values like efficiency, profitability, and optimization, and this creates highly optimistic visions of how good everything can be if one only gets new, better digital tools. In practice, it is, as usual, not so simple. The three examples above—self-service checkouts, digital stopwatches, and control robots—show different ways that the digitalization of working life can change how we work. In all three examples, responsibilities and tasks are transferred from humans to robots because of digitalization; that is, they are *delegated* between human and non-human actors.

In the example of self-service checkouts, digitalization includes a shift in shopworkers' tasks, from scanning goods to surveilling customers who themselves scan goods. As a vision for the future, self-service checkouts fit within the notion of a future characterized by interactions with machines instead of people. But in practice, this is not a question of automating the scanning of goods. Instead, it is a shift in *who* performs this task. The machines don't actually do any more than they did before; they have simply been changed so that the customer can do the work of registering and paying for goods. The technology has the same function but has received a new *script* in which the customer, not the worker, is the user. What was previously paid work is now a task expected of customers—without customers receiving cheaper goods or any bonuses for the work they do. In this way, the shift leads to savings for the store owner, but there are fewer paid positions and there is more work for the customer.

The digital stopwatch used by home care services shows how technology can simplify work tasks, such as ensuring that information is constantly accessible or that reporting can be done on the go. But the example also shows how technology can make the workday more strained. The stopwatch gives home care workers so little freedom that the only option they have, if they are to provide ethical care, is to use counterstrategies, known in script theory as *antiprograms*, that "fool" the technology. To provide the level of care they see as needed, care workers are forced to use the technology in ways that it was not intended to be used, including "white lies" about how long they have been in the homes of care recipients. Even if the technology is sometimes helpful, it shifts focus from care to time, and managing time has become a more important part of the workday.

That craftspeople now build with machines, are controlled by machines, and are trained by machines through VR suggests new ways of working with and within technology (Fyhn & Søraa, 2017). For many tradespeople in the construction sector, automation includes fear of desk work to a greater extent than fear of unemployment. The unpredictable character of construction work implies that human workers will continue to have a role in solving problems in real time (Fyhn & Søraa, 2017), but restructuring processes may be required. Logic, skill, and creativity in the execution of tasks are valuable even when they are combined with digital technologies (Ingold, 2013). The technology's success depends on close and effective interactions between machines and humans—such that the technology is a supplement to rather than a replacement for tradespeople. In addition, it is important to ask who is in control and who has the skills required to interact with the robots who drive around checking the quality of work.

In the example of the self-service checkout, we saw that it was no longer expected that workers scan goods; instead, customers do. Will we all become working customers in the end, and can this be extended to other arenas? Will we, in the future, massage, tattoo, and style our hair ourselves with the help of machines? Which new skills will new workers have? And what about consumers? What will count as "general knowledge and skills" for normal citizens? An example from the USA is the store Amazon Go, where what the customer takes from the shelves is registered and checkout is unnecessary (called "grab and go" [Polacco & Backes, 2018]).

Historically, workers who lost their jobs to machines could move to another sector: farm laborers became industrial workers, who then became service workers, who have since become knowledge workers. But the postindustrial society may run out of sectors workers can move into. The sales and services sector employs the most workers in most industrialized countries. Given the sector's status as a preventer of unemployment linked to deindustrialization, and because of the technological disturbance and effects associated with an increase in digital middlemen (for online retail and online digital services), it is critically important to explore how these workers experience adapting to digitalization and automation.

If we reconsider the fictional examples from the start of this chapter, *Star Trek* provides us with an example of self-service checkout taken to its most extreme potential, where one simply tells a spaceship what to eat and the meal materializes. We see the same on the spaceship in *WALL-E*, where technology ensures everyone is fed at all times. The spaceship's occupants in *WALL-E* follow a sort of stopwatch regime, but only for free time and recreation. Here, what matters is having as much fun as possible and eating as much as possible at the same time. In *Star Trek*, we see that the stopwatch is removed in favor of a slower-paced existence—exploration of outer space takes the time it takes. In the digitalization of building sites, robots check that everything is functioning and report errors. We can see parallels in *Star Trek*, where people's communities of work—that is, the *actor networks* humans and technology create—play an extremely important role in driving progress. On the building site, expert tradespeople are needed to correct errors, and similarly, in *Star Trek*, there is always a mystery that must be solved that require human skills, even when they have access to very powerful computers.

To be able to have a critical perspective on what digitalization does to work, we have to ask: Which work is scripted through the technology? Who develops the script, and what reasons do they have for making it the way they do? How do workers take technologies and automation into use (and nonuse)? Are local adjustments made, and what is lost? Who decides and has power, and who ends up with the "3D jobs" (dirty, dangerous, and demeaning/demanding)? We hope this chapter has encouraged you to reflect on how digitalization, particularly through attempts to automate, will shape our democracies and work environments. Who will decide which jobs should be automated, and what will we do with people whose jobs are "automated away"? What do societies look like if all work is carried out by robots?

During a critical examination of digitalization, it is important not to be technologically deterministic. For example, Wajcman (2017) warns against believing that digital automation is somehow inherently different than other automation and argues for distancing oneself from the typical "Silicon Valley" version of the future to see automation as a social construction that is under negotiation rather than a technological inevitability.

As we saw in Part 1 of this book, a sociotechnical approach to digitalization will require us to ask questions about trends and representations of changes that are described as "natural" or "inevitable," as well as about why and how work is automated and digitalized, who is affected, and who affects the changes. It also encourages us to consider which technologies are involved in the actor networks that are created. Last but not least, there is an interpretive flexibility in the automation and digitalization of work that is important to think about—technology doesn't mean the same things for all actors.

9.8 Conclusion

In this chapter, we have examined how the digitalization of work has created new forms of use for technology, new organizations of work and workers, and changes in trust and communities for employees and employers. The examples of self-service checkouts, digital stopwatches, and construction automation have shown three ways in which digitalization applies to today's methods of work. We have also seen how "work" is a shifting term that has meant (and will mean!) different things in different places and at different times, and we have warned against technological determinism's blind faith that we are moving toward an "inevitable future" we cannot control. Nonetheless, work tasks are increasingly delegated to machines, and there is reason to critically examine how different jobs and workers are affected by automation and robotization, particularly as digitalization includes an increase in registration and surveillance and, as such, increases the chance that technologies will exercise and strengthen the control of employers over employees. Digitalization's tendency to increase the degree of control and surveillance is the theme of the next chapter.

Note

1 For those interested in programming, this may remind you of the "travelling salesman problem" (TMP), a so-called NP-hard programming problem. With only 15 places to visit, there will be at least 653 billion possible routes. One of our computer science colleagues describe this complexity as: "Whoever can solve TSP is guaranteed a Nobel Prize, so important and impossible is this problem!" So you may not expect a municipal home care service app to handle this well! See Klarreich (2013) for an introduction to TSP.

References

Anitsal, I., & Schumann, D. W. (2007). Toward a conceptualization of customer productivity: The customer's perspective on transforming customer labor into customer outcomes using technology-based self-service options. *Journal of Marketing Theory and Practice, 15*(4), 349–363. https://doi.org/10.2753/MTP1069-6679150405.

Asadi, K., Ramshankar, H., Pullagurla, H., Bhandare, A., Shanbhag, S., Mehta, P., ... & Wu, T. (2018). Vision-based integrated mobile robotic system for real-time applications in construction. *Automation in Construction, 96*, 470–482. https://doi.org/10.1007/978-3-030-33540-3_12.

Bergschöld, J. M. (2016). Domesticating homecare services: Vehicle route problem solver displaced. *Nordic Journal of Science and Technology Studies, 4*(2), 41–53. https://doi.org/10.5324/njsts.v4i2.2184.

Bergschöld, J. M. (2018). When saving time becomes labor: Time, work and technology in homecare. *Nordic Journal of Working Life Studies, 8*(1), 3–21. https://doi.org/10.18291/njwls.v8i1.104850.

Brynjolfsson, E., & McAfee, A. (2014). *The second machine age: Work, progress, and prosperity in a time of brilliant technologies.* W. W. Norton & Co.

Dhiraj, A. B. (2018, 14 March). Countries with the most industrial robots per 10,000 employees. *Ceoworld Magazine.* https://ceoworld.biz/2018/03/14/countries-with-the- most-industrial-robots-per-10000-employees-2018-report/

Ford, M. (2015). *Rise of the robots: Technology and the threat of a jobless future.* Basic Books.

Frey, C. B., & Osborne, M. A. (2017). The future of employment: How susceptible are jobs to computerisation? *Technological Forecasting and Social Change, 114,* 254–280. https://doi.org/10.1016/j.techfore.2016.08.019.

Fyhn, H., & Søraa, R. A. (2017). Craftsmanship in the machine: Sustainability through new roles in building craft at the technologized building site. *Nordic Journal of Science and Technology Studies, 5*(2), 71–84. https://doi.org/10.5324/njsts.v5i2.2321.

Geek's Guide to the Galaxy. (2016, 28 May). The economic lessons of Star Trek's money- free society. *Wired.* https://www.wired.com/2016/05/geeks-guide-star-trek-economics/.

Ingold, T. (2013). *Making: Anthropology, archaeology, art and architecture.* Routledge.

Kildal, N. (2005). *Fra arbeidsbegrepets historie: Aristoteles til Marx* [From the history of the concept of work: Aristoteles to Marx]. Stein Rokkan senter for flerfaglige samfunnsstudier.

Klarreich, E. (2013, 30 January). Computer scientists find new shortcuts for infamous traveling salesman problem. *Wired.* https://www.wired.com/2013/01/traveling-sales-man-problem/

Meld. St. 27 (2015–2016). (2016). Digital agenda for Norge-IKT for en enklere hverdag og økt produktivitet [Digital agenda for Norway - ICT for a simpler everday life and increased productivity]. *Kommunal- og Moderniseringsdepartementet.* https://www.regjeringen.no/no/dokumenter/meld.-st.-27-20152016/id2483795/

Olden, A. (2018). What do you buy when no one's watching? The effect of self-service checkouts on the composition of sales in retail. *Institutt for foretaksøkonomi, Norges Handelshøyskole.* https://hdl.handle.net/11250/2490886.

Orel, F. D., & Kara, A. (2014). Supermarket self-checkout service quality, customer satisfaction, and loyalty: Empirical evidence from an emerging market. *Journal of Retailing and Consumer Services, 21*(2), 118–129. https://doi.org/10.1016/j.jretconser.2013.07.002.

Østby, B. A. (2017, 25 September). Vil fjerne stoppeklokkeregimet [Want to remove the stopwatch-regime]. *Sykepleien.no*. https://sykepleien.no/2017/09/vil-fjerne-stoppeklokkeregimet.

Pajarinen, M., Rouvinen, P., & Ekeland, A. (2015). Computerization threatens one-third of Finnish and Norwegian employment. *Etla Brief, 34*, 1–8. https://www.researchgate.net/publication/317089938.

Polacco, A., & Backes, K. (2018). The Amazon Go concept: Implications, applications, and sustainability. *Journal of Business and Management, 24*(1), 79–92. https://doi.org/10.6347/JBM.201803_24(1).0004.

Roddenberry, G. (Writer). (1987-1994). *Star Trek: The Next Generation* [TV Series]. Paramount Pictures.

Schia, M. H., Trollsås, B. C., Fyhn, H., & Lædre, O. (2019). The introduction of AI in the construction industry and its impact on human behavior. *Proceedings of the 27th Annual Conference of the International Group for Lean Construction (IGLC)*, July 3–5, 2019, Dublin, Ireland (pp. 903–914). https://doi.org/10.24928/2019/0191.

Sennett, R. (2008). *The Craftsman*. Yale University Press.

Stanton, A. (Producer). (2008). *WALL-E* [Film]. Disney Pixar.

Susskind, R. E., & Susskind, D. (2015). *The future of the professionals: How technology will transform the work of human experts*. Oxford University Press.

Tøndel, G. (2018). Omsorgens materialitet: Trygghet, teknologi og alderdom [Materiality of care: Safety, technology and old age]. *Tidsskrift for omsorgsforskning, 4*(3), 287–297. https://doi.org/10.18261/issn.2387-5984-2018-03-11.

Wajcman, J. (2017). Automation: is it really different this time? *The British Journal of Sociology, 68*(1), 119–127.

Wisecrack (2019, 28 May). Will *Wall-E* Come True? (vs. *Star Trek*)-Wisecrack Edition [Video]. *YouTube*. https://youtu.be/48mf2QU- tUmg

CHAPTER 10

Digitalization of Control

Surveillance, Automation,
and Algorithms

DOI: 10.1201/9781003289555-13

Digital technology has great potential for control—from the state, from companies, from your boss, and from the people around you. In this chapter, we will examine how control is made possible through digitalization and how surveillance and control are carried out through digital technologies. We are particularly interested in how tracking and attempts to streamline affect the transfer and exercise of power. Which parts of our lives are monitored—and do we already live in a surveillance society? Who is interested in knowing something about you, and why does it matter? We use three examples of groups that have been controlled and surveilled through digital technology—animals, children, and possible criminals—and will consider how different forms of control occur through digitalization.

10.1 Control through Surveillance and Digital Tracking

Big brother is watching you.

This is the warning in George Orwell's (1949) classic *1984*, a book whose story about technology, surveillance, and control is woven into a clear warning: the state sees you, and what it sees will be used against you. Everything you do—where you go, who you talk to, yes, even what you dream—can be used to question your credibility if you do something outside the state's norms for right and wrong. In Orwell's nightmarish vision of a surveillance society, the government even attempts to restrict language use since language can be used against the regime.

A much more recent example of fiction about surveillance is the *Black Mirror* episode "Arkangel" (Brooker, 2017), but in this story, it is family members, not the state, who surveil. The episode follows a mother who has a digital camera inserted into her daughter's eye, an "Arkangel," that with the help of an app, allows parents to oversee everything their children see and do. At first, the technology made the mother feel safe. She particularly liked the pixelating function that allowed her to obscure unpleasant or stressful input, such as violence and sex (so that her daughter only saw a blur). But in classic *Black Mirror* style, it does not end well when the daughter realizes what her mother has done—and all she has missed out on.

These two examples from science fiction tell two different stories about surveillance and technology: the first warns us of state domination, while the second depicts our own families as sources of surveillance and control. Taken together, they illustrate how surveillance has become a much more diverse, widespread, and complex phenomenon through digitalization, as well as how surveillance technology now stretches into new arenas and surveils new groups of users.

Surveillance is to observe, register, and/or gather data on people's behaviors, activities, and bodies with the goal of affecting, manipulating, or managing those who are surveilled. The term surveillance hints at an inequality in the balance of power: that one elevated party monitors another. In the past, surveillance has mainly been a state affair, but the state is now just one of many "big brothers" who wants to have control over what people do. We are also surveilled by large technology companies, by our bosses, by the stores in which we shop, by healthcare companies, and by educational institutions. Science fiction has long prepared us for a society in which technology is used by authoritarian regimes to surveil and control citizens. The warning has come to pass; there is reason to be worried over what types of information the state gathers about you, but reality has shown itself to be far more complex than fiction foresaw.

It is not just large actors who surveil, either; a great deal of surveillance occurs between "normal people." We surveil each other when we follow where people have been and what they have been doing on social media (Duffy & Chan, 2019; Trottier, 2012); when we use GPS tracking to surveil our senile grandparents (Karlsen et al., 2019; Landau & Werner, 2012) small children (Fahlquist, 2016; Hasinoff, 2017); or animals (Paci et al., 2020; Søraa & Vik, 2021); when we check the jogging route of a friend, uploaded by her FitBit; or when we obsessively check whether the last messages we sent to a new flame have been marked as "read"—and how long they took to answer us (Lutz & Ranzini, 2017). For a brief summary of surveillance related terms, see Box 10A. With digitalization, we must therefore broaden our understanding of surveillance and accept that it occurs in many more places and is carried out by many more actors than it used to be.

To be able to understand surveillance, we must also consider how much information we offer "voluntarily" through our use of technologies made for communication and self-expression, such as social media (Brown, 2015). "Voluntarily" is here placed in quotation marks because we must often agree to sharing information that we would prefer to keep private, but don't have the option to refuse sharing if we wish to use the technology in question. In addition, it is important to reflect on what is monitored through digital technology—*digital footprints*.

Box 10A.   Theory: Surveillance, Sousveillance, and Metaveillance

Surveillance doesn't necessarily come from above or from centralized powers. We also have the term "sousveillance," which refers to our own registering of data, about both ourselves and others, through surveillance technologies (Mann et al., 2003). An example is the social movement "the quantified self" (see Chapter 12), in which extensive registration and analysis of personal data is used to improve oneself. It is also possible to carry out mutual surveillance through "metaveillance," which is when two parties surveil each other, like we often do with family and partners through social media, none of whose Facebook posts go unseen or profile pictures go unliked (Mann, 2016). The terms *sousveillance* and *metaveillance* shed light on how we users surveil ourselves and each other. At the same time, we must remember that both national governments and diverse secret police gather data and surveil the population, often with a weak ethical foundation for doing so.

Digital footprints include all forms of electronic information that are created using the internet and can be linked to a concrete person, user, electronic tool, event, or place. *Active footprints* are those we make ourselves: pictures on Instagram, comments on Facebook, posts on Reddit, and the like. *Passive footprints*, on the other hand, are those created and sent (and sometimes saved) automatically through the use of digital technologies. The latter are often used to generate metadata, the most common of which are telephone numbers, email addresses, usernames, genders, ages, locations (where a phone is, for example), time stamps of conversations/emails/files/images, information on the device you are using, and subject lines on emails. Footprints are left in many contexts, both because digital technology is ubiquitous and because it is designed to be dependent on these types of data to function. (With ICBO in mind, we can also think that there must be ways to design technology that is less dependent on data that functions as digital footprints.) The more services and interactions we users of digital technology have, the more footprints we leave. The footprints say something about what we purchase, whom we socialize with, which travel routes we have chosen, and which digital services we use—as well as a number of other large and small data points about ourselves included in everything from healthcare logs to "no fly" lists.

Individually, these footprints say very little, but when they are gathered—and compared with millions of others' footprints— they become so-called *big data,* which can say a surprising amount about societal groups and individuals. Big data is a term referring to how huge amounts of data can be analyzed to indicate contexts, patterns, and trends that are too complex for people to go through individually (see Box 10B) (McDermott, 2017). Examples of this include analyses of people's internet searches, movement patterns, and health data.

Box 10B.   Fact: Characteristics of Big Data

	Big volume	The data set applies to many people and many data points
	Quick collection	Collection is largely automated and happens without input from the people about whom information is gathered
	Large data variation	The data set includes information on everything from food purchases to sleep routines
	Relational data set	Each data point says little individually; it is when they are put together that the data say something
	Large range of focus	Can collect data on almost any subject

Later in this chapter, we will look more closely at how control is digitalized through the tracking, generation, and analysis of big data. You can also use the exercise in Box 10C to investigate your own digital footprint. In the first two examples, we thematize virtual fences, where tracking technology is used to limit certain subjects' environments. The first example focuses on tracking animals, while the second focuses on tracking children. The third and last example examines how big data are used and applied in machine learning in the form of predictive police algorithms. Each example includes a discussion of the affordances and limitations of the technology, including the ethical problems linked to its use.

Box 10C. Exercise: Your Digital Footprint

In this exercise, we ask you, simply and straightforwardly, to search for information about yourself from the point of view of a third party. Use a browser that isn't affected by your earlier searches, for example, DuckduckGo.com. Imagine you don't know anything about yourself. What can you find out about yourself by using the search engine? Examine the following:

- Which personal data do you find, e.g., date of birth, address, partner, relations?
- Which data do you find linked to your own income and finances?
- Which images of yourself can you trace?
- Who owns and is responsible for the data you find? Where are they saved?

If you wish to make the exercise a little bit more like *Black Mirror*, try doing the same search with a friend or peer, and try making profiles of each other based on the information you find.

10.2 Control of Animals Using Virtual Fences

We often think of digitalization as a primarily urban phenomena, but in our first example, we will examine digital control in rural environments. The Norwegian rural landscape includes many fences. They are set up to prevent livestock from wandering off into rugged terrain or eating plants they are not permitted to eat. Keeping track of livestock can be difficult for the farmers who own them and who have a responsibility for managing their movements. Traditionally, fences have taken a lot of time and resources to build and maintain, and once they are put up, they are difficult to move. Animals are also surprisingly talented at finding holes in fences or places where they can jump over them when the grass is greener on the other side. It is here that technology can be used to help—through digital fences.

In 2011, the Norwegian company NoFence launched a new product that aimed to digitalize areas for grazing. By setting up virtual fences in a mapping program on their mobile phones, farmers could demarcate where their livestock could go, and the technology would then prevent the animals from moving outside the virtual fence (Brunberg et al., 2013). This technology is primarily used for goats, cows, and sheep that are outfitted with electronic collars (see Figure 10.1).

If the animals cross the "fence," which they cannot see but which is digitally present, the collar will make a warning sound. If the animals continue in the wrong direction, the sound will get louder and give them an electric shock. It took a relatively long time before the company's system was approved because the Norwegian Food Safety Authority was concerned about the animals' welfare. Studies nonetheless show that animals received less of a shock from the collars

FIGURE 10.1 Goats gracing inside a digital fence. Photo by Roger A. Søraa

than they did from a traditional electric fence—and goats, in particular, showed their intelligence by quickly learning how the technology worked (Brunberg et al., 2013). Søraa and Vik (2021) have examined, for example, how goats who use the technology have taken on a new primary function outside of milk and meat production—as grass trimmers. Some goats can be rented, for example, to trim the grass under power lines, where they are provided with a long, narrow field on which they can walk and graze. This shows how *domestication* of technology can lead to developing new skills for users—even goats! But if the area becomes too small, it limits the original idea of free-range goats. And goats do not necessarily follow the script of the digital fences. For example, some "musical goats" quickly learned that the sounds made by the collar were not in themselves dangerous and that the tones became louder before the electric shock. They could therefore spring over the fence, graze quickly on the other side, and then run back before they were shocked. This is clearly something the goats enjoy, but it wears out the batteries in the collars because they are constantly beeping. In addition, neighbors and hikers might not appreciate the (off-key) symphony made by the cheeky goats!

Through examining the *domestication* of virtual fences for animals, we can see, first, that digital technology makes it possible to surveil new groups in new ways because surveillance technology is so accessible, affordable, and user-friendly. The goats remind us, too, that those who are being surveilled do not always behave as the person surveilling or the technology desires. New consequences can develop out of surveillance (both for those being surveilled and for those doing the surveillance). Goats who learn to "trick" the technology and farmers who gain new opportunities for running small farms or grass-trimming businesses are two such consequences (Søraa & Vik, 2021). One way to reflect on what it is like to be surveilled is to consider the concept of the panopticon (see Box 10D), which demonstrates that when we *know* we might be watched, we will be more likely to regulate our own actions.

Tracking animals makes several interesting aspects of tracking and control visible. First, we ask fewer ethical questions when we are working with animals than we do

Box 10D.   Theory: Panopticon

A surveillance society is characterized by its "functioning, in part, because of the comprehensive gathering, recording, saving, analyzing, and applying of information about individuals or groups in these societies while they live their lives" (Surveillance Studies Network, n.d.). This leads to new forms of control and trust. To reflect on this, one can consider Jeremy Bentham's (1791) term *panopticon*. This thought experiment introduces an institution where inhabitants live in individual cells in a ring around a watchtower. The walls facing the tower are transparent so that the inhabitants can see the tower—but not who or what is in there because the tower has a one-way mirror. As such, a guard can oversee the inhabitants, but the inhabitants cannot see who is watching them. The inhabitants never know if they are being watched; they just know that, in theory, they could be watched at any time. The French philosopher Michel Foucault (1979) was critical of the panopticon. He suggested that constant surveillance forced a form of paranoid self-regulation in which people tried to conform to the possible consequences of being observed by people with more power.

when we are working with people. Animal welfare is clearly subject to strong regulations, but the animals themselves cannot sue the state if they are required to remain within specific areas or if their data goes astray. Secondly, the goat example shows us that surveillance can lead to changes in behavior, which we will explore further in a human-focused and more ethically fraught example of surveillance. While it may not seem problematic to oversee animals' movements, what about overseeing the movements of humans who cannot consent?

10.3 Care, Technology, and the Desire for Boundaries When Surveilling Children

"To lose a child is a parent's worst nightmare."

This is the start of an advertisement for the technology "Jiobit," a GPS gadget about the size of a battery that children can carry and that will provide parents with information about the child's location. In the advertisement, sobbing parents are talking to the police about a missing child, and Jiobit is portrayed as preventing a possible tragedy. Even if the user guidelines explicitly state that Jiobit is for recreational use only and not as a security system (presumably to protect the company from possible lawsuits), the depiction of the product is of an "extra set of eyes" that can follow one's children "no matter how far they go." Jiobit allows parents to create digital fences by marking their address in Google Maps and creating a radius around it to demarcate how far away from home is "safe"— similar to what we saw in the previous example, except with children instead of livestock. If the child wanders out of the "safe" area, the parents receive a warning on their phone. Even if this is not a visible limitation of space, the digital fence becomes a structural facilitator for the collection and processing of localization data (Gilmore, 2019).

However, Jiobit is not *scripted* with children as its imagined users, even if it is children who carry the technology around with them. The product is aimed at parents, who pay for the service and carry out the surveillance. The functionality and aesthetic design suggest safety and control for parents. It is also the parents who agree to the personal data collection agreement—a long document written in incomprehensible legalese—which allows Jiobit to gather information about the child's name, image, and location data, all without a clearly stated reason for doing so and without any information provided about how long this information is stored. And even if Jiobit promises not to use these data for advertising purposes, the agreement requires users' consent to data collection by third parties if new products and services might be of interest. As such, one could understand Jiobit to be not simply a surveillance technology but rather a *capitalistic* surveillance technology that sells data about your child to third parties to make money out of surveilling them.

As a group, children have always been particularly prone to surveillance, from state programs in the form of health checks overseeing their physical development in their first years of life to educational programs that map their progression and level relative to their peers—data that can be used to decide who should or should not be able to serve in the military, for example. The vulnerability of children is strengthened with the introduction of digital technologies because far more modes of surveillance develop and because children are not granted the authority, as they are not considered to have the competence or ability to understand the technologies used to control them. Parents create digital footprints for their children when they share pictures and stories about small and large events on social media—including before their children are born through ultrasound pictures. And a number of passive digital footprints are created by parents who use digital apps to observe their children's sleep habits and growth and various digital tools, such as electronic thermometers or bottles with sensors (Lupton & Williamson, 2017). Technology that gathers information on children's activities with the aim of fostering parents' security is just one more way that childhood is tracked and surveilled through digitalization.

Technologies like Jiobit are a reminder that surveillance also happens between people who know one another; it is not just something done by the state. In this example, it is the parents who oversee their children. Like the "Arkangel" episode of *Black Mirror*, this surveillance is something that happens due to parental care, and it is interpreted not as surveillance per se (at least not initially), but rather as a form of protection and as part of providing a secure upbringing. In contrast to many other tracking and registration technologies used by adults, where measurement and sharing of achievements are central (for example, workout apps) and where terminology like *sousveillance* and *metaveillance* are relevant, children who carry Jiobit have little chance of controlling what, how, and when they are surveilled, or which data about them is shared.

As such, the implementation of technology for tracking children strengthens parents' power over their children. The child's room to maneuver is reduced both metaphorically and literally by the fact that they no longer have anywhere they can go that is outside their parents "gaze," and even their route to school is stipulated by technology that reports "deviations" if the child takes a detour. In addition, the lack of care for personal data is quite common and potentially problematic. This is not just true for technologies made for tracking children but is also true for digital technologies more generally.

In the examples of the surveillance and tracking of children and animals, the collection of data is absolutely essential. It is because the technology constantly gathers data that it can function as a digital fence. And even if the animals' lack of privacy will not keep us awake at night, the sale of children's location data to unknown third parties gives cause for concern. The thematic thread of personal data is one we will continue to follow in the third example. There, we will examine how surveillance technology is used to predict the future through the analysis of data sets (created by various digital footprints) and to calculate the likelihood that a person will break the law.

10.4 Predictive Police Algorithms: Surveillance of Data Sets and Predictions of the Future

What if we could predict who would do something criminal as easily as we predict the weather—a sort of weather report for criminality? In criminology, the term "predictive policing" is used to describe the evaluation of who has the biggest chance of committing a crime, including who has the biggest chance of breaking the law (again) and who should be released from prison. To carry out these evaluations, police use big data and algorithms. Even if this seems like a good idea on paper, the data that has informed the algorithm has been shown to be discriminatory and racist (Kaufmann, 2019; Richardson et al., 2019).

Predictive police algorithms are most often used in the USA, and the problems with such a system become particularly obvious in a land so characterized by socioeconomic differences and systemic injustices (Shapiro, 2017; Asaro, 2019). As #BlackLivesMatter has highlighted, particularly since 2020, the police' handling of Black Americans is both discriminatory and deadly. Black Americans are more often stopped by the police, more often arrested, more often sentenced, more often given longer and harsher sentences, and more often killed when arrested than other groups (Sheehey, 2020). In themselves, these issues are deeply problematic, but they are worsened when the statistics regarding police stops and arrests are made into a data set that is used when prisoners' chances of reoffending are evaluated. The data set suggests that Black Americans are at higher risk of reoffending—even if the real reason that racialized Americans make up a larger proportion of the prison population is because of widespread structural racism within the police state.

Machine learning builds on both big data and algorithms, the latter of which are recipes or programs that carry out specific tasks. By letting computers work with data sets, they can "learn" what the next steps are (predictions), and even learn how a task can be carried out "better." The combination of digital footprints, big data, and machine learning has great potential. As users, we meet the results in the form of recommendations ("See what others who have bought X have also bought!"), digital chat assistants, and custom advertising. Perhaps less visible is how the same technology acts as a foundation for the automatic evaluation of loan applications, rankings of job candidates and applicants to universities, debt collection and credit card offers, and matches made on dating apps—or, within predictive police algorithms, who is considered fit to enter a country. As users, machine learning makes the technologies we meet more customized and personal, but algorithms also have a grimmer side—algorithmic bias (see Box 10E).

Machine learning is used in ever-increasing contexts, and our everyday lives are increasingly permeated by algorithms. We can understand this as a series of *delegations* where we give more and more responsibility and work to technologies, which in turn require something from us. With algorithms,

Box 10E.   Fact: Algorithmic Bias

"Algorithmic bias" does not suggest that computers in themselves are racist, homophobic, or misogynistic but rather that they learn to express forms of discrimination through (1) the data sets they work with, (2) the algorithms that handle the data sets, and/or (3) their interpretation and reproduction of earlier human discrimination. To illustrate this, let's more closely examine face recognition and text-based analyses.

Facial recognition systems can identify people by placing them in groups, analyze feelings, identify gender, age, and race, and more. They are used to open your telephone, during employment processes, to authorize purchases, for security, for surveillance, and for much more, but they often discriminate (Buolamwini & Gebru, 2018). For example, they function best on white men, while everyone else, particularly women and those with melanin-rich skin, are often miscategorized. This has had many problematic results; for example, Google Photos created a furor when their 2015 algorithm incorrectly tagged African Americans as gorillas (Zomorodi, 2015).

Similar problems occur when algorithms are asked to interpret text. Twitter categorized drag queens as more hateful in their language than neo-Nazis (Antonialli, 2019), as well as gay men as women when targeting advertisements (Fosch-Villaronga et al., 2020). Through the term *technological fix*, we warned you that new technology can lead to new problems, and algorithmic bias is a good example of the sorts of problems that can occur when algorithms are asked to categorize and classify humans and human interactions.

this relationship to delegations is somewhat scarier than in other contexts because it can be unclear what is delegated to algorithms and what the algorithms are trying to produce in return.

Researchers who wanted to create an image recognition algorithm to differentiate between wolves and dogs believed for some time that they had succeeded because the algorithm correctly tagged "dog" and "wolf" in images.

However, it was later revealed that the algorithm had learned to recognize snow, which was more often present in images of wolves, and as such could not "see" the difference between dogs and wolves. As such, algorithms can seem to be working as planned, but they may be doing something completely different than we think. An algorithm that appear to be searching for the best candidates for a job may just pick out the "whitest" and "most masculine" applicants because those applicants have been prioritized by people in earlier job searches, and as such, the data set from which the algorithm has learned is biased. Or an algorithm that appears to objectively evaluate the risk factor for who should be examined more closely by border control may be basing its choices on skin color and simply reproducing racist practices.

In sum, we can see that there are many problems with machine learning. The data sets machines are trained with are decisive, and if one gives them historic data, historic problems (like discrimination on the basis of race or gender) will continue to be problems. Discrimination can be difficult to notice in the development process if one is not aware of and therefore does not specifically address the problem, and not even the developers will have clear oversight over what an algorithm does and how it evaluates input. When the rule of law is based on a guess of who could be a criminal produced by algorithms few truly understand, we create a dangerous precedent. That the methods that are used for machine learning today will lead to algorithms' use of skin color, age, gender, sexuality, or other personal attributes when they determine "what you will do in future" is particularly problematic. Algorithms, in other words, are potentially unruly and troublesome actors to have on one's team.

10.5 Life in a Surveillance Society: What Digitalization Does to Surveillance

Digitalization provides more opportunities for surveillance. Most phones and computers have built-in microphones and cameras that can be used against us, as well as programs that gather large quantities of data. Surveillance technology is easily accessible for most people, and we can relatively simply set up systems to surveil our nearest and dearest—whether family members or pets. Even if security has always been a recurring theme when justifying monitoring, also before we developed digital solutions, there is a difference of magnitude between parental worries and national safety. The potentially negative consequences of surveillance must not remain unacknowledged just because surveillance technology is widely available.

When looking at what has been digitalized, it is interesting to note that the technologies that are used to track both livestock and children are almost identical. Tracking children and tracking animals relies on the use of GPS technologies and the creation of virtual fences, and in both cases, the technology is used to generate data about where the subject under surveillance is (that is, localization data). The difference between virtual fences for children and animals is the warning that is sent when the subject goes outside the defined area. (Jiobit sends parents a message, while goats are warned themselves through sounds and, later, electric shocks.) As such, these cases demonstrate how the same technology, with only small changes in design, can be applied differently—and this depends on who uses it and in which ways.

Tracking animals has shown us that the accessibility of surveillance technology is making it easier to surveil and control different areas and actors, including nonhuman actors. Tracking children has shown us how surveillance includes many more actors than the government; here, insight into the subject's movements is provided not just to the whole family but also to unknown third parties who purchase data sets more or less without consent. It is striking how much surveillance occurs outside our control, not just because "Big Brother" (the state) sees us but also because the companies behind the technologies we use for surveillance sell data for profit, and as end users, it is nearly impossible for us to have oversight over which applications and services register what or who has access to these data.

Predictive police algorithms have the opposite geographical premise from the virtual fences used to control goats and children. Here, primary users (the police) are not attempting to keep secondary users (prisoners/suspects) inside a specific area; rather, the aim is to keep secondary users who may undertake criminal actions *outside* areas where they, according to the system, oughtn't to be. The primary users, that is, the rule of law and its enforcers, can therefore ensure that certain areas are kept free of those the algorithm considers undesirable—and this can obviously lead to discrimination.

Because we live in a surveillance society where large amounts of personal data are made available through our use of digital technologies, it is tempting to use these data. But even though it is easier than ever to gather a data set, this does not necessarily mean that these data sets are useful for teaching machines because they already include systematic discrimination—human biases are baked into the data. Predictive police algorithms show what can happen when we think of data sets as true representations of the world or of technologies as neutral and objective. Algorithms are tasked with making independent decisions about what is important in a data set without being remotely capable of understanding the context of the data (a task far outside their capacity).

There is reason to believe that health-related big data, in particular—which is gathered through daily voluntary activities like measuring blood sugar, blood pressure, calorie intake, physical activity, sleep, and more, often together with the use of medicines—could help us to see possible correlations between lifestyles, illnesses, and treatments. However, such traces can cause problems. Who should have permission to gather this information? How should such permissions be given across borders and within varied legal systems? Which rights to our data do we have in practice when use of a platform requires that we agree to the collection of data that is later sold to third and fourth parties? Even if we have laws that give us the right of choice regarding the traces we leave (e.g., in Europe, the General Data Protection Regulation (GDPR)), is there any real consent when end-user license agreements or cookie agreements comprise several thousand words of incomprehensible legal jargon (McDermott, 2017)?

If we compare our examples to those from Orwell's *1984* or *Black Mirror*'s "Arkangel" episode, referenced in the introduction, we can see that surveillance (and surveillance technology) is often introduced as a solution to security and safety concerns. But both in fiction and in real life, the consequences of surveillance are not always immediately visible. In "Arkangel," technology significantly intervenes in the child's life but is presented as an aid for "Big Mother." It is not until the consequences for the child's well-being become visible that the surveillance is interpreted as abusive. As such, "Arkangel" is a reminder that surveillance can be initiated out of love, can occur between people who know each other well (sousveillance), and can have consequences we cannot foresee.

Digitalization makes surveillance significantly simpler, more accessible, and cheaper—and thereby *scripts* both the uses and users of surveillance technology as general purpose. At the same time, it can be difficult to clearly see who the technology is made for, as the design often has many users in mind: both those who use an app every day to surveil family members and those who are potentially purchasing the data generated through both active and passive footprints. There are also limits to how much one who uses these technologies can oppose their *scripts*, since all forms of use result in digital footprints—and in practice, the alternatives available are "to use" or "not to use" the technology. That the surveillance is digital is also a relevant consideration because it makes the data generated much easier to copy and share, which in turn presents new challenges linked to privacy since we have not yet understood nor taken into account the possible consequences of data sharing and sales.

In *1984*'s Orwellian society, citizens are promised that "Big Brother" will take care of them—as long as he knows *everything* about both what citizens do and what they think. Today, we have many "big brothers," including various nations that surveil each other's citizens and commercial actors who want to know everything they can about our lives out of a belief that it will lead to increased sales. Digital footprints are used in large part by the state, for example, in the persecution of criminals, and they have recently been used in attempts to track COVID infections and spread, or how effective we are, how often we take breaks, and what websites we access when we are working from home. At the same time, new forms of surveillance are occurring where family members surveil each other, abusive partners stalk each other, or animals are surveilled by their owners, so our society is perhaps closer to the Orwellian one that we would like to think.

10.6 Conclusion

In this chapter, we have examined how digital technology can be used to manage and control both humans and animals. A digital fence widened the horizons for goats because they found ways to bypass the script, learned new skills, and became "goat lawn mower" rather than simply meat and milk producers. Surveillance over their own children provided parents with increased security but also increased the risk that sensitive data regarding their children would go astray. Predictive police algorithms may appear as if they are working, but they may actually be perpetuating and reinforcing structural discrimination.

Information about where we are and what we are doing is extremely valuable for companies hungry for big data that can illuminate consumption and health trends and thereby allow the companies to sell more things, whether products or political commercials, to more people. Vulnerable groups are particularly subject to surveillance when it is left to algorithms based on skewed historical data. Together, the examples above show that digitalization has created new—and radically different—preconditions for control through data, especially with regard to (1) who can now be controlled because technology is accessible, cheap, and easy to use; (2) who can be surveilled; (3) why we carry out surveillance; and (4) who has access to the information generated by digital surveillance and control.

References

Antonialli, D. (2019, 25 July). Drag queen vs. David Duke: Whose tweets are more "toxic"? *Wired*. https://www.wired.com/story/drag-queens-vs-far-right-toxic-tweets/

Asaro, P. M. (2019). AI ethics in predictive policing: From models of threat to an ethics of care. *IEEE Technology and Society Magazine, 38*(2), 40–53. https://doi.org/10.1109/MTS.2019.2915154.

Bentham, J. (1791). *Panopticon or the inspection house* (2nd ed.). T. Payne.

Brooker, C. (Writer), & Forster, J. (Ed.). (2017). Arkangel (season 2, episode 4) [Episode in a TV series]. In A. Jones & C. Booker (Producers), *Black Mirror*. Netflix.

Brown, I. (2015). Social media surveillance. *The international encyclopedia of figital communication and society*, 1–7. https://doi.org/10.1002/9781118767771.wbiedcs122.

Brunberg, E., Bergslid, R., & Sørheim, K. (2013). The virtual fencing system Nofence-trials 2013. *Bioforsk-rapport, 8*(176). https://hdl.handle.net/11250/2445612.

Buolamwini, J., & Gebru, T. (2018, January). Gender shades: Intersectional accuracy disparities in commercial gender classification. *Proceedings of the 1st Conference on Fairness, Accountability and Transparency, PMLR 81*: 77–91 (pp. 77–91).

Duffy, B. E., & Chan, N. K. (2019). "You never really know who's looking": Imagined surveillance across social media platforms. *New Media & Society, 21*(1), 119–138. https://doi.org/10.1177/1461444818791318.

Fahlquist, J. (2016). Ethical concerns of using GPS to track children. In E. Taylor & T. Rooney (Eds.), *Surveillance futures: Social and ethical implications of new technologies for children and young people* (p. 122). Routledge.

Fosch-Villaronga, E., Poulsen, A., Søraa, R. A., & Custers, B. H. M. (2020). Don't guess my gender, gurl: The inadvertent impact of gender inferences. In *Bias and Fairness in AI: Workshop at ECMLPKDD 2020*, Ghent, Belgium, September 18, 2020 (pp. 1–9). Springer.

Foucault, M., & Sheridan, A. (1979). *Discipline and punish: The birth of the prison*. Peregrine Books.

Gilmore, J. N. (2019). Securing the kids: Geofencing and child wearables. *Convergence: The International Journal of Research into New Media Technologies*. https://doi.org/10.1177/1354856519882317.

Hasinoff, A. A. (2017). Where are you? Location tracking and the promise of child safety. *Television & New Media, 18*(6), 496–512. https://doi.org/10.1177/1527476416680450.

Karlsen, C., Moe, C. E., Haraldstad, K., & Thygesen, E. (2019). Caring by telecare? A hermeneutic study of experiences among older adults and their family caregivers. *Journal of Clinical Nursing, 28*(7–8), 1300–1313. https://doi.org/10.1111/jocn.14744.

Kaufmann, M. (2019). Who connects the dots? In M. Hoijtink & M. Leese (Eds.), *Technology and agency in international relations*. Taylor & Francis.

Landau, R., & Werner, S. (2012). Ethical aspects of using GPS for tracking people with dementia: Recommendations for practice. *International Psychogeriatrics*, *24*(3), 358–366. https://doi.org/10.1017/S1041610211001888.

Lupton, D., & Williamson, B. (2017). The datafied child: The dataveillance of children and implications for their rights. *New Media & Society*, *19*(5), 780–794. https://doi.org/10.1177/1461444816686328.

Lutz, C., & Ranzini, G. (2017). Where dating meets data: Investigating social and institutional privacy concerns on Tinder. *Social Media + Society*, *3*(1), 1–12. https://doi.org/10.1177/2056305117697735.

Mann, S. (2016, June). Surveillance (oversight), sousveillance (undersight), and metaveillance (seeing sight itself). In *2016 IEEE Conference on Computer Vision and Pattern Recognition Workshops (CVPRW)* (pp. 1408–1417). IEEE.

Mann, S., Nolan, J., & Wellman, B. (2003). Sousveillance: Inventing and using wearable computing devices for data collection in surveillance environments. *Surveillance & Society*, *1*(3), 331–355. https://doi.org/10.24908/ss.v1i3.3344.

McDermott, Y. (2017). Conceptualising the right to data protection in an era of Big Data. *Big Data & Society*, *4*(1). https://doi.org/10.1177/2053951716686994.

Orwell, G. (1949). *Nineteen eighty-four: A novel*. Secker & Warburg.

Paci, P., Mancini, C., & Price, B. (2020). Understanding the interaction between animals and wearables: The wearer experience of cats. *Proceedings of the 2020 ACM Designing Interactive Systems Conference*, July 6–10, Eindhoven, Nederland (pp. 1701–1712). Association for Computing Machinery. https://doi.org/10.1145/3357236.3395546.

Richardson, R., Schultz, J. M., & Crawford, K. (2019). Dirty data, bad predictions: How civil rights violations impact police data, predictive policing systems, and justice. *NYUL Review Online*, *94*(15). https://www.nyulawreview.org/online-features/dirty-data-bad-predictions-how-civil-rights-violations-impact-police-data-predictive-policing-systems-and-justice/

Shapiro, A. (2017). Reform predictive policing. *Nature*, *541*(7638), 458–460. https://doi.org/10.1038/541458a.

Sheehey, B. (2020). Ethics beyond transparency: Resisting the racial injustice of predictive policing. *Techné: Research in Philosophy and Technology*, *24*(3), 256–281. https://doi.org/10.5840/techne202087128.

Søraa, R. A., & Vik, J. (2021). Boundaryless boundary-objects: Digital fencing of the CyborGoat in rural Norway. *Journal of Rural Studies*. *87*, 23–31.

Surveillance Studies Network. (n.d.). *An introduction to the surveillance society*. https://www.surveillance-studies.net/?page_id=119

Trottier, D. (2012). Interpersonal surveillance on social media. *Canadian Journal of Communication, 37*(2), 319–332. https://doi.org/10.22230/cjc.2012v37n2a2536.

Zomorodi, M. (Host). (2015, 30 September). Why Google "thought" this Black woman was a gorilla. Note to self. *WNYC Studios*. https://www.wnycstudios.org/podcasts/notetoself/episodes/deep-problem-deep-learning

CHAPTER 11

Digitalization of Culture

*Remix, Community,
and Prosumers*

DOI: 10.1201/9781003289555-14

Culture is thoughts, communication, norms, values, artifacts, and patterns of behavior that are shared between many people—in groups of varying sizes. Culture can also be understood as the creations we make to explore what it means to be human, to entertain ourselves, to inform, and to bond. In this chapter, we will dive deeper into how cultural expressions have evolved together with new technology and, especially, how the digitalization of culture has made users and audiences into *prosumers* (both producers and consumers).

Digitalization affects cultural expression by (1) shaping how culture is created and shared, (2) challenging established ideas about who are the makers of culture, and (3) changing the artifacts themselves—that is, changing what culture can look, sound, and feel like because it is now made and accessed with digital technologies. Examining the digitalization of culture is a way to study digital technologies as tools for culture as well as how cultural expressions are created and shared through innovative user practices and communities. In this chapter, we will examine how culture is created, shared, and transformed (remixed) digitally through three examples: memes, fan fiction, and game streaming.

11.1 *SKAM* and Transmedia Storytelling

To tease out how digitalization is changing culture, we want to start with the Norwegian hit series *SKAM* (Andem, 2015) as an example of how new technology affords new ways of telling and engaging with stories. In *SKAM*, we meet a group of high school friends, and the show details their experiences of love, friendship, betrayal, and shame. The series' themes are typical for a teen series, with drama linked to school, friends, identity, parents, and the future. However, even if the themes are what you expect, *SKAM* is not a traditional series. Instead, it is a real-time, transmedia online series comprised of short daily video clips (that were put together and aired as weekly episodes) and a whole range of different interactions on social media, where the story unfolded through chat messages, Instagram posts, and YouTube videos from the series' fictional characters.

While streaming platforms have hailed "on demand viewing" as a benefit of digital broadcasting, allowing viewers to "binge" entire seasons and rewatch as they please, *SKAM* instead made a fictional world that operated in "real time" through transmedia storytelling, where the story progressed just as much through what the fictional characters posted on social media as it did through the episodes. In other words, Monday afternoon in the real world was also Monday afternoon in the series, and the plot developed in real time through different platforms and content as the characters "posted" about their lives. That the story was told through social media meant that "watching" the show was integrated into and blended with daily internet use (Magnus, 2016).

On different social media platforms, fans discussed the themes of the series, speculated about what would happen, and shared gossip, memes, and fan art. Fans' engagement can be partially explained by how the series facilitated their participation and motivation. First, the series went through comprehensive preparatory studies to ensure that the themes selected were relevant for the (young) audience. Secondly, the series was peppered with "easter-eggs," hints, references, and symbolism that fans could detect, share, and decode. For example, the season three tagline was "everything is love," and the advertisement for the season featured Isak being showered with milk by other boys in a locker room. This was a clue to how the season would focus on LGBTQ+ stories and turned out to center on the romance between the characters Isak and Even (Magnus, 2016).

Both as a series and as a (fan) phenomenon, *SKAM* challenged contemporary conventions about how to make compelling drama. *SKAM* is an interesting example of digitalization of culture, not because of *which* stories are told but rather due to the *ways* in which they are told: in different formats and media, across different platforms, in real time, with a close connection with the audience's daily lives and habits. *SKAM* showcases how digitalization affords new ways of creating and experiencing cultural artifacts and expressions, as well as how digital technology is shaping how audiences can engage with culture. The latter is of particular interest.

By orienting cultural expression toward what users do, both within and outside of the visions of platform designers and developers, we capture technological and cultural practices that are unexpected yet made possible because every technology is open for multiple interpretations (*interpretatively flexible*). Through digitalization, many cultural expressions have become faster, easier, and cheaper to create, and through the internet, they are also faster, easier, and cheaper to share. However, speed and cost are not the only changes that matter.

11.2 Remix Culture as the Foundation of Digital Culture

The first aspect of digitalization we want to highlight is how it is democratizing several creative practices simply by making the tools needed for creating and sharing one's own cultural expressions accessible to more people. For example, only a few decades ago, video recording equipment cost an arm and a leg to purchase and required specialist knowledge to operate. As such, it was, in practice, reserved for professionals and wealthy enthusiasts. Today, filming something is easily done on our smart phones, and it is simple to edit those videos with the help of free apps. That these creations can also easily be shared through already-established networks on various digital platforms also indicates that the ways in which digital culture spreads (and how the public engages with culture) have changed. Digitalization has changed who can express their ideas, stories, and visions through film, and we see similar patterns for other formats like text, audio, and images.

That digital tools result in cultural artifacts made in digital *formats* is also worth noting, as it has consequences for how those artifacts can be used and by whom. Following a sociotechnical approach where we take materiality seriously, we must reflect on how digital cultural expressions differ from non-digital ones. For example, a painting in a gallery or a performance at the local theater have different possibilities for transformation and sharing than a digital image or a digital recording of a play. The non-digital examples are bound to time and place in a way digital formats are not, placing limits on, among others, how many people can view them and when. More interestingly, while art has always been about borrowing and commenting on the works of others, a digital format affords remixing in new ways. Since the digital format flattens any and all content into lines of machine-readable information, it can be (re)mixed in ways earlier modes of expression could not. That a digital format is so easy to copy, transform, or combine in new ways is the material foundation for what we can describe as *remix culture* (Lessig, 2008).

There are no books, films, songs, games, or other cultural artifacts that are not affected by earlier works, a point that is well summarized by the phrase "everything is a remix" (Meikle, 2016, as illustrated in Figure 11.1) from the

THE BASIC ELEMENTS OF CREATIVITY

COPY   TRANSFORM   COMBINE

FIGURE 11.1 The basis elements of creativity.

documentary with the same title. Remixing is, as such, a key characteristic of culture in general, although it is one that has become much more pervasive through digitalization—both because we have tools available that allow us to be cocreators of culture and because we have developed an understanding of these tools that encourages our creativity and playfulness. Rather than idealizing cultural expressions based on their "originality," remix culture embraces creativity and cultural expression as something characterized by copying, transforming, and combining known elements to make something new (Navas & Gallagher, 2014; Baron, 2019).

Although some criticize remix culture for producing simple imitations or derivative work, those who take part in it argue that it represents a democratization of culture that, through innumerable contributions by users, creates a richer and *more diverse* culture. In line with the idea of the active user as a coproducer of both technology and culture (see Chapter 4), remix culture invites us to think of cultural artifacts as unfinished when they are sent out into the world. Books aren't there simply to be read but rather to provide stories to build on and share, and songs aren't just to be listened to but are also beats we can play with when making our own. In a sociotechnical perspective, remix culture is also interesting because remixing destabilizes the division between users and producers by making users into producers—or so-called *prosumers* (see Box 11A).

Box 11A. Theory: Prosumers

Prosumers are both producers and consumers. In the digital world, the term was first used to describe how "dot-com communities" appeared to be fully saturated by mass-produced goods and needed normal users to act as active cocreators and producers of design, including among other things, redesigning products to better suit themselves and the subcultures of which they were a part. Within research, the term is used to describe many things, including energy systems, such as how placing a solar panel on one's roof can make one a "prosumer" of energy, as well as robotics and science fiction studies.

The remixed artifacts we will examine more closely in this chapter—memes, fan fiction, and livestreamed games—have developed in user-driven online communities, often against the developers' visions (and even wishes) about how they should be used. Common to these artifacts is how they are created through copying, remixing, and sharing on digital platforms. However, before we dive into the examples, let us first consider the material and cultural preconditions for a remix culture through the concepts of *participatory culture* and *networked publics.*

11.3 Understanding Where Remix Culture Comes From: Participatory Culture and Networked Publics

Participatory culture describes online communities for artistic expression and social engagement. The term has been used to describe the enthusiasm and productivity of gaming and fan communities (Jenkins, 2006). Participatory cultures are characterized by their supportive and collective approach to creation, where members cheer each other on and share their creations freely. From encouraging others in the community to establishing practices that facilitate creative output (for example, informal competitions, workshops, and hackathons), participatory cultures create a supportive environment with a low threshold for participation. New members are initiated through informal mentorships, whereby experienced users share knowledge with newcomers both by creating content that explains the community's interests and rules and through one-on-one interactions.

The boundaries between producers and users are unclear because everyone is understood as a contributor (even if some voices are clearly better heard than others; the voice of a famous author, for example, goes farther and is heard by more people than the beliefs of an unknown fan). Members can contribute in different ways: writing texts, managing a website, making gifs, or perhaps "just" commenting or sharing content. Either way, members experience this participation as meaningful. There is no member registry or official list of participants, but through shared interests, members experience community and belonging (Jenkins, 2009).

The term participatory culture was coined by Henry Jenkins (1992), a pioneer in research on fan cultures. The term describes characteristics of supportive and creative online communities but is also a critique of traditional understandings of media, learning, and citizenship, where engaging with pop culture is considered a meaningless hobby. Instead of labeling media use as mindless consumption by a passive audience, members of participatory cultures invite us to think of everyday users as active coproducers of culture who create and shape their experience of media—in line with the term *prosumer*, above. Spending time on media, and particularly popular culture, is not, from this perspective, a "waste of time," but rather a way of showing engagement, developing critical perspectives, and building community (Edutopia, 2013).

Participatory culture also demonstrates that learning is not limited to classrooms and political engagement is not limited to political parties. Learning can just as well take place in meetings between enthusiasts who form informal mentorships, undertake their own interest-based explorations, and desire to develop new knowledge for themselves and their fellow fans. Democratic participation can be more than just becoming a member of a political party and writing opinion pieces in national papers (even if these are still important democratic tools). In participatory culture, the path from fandom to political activism is short. For example, in spring 2020, K-pop fans took over several Nazi hashtags and thus "drowned out" opponents of #BlackLivesMatter in social media (Lorenz et al., 2020). Another example is when various groups of fans used the hashtag #oscarssowhite to demand that Oscar nominations become more diverse and representative of various ethnoracial groups. It can also be remixing pop culture to share one's own stories and ideas—and through them, challenge societal norms and diversify what stories we tell (Jenkins & Shresthova, 2012; Brough & Shresthova, 2012). See a brief summary of participatory culture in Box 11B.

Box 11B. Characteristics of Participatory Culture

	Low thresholds	Low thresholds for creative and social engagement make it easy to participate, and activism is supported.
	Informal mentorship	Knowledge is exchanged through informal mentorships, and experienced members initiate new members.
	Digital expression	Remix culture is expressed in new and creative forms of production such as modding, machinima, fan fiction, zines, mashups, and so forth.
	Shared problem-solving	Community members work cooperatively toward shared goals like developing a dedicated Wikipedia page or exploring a fictional universe. This can also include political engagement, such as fan activism.
	Spreadable media	Support is provided for creating and sharing what is made with others; the circulation of opinions and content in and across platforms characterizes the spread of media.
	Meaning making	Members have the experience that "their contribution" plays a role, as well as feelings of community and belonging, even if there are no requirements for membership or no defined organization.

In addition to having established networks that can be quickly deployed when a pressing issue arises fans also routinely engage with social issues through their fandoms. Fans in participatory cultures have long been champions of more diverse stories, characters, and actors. A pertinent example is the racebending community that developed in protest to the whitewashing of the popular anime series *Avatar: The Last Airbender* (Gilliland, 2016) in the film adaptation, and has continued their work by re-envisioning the fictional universe as more diverse. Another example is how *Supernatural* fans, led by *Supernatural* star Misha Collins, dedicate 1 week every year to doing good deeds and undertaking creative activities through taking part in the world's biggest scavenger hunt, GISHWES (The Greatest International Scavenger Hunt, 2020).

To understand how participatory culture is materially supported—that is, how technology facilitates or hinders certain actions—the term *networked publics* can be useful. Coined by internet researcher dana boyd (2010), the term networked publics is used to describe how new publics are made possible through digitalization. Networked publics are constructed through network technologies (such as the worldwide web [www], social media, and diverse platforms) and new configurations of people, technologies, and practices. The term *publics* refers here to gatherings of people with shared understandings of the world, shared identities, and shared interests. By linking publics to their material preconditions, that is, how technology shapes what can happen and how it can happen, the term networked publics emphasizes how bits and bytes function as architectures and infrastructures that make certain processes possible while preventing others. The material preconditions for network technologies are shown in Box 11C.

In a remix culture, these material limitations are central: because what we share is saved, it can also be seen by others long after it was shared (persistence). That digital content can be copied is central to remixing and sharing (replication). Because it is shared online, it has the potential to reach a wide audience (scalability and spreadability), and the source material used in remixing is made accessible across time and space (searchability). We can understand these qualities as the overarching *script* for digital platforms, in which the imagined user is interested in both finding and sharing content (potentially on a large scale), and use is linked to searching, producing, and sharing content.

The combination of networked publics and participatory cultures is a mix that has, over the past few decades, shifted how we engage with culture. These technologies and practices have moved from subculture to mainstream, and now affect how we think about culture, creativity, and

Box 11C.   Theory: Characteristics of Networked Publics

	Persistence	Expressions and statements online are automatically saved and archived—they persist. This means that you don't need be present "when it happens" to be able to see/read/play/hear/experience culture.
	Replication	Content made of bits can be copied and moved to various devices and platforms. Both those who save content and those who use it (the public) can make copies.
	Scalability	Since the cost of sharing is low, a picture can just as easily be shared once as a million times.
	Spreadability	New content can easily be shared by a large number of users, and sharing functions (both within and between platforms) support this.
	Searchability	Content is organized so that it is searchable (for example, by keyword or hashtag), and it is thus also accessible outside the platforms and contexts in which it is shared.

community more broadly. We will explore this further in the three empirical examples of memes, fan fiction, and livestreaming games, which demonstrate how creativity can be a collective project as well as how digital materiality changes the relationships between users and producers.

11.4 Memes: Collective Creativity, Both Serious and Humorous

In daily speech, the term *meme* is used to describe text, images, videos, sounds, and links—often humorous in character—that are shared via social media. For a more precise definition of internet memes, we can turn to Shifman

(2013), who defines memes as (1) a group of digital objects with common features in content, form, and/or stance; (2) that are made with awareness of other memes; and are (3) shared, imitated, and/or changed online by many different users. As such, memes are best understood not as single jokes or ideas shared on social media but rather as a "community" of small, shareable stories that reference each other. Memes exist on all platforms, are found in both artistic and simple formats, have local and global variations, and are generated and shared in a number of different settings. Memes are just as easily used to demonstrate political affiliation as they are to poke fun at a close friend.

We tend to think of memes as being born out of internet culture, but memes actually existed before the internet and social media. Take, for example, "Kilroy was here" from World War II, illustrated in Figure 11.2. As far as we know, the text was first used by a ship inspector, James J. Kilroy, to mark the boats he had inspected before they were sent into battle. Soldiers noticed the signature and made a game of scribbling it on all possible surfaces. Along the way, someone added a simple drawing of a man with a big nose, and the meme became a recognizable figure that remained popular long after the war (Shifman, 2013).

Other examples of non-digital memes are friendship books and graffiti tags, where short texts and artistic signatures are made again and again as signs of both unity and protest. As such, memes were not created on the internet. However, the huge number of memes that now exist and their complexity, as well as how quickly they appear and disappear, make

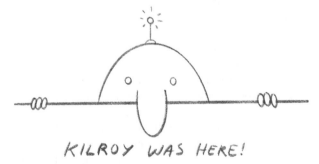

FIGURE 11.2 Illustration of the Kilroy-meme. A line drawing of a large nosed figure popping his head above the horizon. Illustration by Nienke Bruijning

internet memes significantly different than their non-digital forebears.

Memes exemplify how digitalization of culture can be a democratizing process where all users have access to technologies for production and sharing. Even if you obviously need to know a variety of memes to "master" the genre and make your own, they require few technical skills and no specialized equipment to make. There are many free image meme generators available where you can choose between known templates, and all you need to do is write in the text you want. Platforms like TikTok have functionality that supports the saving of (memetic) sounds and the creation of new content using them. As such, the threshold for making memes is low. The material preconditions for networked publics are made clearly visible through memes, as they are easy to make, copy, and share precisely because they are digital.

If we look at memes from a *user perspective*, that is, if we consider what making and sharing memes means for users, we see that using memes often relates to several different things at the same time. Sharing memes demonstrates being on the "inside" of a group, someone who knows the internal jokes and jargon and understands "what's up" (Miltner, 2014). Memes are also used to demonstrate knowledge about popular culture, subcultures, and meme culture, to express ideas, political stances, and life experiences, and as a way to create collective identities and strengthen communities.

Memes are great at expressing emotions. Since a great deal of our online communication happens via text—and often through a few words written in a short space of time—it can be difficult to communicate nuances and feelings compared to face-to-face conversations since we cannot rely on tone of voice or body language. To show the moods or feelings linked to a comment, memes are used (together with emojis and other slang) to indicate the tone of communication. Negative feelings may be particularly difficult to express online due to social media norms that expect us to post and showcase our best sides (see Chapter 12). Memes are thus often used to express dark, painful, or shameful reactions or feelings. As such, we *delegate* the responsibility of digitally showing and expressing our feelings—particularly the negative ones—to memes.

Even if memes have democratizing traits, the format is also potentially limiting. This duality became clear in an analysis of the subgenre of memes about students' lives called *student problem memes* (SPM) (Ask & Abidin, 2018). Through SPM, students used humor to express, share, and find support for problems related to their lives as students. They shared worries about the future, shame about procrastination, struggles with balancing their studies with free time, and issues related to mental health. In contrast to the polished and idealized stories that are the norm on platforms like Instagram, SPM expressed and emphasized flaws and failures. As such, SPM memes contributed to creating a shared student identity that showcased how student life can be a difficult experience, see examples in Figure 11.3.

While SPM in some ways opened up the discourse about student life by expressing dissatisfaction and worries, the format was also limiting regarding what challenges were represented and who's challenges were made visible. It was striking that in the study sample, none of the student problems were linked to structural inequalities, such as discrimination on the basis of gender, sexuality, skin color, or ability. The absence was particularly notable, as in the same period, there were plenty of news stories that addressed sexism and racism in higher education, difficulties faced by

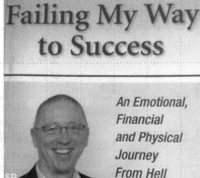

FIGURE 11.3 Examples of student problem memes about procrastination, stress and worries about student life from the Facebook group "Student Problem Memes"

queer students, as well as campuses and programs of study that were not universally designed. Since both relatability and humor are important drivers for sharing, there is an expectation that memes should present easy-going and widely relatable content, which means that both critical and marginalized voices rarely reach the same level of shareability—and they thus *remain* marginalized in meme culture. SPM are therefore both inclusive, in that they aim to strengthen a collective student identity, and exclusionary, since they exclude student problems based on structural inequalities.

This example shows how remix culture can allow important stories to be shared in (a networked) public and how memes can express important feelings and ideas that would otherwise remain invisible. It also shows that a user-driven culture, which we tend to frame as more democratic, does not automatically mean equal opportunity to be heard or represented. That users are active coproducers does not mean that all users have the same power and possibilities. If we understand SPM as a *domestication* of memes and meme-related technology, they emphasize how important *interpretation* is for use: the expectation that memes be used for light-hearted content establishes a norm for use that emphasizes everyday problems at the cost of ignoring structural challenges. Test and challenge this yourself in the Box 11D exercise. In the next example, remixing and user-generated content are also in focus, but our emphasis is on fictional universes and story writing rather than everyday life and humor.

Box 11D.   Exercise: Make Your Own Memes

Search for a meme generator and attempt to make some of your own memes. Reflect over:

- Which formats/templates appeal to you—and why?
- Which knowledge is required to understand, and thus create, different memes?
- How one develops such knowledge?
- Where and with whom would you share the memes you create—and why?
- Who would you *never* share them with—and why?

11.5 Fan Fiction: When Fans Take Ownership of the Story

Fan fiction is genre of stories about worlds and characters established by someone else (Hellekson & Busse, 2006). In contrast to other fiction, where the making of a new fictional setting, people, and events is a given, fanfiction is stories written by fans about an existing universe. The stories continue and expand on the original work to tell stories that the fan fiction writers felt were missing in the original materials, or just as commonly, because fans want to play with ideas and genres in a fictional universe they are invested in. Perhaps you yourself have wanted a story to continue after the book/series/game/film is over and wondered what happened *after* the end credits. Perhaps you have wished for a side character to play a more central role, that a love triangle had a different outcome, or that your favorite character could explore another fictional universe (Pande, 2015). In fan fiction, these are common motivations for fans' remixing fictional universes and writing their own versions and stories.

Fans are, of course, not the only ones making stories by remixing existing materials. Consider how many times Sherlock Holmes has been reinterpreted for TV (21 times, according to Wikipedia) (Adaptations of Sherlock Holmes, 2020), with *Elementary* (Doherty et al., 2012–2019) and *Sherlock* (Vertue, 2010–2017) as recent examples, and popular series like *House* (Attansio et al., 2004–2012) providing a medical version of the character. Or think of how Alice has traveled from Wonderland into books like *The Looking Glass Wars* (Le Carré, 2013), TV games like *American McGee's Alice* (Rouge Entertainment, 2000), and restaurant concepts in Tokyo and elsewhere. Fan fiction nonetheless differs from such commercial adaptations both because fan fiction is not written to make money and because it is primarily motivated by love for the work in question or other members of the fan community. The participatory cultures that support writing fan fiction are characterized by gift economies, where giving and receiving textual "gifts" has a value in themselves and placing a monetary value on them is seen as lessening the giving (Turk, 2014).

Some early examples of fan fiction come from the *Star Trek* fandom in the 1960s, where alternative visions of *Star Trek*'s characters and adventures were written and distributed in "fanzines" (fan-run magazines that were photocopied and distributed by mail). Fans were also early adopters of mailing lists and digital forums, and early social media platforms like LiveJournal were characterized by fan fiction writers' creative contributions and strong communities (Jenkins, 1992). Today, fan fiction is found on dedicated databases and platforms (e.g., www.fanfiction.net, www.archiveofourown, www.wattpad.com, www.commaful.com), as well as on smaller websites and blogs (e.g., on Tumblr).

It is impossible to determine how many fan fiction stories have been written, but those who worry that digitalization will result in the end of reading and writing in culture might be comforted by fan fiction. Archive of Our Own (AO3), one of the most popular platforms for sharing fan fiction, hosts over 10 million stories (per January 2023). The stories that are written include everything from short novellas to epic works that would fill multiple volumes. For example, the series *Austraeok* (Imploding Colon, 2012), a *My Little Pony: Friendship is Magic* fan fiction, is 212,744 words long. (To compare, Tolkien's *Fellowship of the Ring* is only 187,000 words long.)

Fan fiction is thus an excellent example of remix culture, where existing fictional universes are copied, expanded upon, and pasted together in new ways. The term *participatory culture* has to a large degree been developed through the study of fan cultures, in which fan fiction plays a central role and characterizes how fans make such stories because they matter to them and how the community supports this effort through competitions, challenges, and critical or supportive comments. As readers and writers, these fans have taken ownership over the digital format and have developed innovative uses of digital technologies to support their creative expressions. In a *sociotechnical perspective*, we can understand fan fiction as a protest of mass media's *script* that posits the audience as passive consumers, where fans instead have written their own script (a user script), in which the public is a coproducer of media content. We can also understand fan fiction as a *domestication* through which users "tame" media so that it has meaning in the everyday lives of fans by (quite literally) making the stories their own.

Fan fiction is particularly interesting because of how often it depicts stories from marginalized perspectives. So-called *slashfics*, in which fans write same-sex romances, have been an established and popular genre since the start (Jenkins, 1992; Bacon-Smith, 1992). While commercial storytelling have long sidelined and avoided LGBTQ+ relationships, focusing instead on heterosexual couples, fan fiction was an early space in which other forms of love were celebrated (Tosenberger, 2008; Isola, 2010). Fan fiction is, as such, not simply a space in which fans can further develop the fictional universes they love but also a place in which to explore other ways of thinking about gender, sexuality, ethnicity/race, and (dis)ability. The radical reinterpretations of both the audience's role and the fiction's frames remind us of *antiprograms*, where radical new interpretations of *scripts* are made by users. However, making stories based on an established fictional universe is not without its problems.

Since fan fiction, by definition, makes use of someone else's materials, it challenges both ideas about and laws related to copyright. It has been an established norm in fan cultures that fan fiction ought not to result in income; it is fiction written by and for fans and shared in a gift economy (Turk, 2014). Because money does not change hands and because it strengthens the fan community—something many authors and filmmakers find useful—fan fiction has often avoided the strongest interpretations of copyright. The Organization for Transformative Works (n.d.), an interest organization dedicated to fan productions, believes that fan fiction falls under "fair use" within copyright laws and that fan fiction is thus protected and legal. However, there are authors and producers who actively threaten to sue fan fiction writers and websites for breach of copyright using so-called cease-and-desist letters, which require that the stories be removed from the internet.

Even though the acceptance of fan fiction has increased dramatically, not least because the value of an active and creative fanbase has become more obvious with the mainstreaming of nerd culture in recent decades, there are still authors who want their fictional worlds left in peace.

The fan fiction platform Fanfiction.net has therefore published a list of authors who have stated they do not wish fans to write fan fiction based on their works. One of the best-known examples is the vampire author Anne Rice, who has stated, "I do not allow fan fiction. The characters are protected by copyright. It upsets me just to think of fan fiction with my characters." She has vehemently opposed fans' use of her characters with the help of harassment and threats (Jackson, 2018).

The interest in fan fiction has not gone unnoticed, and as such, there have been more and more attempts to monetize fan fiction. These include relatively unsuccessful attempts, like Amazon's Kindle World, which was created in 2013 (and shut down in 2018) and aimed to make fan fiction purchasable (Robertson, 2013). Even if the idea seems obvious, Amazon misjudged how fan fiction and fanfiction communities function. They underestimated how important the collective aspect of writing fan fiction is, as the stories often develop through conversations between readers and writers—and they also ignored how the motivation for writing is not to become rich but rather to enjoy a shared interest and share it with a likeminded community. A ban on pornographic content is also likely a factor, as a considerable amount of fan fiction has sexual elements or is straight-up porn (known as PWP: Porn Without Plot). Other attempts to commercialize fan fiction have been much more successful. The best-known example is the bestselling book (and, later, film) *50 Shades of Gray* (James, 2011), which started out as a *Twilight* (Meyer, 2005) fan fiction and was (minimally) rewritten before being released as an original work.

Finally, it should be noted that while fanfiction in many regards challenges social structures, the way women and minorities are portrayed in media is not always the case. Fanfiction can also reproduce stereotypes and tropes about, for example, gay relationships in slash fiction (Coleman, 2019).

In sum, fan fiction shows us that in a remix culture, it is difficult to say who is the "true" producer/author/creator as the work carried out by fans makes an undeniable difference in how a creation is interpreted—and what status it has (explore this yourself in the Box 11E exercise). After all, who

Box 11E. Exercise: What Fan Fiction Is Written about Your Favorite Work?

Choose one of your favorite books, films, series, or games. Go to fanfiction.net or archiveofourown.org and search for it. Explore a little:

- How many fan fiction stories have been written? Is this many or few compared with other fictional worlds on the platform?
- Which themes and characters are popular? What have the fans done to the main characters?
- Read comments on the stories: which aspects of these fan-authored stories resonate with readers? What types of comments do they give authors? Does it seem like a participatory culture?

Finally, try reading a couple of fan fiction stories. Choose, for example, the most read stories from your chosen fandom or, perhaps best, a story that matches your desires for expansions of or changes to this fictional universe.

gets to decide when a story is finished? In the next example, users' innovative approaches to digital technology are also crucial to their expression of passion for their hobby, but we will move from the textual to the "livestreaming" of video.

11.6 Twitch.tv and Livestreaming Games: How Innovative Gamers Made One of the World's Biggest Platforms

The third and last example of the digitalization of culture is the livestreaming of games and the development of the Twitch.tv platform. This extremely popular platform is best known for the livestreaming of games and has been crucial to the popularity of the livestreaming phenomenon. Even though the platform is rarely discussed in traditional news media (newspapers, TV, and radio), Twitch.tv is among the top 30 most visited websites globally, well ahead of sites like Pinterest or eBay. Those who are still scratching their heads over why people spend time playing games will have real trouble understanding why anyone would spend their time *watching* other people play. However, the explanation is pretty simple from a user perspective, and the user perspective is also useful for understanding the platform's development.

Twitch.tv shares many characteristics with sports, through which one finds joy by watching others perform great feats, following competitions, or just being a part of a wider community. For audiences, the social aspect of the platform is also central in that they can chat with other audience members, participate in polls, learn new strategies for gaming, provide strategy suggestions to the streamer, and shape the content that is created in many other ways (Sjöblom & Hamari, 2017). Because of the social aspect, we may consider Twitch.tv to be a "third space," a place outside of work and home characterized by belonging, informality, volunteerism, and enjoyment (Hamilton et al., 2014).

Where small channels of up to 20 viewers on Twitch.tv are characterized by close bonds and interactions between the streamer and their audience, larger channels with thousands of viewers are more akin to large concerts or sporting events. The chat is total chaos (it moves so fast it's barely readable) but nonetheless gives the feeling of being part of something happening "here and now." As such, switching between small and large channels becomes a way to shift between different modes of viewing, where the shift marks a move between the intimate and the grandiose (Spilker et al., 2020).

The social aspect of livestreaming is key to understanding its appeal, and users, both broadcasters and audiences, point to interactions and community as strong motivators. Sociability is also *scripted* into the platform, as the platform envisions a user that is highly involved with other users and creators. However, just because sociability is important, it does not mean that the audience is glued to the screen at all times. In fact, it is common to have Twitch.tv playing in the background, in the same way one might put on the radio for atmosphere or company. If something exciting happens in the stream, it is easy to sit back down and reengage. Changing between active and passive viewing are different ways of using Twitch.tv and shows that one platform and one type of content can be used and experienced in different ways (Spilker et al., 2020; Hansen, 2017). These variations in use can be understood as different kinds of *domestication* through which the platform is adapted to everyday routines through different patterns of use, but they can also be understood as an expression of the *interpretive flexibility* where the same platform holds different meanings and associated practices—even for a single user.

Like both memes and fan fiction, livestreaming of games has developed from the bottom up; that is, it is a development emerging from users' innovative engagement with technologies rather than from producers, owners, or developers. Twitch.tv was started by the American internet entrepreneur Justin Kan in 2007. He chose to livestream his everyday life, 24/7, and became central to the popularization of the phenomenon that came to be known as *lifecasting*. Within a year, more than 3,000 people had joined the trend, and with more streamers came more themes; food, animals, travel, and technology news found space on the platform known as Justin.tv. The platform grew in popularity over the following years, but its success also caused several problems. Many streamers used the platform to share copyrighted materials, especially sports games, through so-called guerilla rebroadcasting. In addition, the platform suffered from a lack of moderation, and content that was not in line with investor values was uploaded, causing them to pull out. This marked the end of phase one of the platform's history.

To everyone's surprise, one of the platform's subgroups— *gaming*—grew massively during the same period. The gaming section sported several different games and play styles and did not have issues regarding copyright-protected materials. In 2011, the streaming of games became the platform's flagship, and soon the platform grew and became one of the biggest gaming communities in history (phase 2).

The third and final phase started when Amazon purchased Twitch Interactive for $970 million and created a business-focused mixture of Amazon's products/subscriptions and

Twitch.tv's own. Even if livestreamed games are still the platform's most popular content, the new owners pivoted toward more general content to be streamed, such as food, creativity, music, and IRL (in real life). In the course of the three phases, the platform has gone from general content to focusing specifically on games and back again. The development of the platform was characterized by both unregulated and innovative forms of use, first through guerilla rebroadcasting, which caused problems, and later through the livestreaming of games, which showed itself to be both popular and lucrative. At the same time, the platform is also shaped by ownership, legal frameworks, and technical developments that have emphasized both quality and user-friendly streaming, something that shows how nonhuman actors in various *actor networks* take part in shaping digitalization processes.

The three phases of Twitch.tv can be understood as three different scripts with different notions of both use and users, from general streaming for all, to the streaming of gaming for gamers, and back again to general streaming for all (even if gaming is still the most popular use of the platform). The script has developed as a back-and-forth between users' practices and changes in the owners' visions for the platform. "Collaboration" between users and producers is not limited to the development of and response to emerging user practices; there are also debates on forums, changes in the content produced, the making of mods, and the generation of metadata. That both the producers and the users had such an active role in *scripting* the platform—and that it occurred simultaneously through digital channels and data—marks this development as an example of *co-scription*, where both partners are involved in creating a technology's *script* (Ask et al., 2019).

Even if Twitch.tv is a good example of how users co-create technology, we should not equate co-creation with fairness or equality, as users can also contribute to the making of unfair or unjust technologies and technological practices. In the case of Twitch.tv, there are widespread issues with harassment, where particularly women streamers and non-white streamers are targeted (Ruvalcaba et al., 2018, Taylor, 2018).

The story of Twitch.tv shows how important the *user perspective* is to understanding not just what actually happens during a digitalization process but also how technological innovation happens. There was no "genius techbro" in Silicon Valley behind this highly popular platform; there was no single vision that made this technology dominant. What we today know as Twitch.tv is the result of creative enthusiasts who, through a more or less defined community, established new ways of using the technology, which in turn formed how the technology further developed.

11.7 Discussion: Prosumers' New Cultural Expressions

The examples of memes, fan fiction, and the livestreaming of games show how innovation and creation can happen outside of established institutions and streams of income. They also demonstrate that users can do more than just adapt the technology to their own needs; they can also give the technology radical new areas of use, and change both how we perceive the technology and its developmental trajectories. In addition to developing new interpretations and areas of use, the above examples also include the development of new knowledge (from how to interpret memes to how to write good fan fiction) and the appropriation of new technologies such as software to create memes or add-ons that improve the functionality of the platform being used (e.g., to help moderate the chat on Twitch.tv). In contrast to many other examples in this book, digitalization in this chapter is not a consequence of clearly articulated plans or political visions but rather a series of small innovations that have occurred in bits and pieces and have spread from one subculture to another as both users and ideas circulate.

The emphasis on interest-based online communities as drivers of technological change resonates with early visions of the internet, where the production and sharing of culture and knowledge were based on communality, equality, and equal participation (see Chapter 7). However, even if remix culture is exciting and creative, it is not exclusively a force for good. The same mechanisms of participatory culture and networked publics that have been potent catalysts for democratizing communities and cultural expression have also been an effective way for more reactionary groups like "men's rights" activists, the alt-right, and neo-Nazis to organize. In the chosen examples, we have seen that the "student problem meme" format did not provide space for discussions of structural inequalities, fan fiction can reproduce heteronormativity and marginalize racialized fans (Gatson & Reid, 2012), and Twitch.tv has a widespread problem with the sexual harassment of female streamers (Taylor, 2018).

Nonetheless, across the examples of memes, fan fiction, and livestreamed games, we see a recurring motivation and drive for use: a desire to *share*. Culture is, per definition, social, and in these examples, we can see how passion, creativity, community, and the desire to share one's own creations have produced innovative and productive ways of appropriating digital technology. Digital platforms allow us to avoid traditional gatekeepers like editors as well as economic and logistical limitations linked to distribution, but they are as much spaces and communities to belong to as they are ways of communicating and distributing.

What is digitized in these examples? Memetic expression (that is, how they look and what they discuss) is deeply characterized by the digital format. That digital objects can be so easily copied, remixed, and shared is a necessary precondition for memes to exist as we know them today. The qualities of networked publics linked to replication and scalability are particularly important. For fan fiction, the way stories are published (on various digital platforms) and the interactions around them (comments, contests, events, and more) are digitalized. However, the stories largely remain textual without images or hyperlinks, meaning they are very similar to the early fan fiction stories that were written on typewriters, collated, and sent by mail in fanzines. Nonetheless, that the internet allows interactions between fans to be instantaneous is essential, as readers' input and wishes often help to form the story; authors sometimes choose to write stories based on suggestions from other fans.

The livestreaming of games, on the other hand, is entirely dependent on digital technology. Even though there are extremely popular non-digital games, like chess and GO, that have international tournaments that were broadcast on TV long before the internet, livestreaming of gaming differs in important ways. This is both because gaming is in itself dependent on digital technology and also because creators are both performers (gamers) and streamers (broadcasters) at the same time.

The three examples show us that during digitalization processes, the boundaries between producers and consumers can shift or even be erased (in that users become prosumers). Instead of having clear and predictable categories that separate broadcasters from their audiences, designers from their clients, or producers from consumers, the production and use of memes, fan fiction, and streams are characterized by shifts in these roles. Memes will rarely have an identifiable origin (and thus creator/producers) and emerge as memes through collective remixing and use in various contexts. Fan fiction challenges what it means to be an author and raises important questions about ownership as fans make new stories based on established fictional universes and characters. On Twitch.tv, the path from audience member to streamer is supported and desired by the platform, and all that is needed to switch between the roles is to click on the "stream" button. How to be successful as a streamer is however another issue entirely, that we do not have time to cover here. All three examples showcase how important the user perspective is if we wish to understand what happens during digitalization and, not least, how technology—through use—can develop new and unforeseen meanings and areas of use. This transformation can be understood both as an opposition to a technology's *script* and as *domestication*, during which the technology's functions are developed through use.

If we return to *SKAM*, which we discussed in the introduction, we can see similarities between how *SKAM* was distributed via various channels and the ways online communities create and share cultural artifacts. Neither stories nor communities are limited to one format or one platform. Rather, a whole host of platforms, expressions, and users act together.

SKAM was, in many ways, built with meme culture, fan culture, and coproduction in mind. The series had clips that were shared in channels where one could comment and "memeify" episodes, mysteries and hints that invited fans to speculate, and a format that was easy to copy, remix, and make one's own.

Culture has always been shared. It is something that is created and experienced together (if not always at the same time or in the same place). With digitalization, new cultural expressions that play with the material prerequisites of the digital have emerged, along with communities that collectively create stories (whether in the form of memes, fan fiction, or streams). The above examples of innovative digital cultural expressions also demonstrate that it is both possible and meaningful to engage in cultures that exist outside of established cultural institutions and revenue streams. Gift economies, genuine enthusiasm, and low production costs have made communities possible where creation and sharing are goals in themselves.

11.8 Conclusion

In this chapter, we have seen how the digitalization of culture is a process of change characterized by remixing and that the collective cultural expressions of memes, fanfiction, and livestreaming of games are shaped by participatory cultures and the material prerequisites for networked publics. First, memes create community online through sharing, imitating, and remixing at many levels and with many different users. Second, fan fiction shows how fans take established works and transform them into new, remixed narratives—which often tell stories from different perspectives than those centered in the original work and thereby challenge established narratives and make space for alternative voices and experiences. Finally, the livestreaming of games on Twitch.tv developed due to innovative gamers and a platform that capitalized on new user practices. All three examples demonstrate how the digitalization of culture creates *new forms* for production and use, as well as eroding the boundaries between producers and consumers.

References

Adaptations of Sherlock Holmes. (2020, September). *Wikipedia*. https://en.wikipedia.org/w/index.php?title=Adaptations_ of_Sherlock_Holmes&oldid=977975897. Last edited 23 October 2023.

Andem, J. (Producer). (2015). *SKAM* [TV series]. NRK.

Ask, K., & Abidin, C. (2018). My life is a mess: Self-deprecating relatability and collective identities in the memification of student issues. *Information, Communication & Society, 21*(6), 834–850. https://doi.org/10.1 080/1369118X.2018.1437204.

Ask, K., Spilker, H. S., & Hansen, M. (2019). The politics of user-platform relationships: Coscripting live-streaming on Twitch.tv. *First Monday, 24*(7). https://doi.org/10.5210/fm.v24i7.9648.

Attansio, P., Jacobs, K., Shore, D., Singer, B., Moran, T. L., Friend, R., Lerner, G., Yaitanes, G., & Laurie, H. (Producers). (2004–2012). *House* [TV series]. NBC Universal Television Distribution.

Bacon-Smith, C. (1992). *Enterprising women: Television fandom and the creation of popular myth*. University of Pennsylvania Press.

Baron, R. J. (2019). Remix Culture. In R. Hobbs & P. Mihailidis (Eds.), *The international encyclopedia of media literacy*. https://doi.org/10.1002/9781118978238.ieml0196.

boyd, d. (2010). Social network sites as net- worked publics: Affordances, dynamics, and implications. In Z. Papacharissi (Ed.), *A networked self: Identity, community, and culture on social network sites* (pp. 47–66). Routledge.

Brough, M. M., & Shresthova, S. (2012). Fandom meets activism: Rethinking civic and political participation. *Transformative Works and Cultures, 10*. https://doi.org/10.3983/twc.2012.0303.

Coleman, J. J. (2019). Writing with impunity in a space of their own: on cultural appropriation, imaginative play, and a new ethics of slash in Harry Potter fan fiction. *Jeunesse: Young People, Texts, Cultures, 11*(1), 84–111. https://doi.org/10.3138/jeunesse.11.1.84

Doherty, R., Timberman, S., Beverly, C., Coles, J., Polson, J., & Tracey, J. (Producers). (2012–2019). *Elementary* [TV series]. CBS Television Distribution.

Edutopia. (2013, 7 May). Henry Jenkins on participatory culture (Big Thinkers Series) [Video]. *YouTube*. https://www.youtube.com/watch?v=1gPm-c1wRsQ&feature=youtu.be.

Gatson, S. N., & Reid, R. A. (2012). Editorial: Race and ethnicity in fandom. *Transformative Works and Cultures, 8*(1). https://doi.org/10.3983/twc.2011.0392.

Gilliland, E. (2016). Racebending fandoms and digital futurism. *Transformative Works and Cultures, 22*. https://doi.org/10.3983/twc.2016.0702.

Hamilton, W. A., Garretson, O., & Kerne, A. (2014). Streaming on twitch: Fostering participatory communities of play within live mixed media. *Proceedings of the 32nd Annual ACM Conference on Human Factors in Computing Systems* (pp. 1315–1324). https://doi.org/10.1145/2556288.2557048.

Hansen, M. (2017). *Domestiseringen av Twitch TV* [Master's thesis]. Norwegian University of Science and Technology. https://ntnuopen.ntnu.no/ntnu-xmlui/handle/11250/2454403.

Hellekson, K., & Busse, K. (Eds.). (2006). *Fan fiction and fan communities in the age of the internet*. McFarland & Company.

Imploding Colon. (2012, 12 May). *Austraeoh*. FIM Fiction.

Isola, M. J. (2010). Yaoi and Slash Fiction. In A. Levi, M. McHarry, & D. Pragliassotti (Eds.), *Boys' love manga*: *Essays on the sexual ambiguity and cross-cultural fandom of the genre* (p. 84). McFarland.

Jackson, G. (2018, 17 May). It used to be perilous to write fanfiction. *Kotaku*. https://www.kotaku.com.au/2018/05/it-used-to-be-perilous-to-write-fanfiction/.

James, E. L. (2011). *Fifty Shades of Grey*. Vintage.

Jenkins, H. (1992). *Textual poachers: Television fans and participatory culture*. Routledge.

Jenkins, H. (2006). *Fans, bloggers, and gamers: Exploring participatory culture*. NYU Press.

Jenkins, H. (2009). *Confronting the challenges of participatory culture: Media education for the 21st century*. MIT Press.

Jenkins, H., & Shresthova, S. (2012). Up, up, and away! The power and potential of fan activism. *Transformative Works and Cultures, 10*. https://doi.org/10.3983/twc.2012.0435.

Le Carré, J. (2013). *The looking glass war: A George Smiley novel*. Penguin.

Lessig, L. (2008). *Remix: Making art and commerce thrive in the hybrid economy*. Penguin.

Lorenz, T., Browning, K., & Frenkel, S. (2020, 11 July). TikTok teens and K-Pop stans say they sank Trump rally. *The New York Times*. https://www.nytimes.com/2020/06/21/style/tiktok-trump-rally-tulsa.html

Magnus, M. (2016). *SKAM*-når fiksjon og virkelighet møtes. *Nordicom Information, 38*(2), 31–38. https://www.nordicom.gu.se/sites/default/files/kapitel-pdf/nordicom-information_38_2016_2_31-38.pdf

Meikle, G. (2016). *Social media: Communication, sharing and visibility* . Routledge. https://doi.org/10.4324/9781315884172.

Meyer, S. (2005). *Twilight*. Little, Brown and Company.

Miltner, K. M. (2014). There's no place for lulz on LOLCats: The role of genre, gender, and group identity in the interpretation and enjoyment of an internet meme. *First Monday*, *19*(8). https://doi.org/10.5210/fm.v19i8.5391.

Navas, E., & Gallagher, O. (Eds.). (2014). *The Routledge companion to remix studies*. Routledge.

Organization for Transformative Works. (n.d.). *Welcome!* https://www.transformativeworks.org/.

Pande, R. (2015, 7 October). Explainer: What is fanfiction? *The Conversation*. https://theconversation.com/explainer-what-is-fan-fiction-48150

Robertson, A. (2013, 4 June). How Amazon's commercial fan fiction misses the point. *The Verge*. https://www.theverge.com/2013/6/4/4392572/does-amazon-kindle-worlds-miss-the-point-of-fanfiction

Rouge Entertainment. (2000). *American McGee's Alice*. (Xbox 360, Playstation 3, Microsoft Windows, macOS) [Game]. Electronic Arts.

Ruvalcaba, O., Shulze, J., Kim, A., Berzenski, S. R., & Otten, M. P. (2018). Women's experiences in eSports: Gendered differences in peer and spectator feedback during competitive video game play. *Journal of Sport and Social Issues*, *42*(4), 295–311. https://doi.org/10.1177/0193723518773287.

Shifman, L. (2013). *Memes in digital culture*. MIT Press.

Sjöblom, M., & Hamari, J. (2017). Why do people watch others play video games? An empirical study on the motivations of Twitch users. *Computers in Human Behavior*, *75*, 985–996. https://doi.org/10.1016/j.chb.2016.10.019.

Spilker, H. S., Ask, K., & Hansen, M. (2020). The new practices and infrastructures of participation: How the popularity of Twitch.tv challenges old and new ideas about television viewing. *Information, Communication & Society*, *23*(4), 605–620. https://doi.org/10.1080/1369118X.2018.1529193.

Taylor, T. (2018). *Watch me play*. Princeton University Press.

The Greatest International Scavenger Hunt! (2020). *What is GISH?* https://www.gish.com/what-is-gish-2020/.

Tosenberger, C. (2008). Homosexuality at the online Hogwarts: Harry Potter slash fanfiction. *Children's Literature*, *36*(1), 185–207. https://doi.org/10.1353/chl.0.0017.

Turk, T. (2014). Fan work: Labor, worth, and participation in fandom's gift economy. *Transformative Works and Cultures*, *15*, 1–8. https://doi.org/10.3983/twc.2014.0518.

Vertue, S. (Producer). (2010–2017). *Sherlock* [TV series]. BBC.

CHAPTER 12

Digitalization of the Self

Selfies, Influencers, and the Quantified Self

DOI: 10.1201/9781003289555-15

How is digital technology changing how we understand ourselves and express our identities? In this final thematic chapter of this book, we turn our attention to the individual and how digitalization is changing our relationship with ourselves. Central to our inquiry is whether we can understand self-representation through digital technology as "real" and how the self is changed through digitalization processes. In this chapter, we explore how identity changes, specifically how we understand and represent ourselves, through three examples: *selfies*, *influencers*, and *the quantified self*.

12.1 Picture Perfect? What "Instagram vs. Reality" Can Teach Us about Being Fake and Authentic Online

To start off our exploration of identity as it relates to technology, let us consider the meme *Instagram vs. reality*. The meme format compares two images: the first will typically show a buff body, flawless skin, and luxurious clothing and surroundings, while the second "reveals" that the same person actually has love handles, wrinkles, pimples, and dirty laundry heaped over their bed. In this way, the meme directs attention to the discrepancy between the idealized way people present themselves on Instagram and how they look "in reality"—without makeup, filters, or flattering camera angles (Instagram vs. Reality, 2019).

The Instagram vs. reality meme (see Figure 12.1 for an example) pokes fun at the unrealistic beauty standards found on social media and is also used to raise critique about the consequences on self-image and the appropriateness of influencers as role

INSTAGRAM   REALITY

FIGURE 12.1   Instagram vs. reality, made by Nienke Bruijning.

models. In this way, the meme is used to critique influencers who freely promote beauty products and plastic surgery to their followers and how their portrayal of an impossibly perfect life relies on comprehensive image editing. These worries are well summarized in an article on the BoredPanda blog about this type of meme:

"We all know that most people share an idealized version of themselves on social media, cherry-picking only the best images, thoughts, and experiences to share with the world. But some Instagram celebrities have taken this concept to the extreme. They bombard their followers with photoshopped images that are so far from reality that they can sow seeds of doubt in some people's minds, leading them to strive for unrealistic body image at great cost to their self-esteem and mental health."

(Caunt, 2019)

The critique raised in the Instagram vs. reality meme is not just directed at influencers. As the above quote points out, it is not just internet celebrities who share idealized versions of themselves online. That it is both easier and expected of us to share flattering versions of ourselves on social media is common knowledge and, for most, something we have experience with. Sharing successes is an established norm in social media (although there are differences between platforms). It is easier to make a post about a successful summit hike than the times we stayed on the coach, to share photos from a fancy homemade dinner than one made of canned soup, just like it is easier to post about getting top grades than failing exams. While some have interpreted this as people being "fake online," we might consider the emphasis on positive and idealized self-representation online as reasonable, given that posts on social media are often visible to people far outside a close circle of friends or family (Aalen, 2015).

Instagram vs. reality critiques unrealistic and unhealthy beauty ideals, but on a deeper level, the meme is also about *authenticity*. By contrasting the Instagrammable with "reality," it draws attention to how staged and idealized posts show a "fake" image of ourselves and our daily lives—that the artificial, glamorous style that characterizes images in social media is a glorification of the false, the manipulated, and the *in*authentic self. It is, as such, not just about body ideals and role models but also to what degree we can trust that people are their "true self" on social media. *Instagram vs. reality* thus gestures toward a large and ongoing debate about authenticity and the internet that asks if we are real when we are online, and what makes us consider some digitalized self-expressions as "real" and others as "fake"? To answer these questions, we need to understand how identity relates to technology, specifically the internet.

12.2 From Anonymity to Persistent Identities on the Internet

How we think about identity and digital technology has changed drastically over the past 30 years. A brief retrospect can be useful to understand why authenticity is such a central question, as well as to show how today's norms of self-expression online (like sharing successes and not failures) have not always existed—and thus, that what we perceive as normal "could be otherwise" and that other norms may develop in the future.

Anonymous and semi-anonymous (pseudonymous) interactions characterized internet communities and forums in the 1990s and early 2000s. Unsurprisingly, early internet studies attempted to understand internet identity by making sense of anonymity. The freedom that came with being able to choose your own name/pseudonym, particularly at a time when online presence was barely regulated, allowed the internet to become a playground for experimenting with new identities. The idea was that on the internet, you could be anyone you wanted to be, free from the boxes society had made for you (Turkle, 1995), a way of thinking you may recognize from Barlow's "internet manifesto" (see Chapter 7).

Later studies of online communities show that even though anonymity was an option, it was unusual to create a radically different identity for ourselves online. Even though we could create new accounts and new pseudonyms to avoid responsibilities and consequences for our actions, it turned out that internet users were more concerned with belonging to a community, which meant building good reputations by following community norms and rules (Taylor, 2006). In addition, our physical identities—our genders, sexualities, skin colors, ethnicities, class identities, and levels of education—continued to strongly influence which roles we could choose between online and where we might feel at home (Phillips, 2019). The internet was, as such, neither a blank page where you could choose to be anyone at all nor a place where you could do precisely what you wanted without consequences—even if the technology allowed it.

With the advent of social media and Facebook in particular, online identity norms changed dramatically. We are no longer expected to be anonymous online; instead, we are expected to present our full names, jobs, and places of study, along with a pile of pictures that make it clear that we are precisely who we claim to be. Instead of expecting online interactions to be with anonymous people who share our interests, it became an expectation to connect with people we knew in real life. Facebook's founder (now Meta), Mark Zuckerberg, went as far as to say that "Having two identities for yourself is an example of a lack of integrity" (Ingram, 2014). In this vision, an online identity should be an accurate and direct reflection of one's offline identity, for the identity to persist across the online/offline divide and be a permanent online representation of the self.

The transition to persistent online identities has also been justified as a way to combat online harassment, claiming that anonymity is the cause of poor behavior, even if research shows that both online harassment and trolling are more complex phenomena than straightforward side-effects of anonymity

(Chui, 2014; Bishop, 2014). Others have argued that anonymous spaces online have value in themselves. Christopher "Moot" Poole, the founder of the anonymous discussion board 4chan, has warned against eradicating anonymity online. Even though anonymity has caused problems (mostly relating to accountability), it has also created fertile ground for creative expression and modes of communication (Poole, 2010).

In hindsight, Facebook's shift from pseudonyms to persistent identities and networks probably had less to do with concerns about integrity and more to do with earning potential for the platform's owners, as data about user behavior has much higher value for advertisers if it comes with indicators like gender, age, and location. Zuckerberg's statement is nonetheless representative of the shift away from anonymity in favor of persistent online identities.

As the reign of Facebook is ending, so too is perhaps the idea that online identities need to be accurate reflections of offline identities. Instead, it is common to have accounts on many platforms at once and to let the platforms' varied cultures and norms form what is shared. For example, Snapchat is more commonly used for everyday events and unstaged images, while Instagram is geared toward carefully selected and stylized images (Schreiber, 2017). With newer platforms like TikTok, identity work is changing once more as creators are not just communicating with an audience; their self-representations also must engage the algorithm if their content is to be visible, and users experiences of intimacy and authenticity are also shaped by interactions with the algorithm (Şot, 2022).

By looking back at the history of the internet and identity, it becomes clear that what seems "totally normal" today when it comes to expressing yourself online is a specific constellation of technology and culture that is also likely to change in the future. To gain some perspectives on identity and technology that have a better shelf life than the latest platform trend, let us take a closer look at how we can understand identity more generally—and particularly as it relates to technology.

12.3 Frontstage, Backstage, and the Cyborg's Theater

Identity is a set of characteristics and traits that define who we are (Leary & Tangney, 2011). Identity describes how we understand ourselves (who we experience we "are") and how we express our self-understanding (how we show who we "are"). Identity is also concerned with associations—which groups we belong to and what categories we are assigned. The sociologist Erving Goffman (1978) has described identity as a kind of theater where meetings between people are characterized by impression management. That is, we work actively to present ourselves in specific ways and to be perceived in ways we desire. Central to this theory is the idea that we have a *frontstage*, where we are observed by others and where our behavior is formed by established norms and conventions, and a *backstage*, where we let go of these roles without much thought to how we are perceived. Even if the theory was developed long before the internet, it resonates with our everyday digital lives: we show awareness about what we are willing to post on social media and how it makes us look (frontstage), and we actively hide everyday clutter, pimples, unfinished dishes, and other less-than-flattering aspects of our lives (backstage) when we are choosing our next profile picture.

From the idea of identity and interaction as a kind of theater, we can understand identity as *performative*. That is, identity is something we *do* rather than something we *are*. Identity is not the outcome of some unchanging, immutable "soul," but rather something that is constructed by the actions you take to express yourself. "Doing" identity means also linking yourself to and displaying different identity markers. Some identity markers draw attention, some we take for granted, and others are hidden. Which markers are considered acceptable can also vary widely from place to place, from subculture to subculture, and from platform to platform. Widespread use of memes is considered normal on Tumblr but would be seen as strange on LinkedIn. Similarly, emojis are central to communications on both Snapchat and TikTok but are disdained on Reddit. Identity markers are thereby linked to the social rules of different arenas.

To argue that identity is performative may sound like a claim of fakeness—that identity is "just a show." However, the point is not that our identities are fake or that we can freely choose how we identify. The concept of performativity instead emphasizes how identities are created in cooperation with society and the people around us—and challenges us to critically evaluate which roles society defines for us, which identity markers are available to us, and whom various identity markers are (or are not) available to.

Goffman's terms, frontstage and backstage, help us understand the work of impression management in social media. There is work put into choosing the "right" profile picture, formulating an appropriate comment, and deciding which posts get liked. Work that is carried out with awareness that our actions are being observed by others. Correspondingly, it also becomes clear that there is a great deal we choose not to show, that we have a kind of backstage access to our stories and experiences that we choose not to share because we want to make a specific impression on friends, followers, and our audience (Shulman, 2016). However, we should show caution when we apply Goffman's frontstage/backstage to understand our digital lives (Pinch, 2010), lest we end up with social determinism (see Chapter 3), where technology's effects are made invisible.

To include material actors in the analysis, we must account for the various "stages" in which identity is performed, what kind of performances the technology is catering to, and how the technology allows some actors and actions more opportunities than others. This also includes consideration of how platform use is also influenced by factors outside our control, such as hidden algorithms that promote certain content or that our representations are shared with third parties against our will (Mariabelli & Page, 2018). This can make it difficult to know which audiences we are actually addressing when we post something, which complicates the work of managing impressions.

To account for technological agency and how material actors form what is or isn't possible to do—both frontstage and backstage—we need a *sociotechnical* conceptualization of identity. A sociotechnical perspective of identity takes for granted that our self-understanding and the unfolding of the self occur with and through technology. Rather than seeing technology as something outside ourselves, we can think of technology as an extension of the self (Case, 2010). Instead of seeing social media as a "place" where we "do" our identity, social media can be seen as an extension of both our bodies and senses that provide different opportunities (and limitations) for expressing identity. Rather than clearly delineating between the human and the technological, we can think of them as melting together, as a *cyborg*.

As discussed in Chapter 7, a cyborg is a merging of human and machine, of fiction and fact, and of myth and material reality (Haraway, 1987; Moser, 1998). The cyborg can therefore say something to us about how the boundary between humans and technology is in constant flux. It is not a stable or immutable divide, but rather a delineation made up of fluid and intricate intersections. One of the most important properties of the cyborg concept is how it destabilizes boundaries—between nature and culture, between human (body) and technology—as a hybrid creation that is not "either or" but "both."

With the cyborg as a starting point for understanding identity, we can think beyond and outside categories like "true" and "false" self-representations because the cyborg destabilizes these boundaries. In the cyborg's world view, there are no "real" identities that are made "false" through digital manipulation or play; it is taken for granted that we humans are always transforming and manipulating ourselves with the help of technology. Whether this occurs through a photo filter, birth control, or a pulse watch, the cyborg is not concerned with whether these technologies make us less human or less real but rather with what we can accomplish together. The question is then not whether you are "real" online, but rather how a cyborg creates something we find authentic.

If we think of ourselves as cyborgs, as beings comprising bodies, minds, and technologies, what can selfies, influencers, and the quantified self (QS) teach us about identity—about our lives as both humans and machines?

12.4 Selfies: The Cyborg's Self-Portrait?

It is tempting to define selfies simply as "digital self-portraits." Selfies are, after all, images of ourselves, and like self-portraits, they are used to explore and express our identities. However, selfies and self-portraits differ in important ways; in particular, selfies are representations of the self "here and now," and sharing them through digital networks is integral to their meaning. So, rather than thinking of selfies as self-portrait photography, we may consider them visual communication about ourselves: an expression that says something about who we are, where we are, and what is happening around us. Selfies as an expression are made possible and formed by the technology being used, as well as our relationships with intended and unintended recipients (see Box 12A).

As an alternative to self-portraits as a mental image of what selfies are, we can think of selfies as an *actor network* of bodies, identities, relationships, and technologies. Hess (2015) describes selfies as comprising a staged self, the place the selfie is taken, camera technology, and digital platforms. Hess's description of selfies draws strongly on Goffman's ideas of staging and impression management, and it emphasizes how selfies are anchored in time and space.

Box 12A.   Fact: What Makes Up a Selfie?

	A staged self	A selfie includes the purposeful positioning of the self. The background, angle, and expression are chosen to say something about who one is. As such, a selfie can just as easily express that one supports a political issue as it can show that one is on vacation.
	The place where the selfie is taken	A selfie links the person in the picture to a specific place and a specific time, whether they are at home or out in the world. As such, a selfie is a picture of the self in relation to the place in which it is taken.
	Camera technology	A selfie is made with the help of a smartphone that, with its forward-facing camera, scripts a form of use in which one takes pictures of oneself. This is supported by other technologies like selfie sticks, filters, and image-editing apps.
	Digital platforms	A selfie is made to be shared (even if not all selfies are shared), and as such, it is inextricably linked to the digital platforms that are used to share, view, and be integrated with selfies.

If we think of selfies first and foremost as self-portraits, taking pictures of yourself on vacation with exotic backgrounds can appear like self-involved bragging. If we instead think of selfies as a form of communication through which we depict something about ourselves to others, it makes sense to share your time on vacation and how you enjoyed the good weather by showing sun and beach in the background (or snowstorms and the northern lights if you are on vacation in Norway; what counts as "exotic" is, after all, subjective). Instead of thinking of the staging of a selfie as manipulation or manufacturing a fake self, we should instead consider what the selfie communicates through its choices of angles, filters, locations, and publication. Studies also show how self-obsession and self-glorification are themes that are frequently brought up in news stories about selfies but do not accurately reflect the process of taking and sharing selfies.

In contrast to discourses about selfies as rampant narcissism, user studies show how the visibility gained through selfies is a source of both happiness and discomfort. The aesthetic of selfies, which tend to signal success, playfulness, and an unpretentious "see how much fun I'm having" vibe, is not necessarily reflective of the process of making them. A study of young users (Cambre & Lavrence, 2019) showed that taking a selfie could give positive feelings of control as the technology allowed users to dictate how they appeared through careful staging, edits, and filters, as well as having the option of taking many images and deleting the bad ones. While users felt control while taking the selfie, they had little control over the selfie after it was shared with an audience whose cruel comments or lack of likes made them look at themselves more critically. As such, taking selfies is a practice characterized by ambivalence.

The way we stage our lives for presentation on the internet is criticized through the meme *Instagram vs. reality*, which equates the idealized with the fake. The implication is that the less staged an image is, the more authentic it is—and the less self-obsessed the person shown is. But are authenticity and narcissism truly useful ways to think about self-depiction in social media? If we follow Goffman's idea of frontstage/ backstage, the selfie that is shared represents the frontstage. The work that is put into positioning the body, choosing the right scene (and context) for the image, deciding on which filter to use and on which platform to post the image—not to mention which hashtags to use and what time of the day would best suit the algorithm—is hidden backstage. Using frontstage/backstage as a framework helps us acknowledge that a selfie shared via social media is a conscious, constructed, and idealized representation of the self. You can test this yourself in the selfie exercise in Box 12B.

At the same time, such a division can lead to thinking that what happens backstage is more "real" than what happens frontstage and that selfie culture is a glorification of the "false" precisely because so much work is undertaken backstage. If we instead use the cyborg to understand selfies, selfies become representations of the cyborg without being so focused on whether this is a "real" representation because technology is involved. We may instead direct our attention to what message is expressed in a selfie and how it is told, rather than being stuck judging its morality based on its appearance as "real" or "fake."

Box 12B.   Exercise: Take a Good Selfie!

Take a selfie that you think is good and that you could share on Instagram—or on other social media where idealized self-representation is the norm. Reflect on what you must do and how you experience the process.

- What backstage work needs to be done? How did you adapt your surroundings to get the picture? What technologies other than a camera did you use?
- What is your assessment of a "good" selfie built on? Do you want to follow a norm, or is it more important to seem original? Is your image stylized or unpolished?
- What did you feel while you were taking the selfie—control, fear, happiness, or uncertainty?
- Last but not least, do you see the selfie as an authentic representation of yourself?

To take a good selfie requires time, resources, and expertise. Which angles are good, what lighting, which filters, and which hashtags and emoticons should be used are all examples of knowledge that is used when taking selfies. In the next example of influencers who have made careers out of looking good on social media, the work of appearing relaxed and authentic comes into focus.

12.5 Influencers: The Professionalized Digital Self

Influencers are often accused of being "known for nothing," of being self-involved, and of cynically taking advantage of a lack of laws and impressionable youths through shady sponsorship agreements and hidden marketing. The meme *Instagram vs. reality* has largely taken aim at influencers and the ways in which they depict themselves in *overly* idealized images. Independent of whether we think this critique is justifiable, a critical analysis of the work influencers put into self-representation can be useful in helping us understand how authenticity is not an inherent quality but rather the result of a conscious process. But first, what precisely is an influencer?

In short, an influencer is an internet celebrity. The word "celebrity" invokes images of glamorous Hollywood actors and red carpets, or perhaps rock stars in large stadiums filled with thousands of wild fans. Others are celebrities by virtue of holding visible public positions, like presidents, queens, or authors. When influencers are derided for being "famous for nothing," it is implied that before the internet, fame was linked to an achievement, a talent, or a position. However, a more critical analysis of celebrity as a phenomenon shows that it is not necessarily the most successful, smartest, or prettiest people who become famous, and what counts as an achievement is shifting. Instead, fame is created through different strategies and measures (and many coincidences), and as such, anyone could potentially become a celebrity.

However, even if "normal people" and "anyone at all" could, in theory, become famous, it is rare that "normal" or "typical" characterize those who become known for "being themselves." They become famous because they have first-hand knowledge about an important event, are willing to share something private, or, in other ways, manage to capture the interest of an audience.

Before influencers, reality stars and people who took part in TV shows like *Dr. Phil* are examples of people becoming famous by sharing intimate stories or personal information. Other precursors to influencers were microcelebrities, discussed in early Web 2.0 histories (Senft, 2008). In contrast to traditional celebrities, who, to a greater degree, were expected to have unusual and exceptional lives, microcelebrities were expected to demonstrate that they were "real people" with "real problems"—and to do so in close relation to their audience, who expected answers to comments and messages on the platforms on which they operated.

This is also the case for influencers today, but some important changes have occurred over the last 20 years: *influencers'* fame is no longer limited to a subculture online as influencers can be as famous as traditional celebrities; influencers are not linked to a single platform but operate across platforms; while microcelebrities "worked" online as a hobby, being an influencer is a career; and while microcelebrities were more or less dependent on intimacy with their audience (developed by sharing personal information), influencers switch between thematic content where they demonstrate their talents and "fillers" that provide small glimpses into their everyday lives—and thus make them appear "normal" (Abidin, 2018).

Influencers must continually balance being exceptional (and thus worth following) and relatable (and thus like everyone else). They make a living rendering their everyday lives into a format that appears both exciting and recognizable, and they are dependent on having a credible and authentic persona to succeed. Due to the dependency on authenticity, it is not surprising that influencers have become experts at appearing unkempt and down-to-earth when they need to. Internet researcher and expert on internet celebrities Crystal Abidin (2017) uses the term "calibrated amateurism" to describe the aesthetics and practice of appearing unfiltered, amateurish, and spontaneous, for example, through small stories that show the set of a recent photoshoot or a "no-makeup selfie" early in the morning. Even if the images appear improvised and "spur of the moment," they are actually the result of careful staging and deliberately chosen camera angles, lights, outfits, and backgrounds. The way influencers show themselves to be unglamorous and "real" can be understood as a conscious depiction of *backstage* in an attempt to appear authentic. As backstage is staged and shared, it is made into a *frontstage*, but the way the different aesthetics are blended to create an authentic expression demonstrates how skilled influencers are in navigating self-representation on various stages.

That influencers have conscious strategies for appearing authentic and real, and are largely successful in this, shows that authenticity is not something that simply exists; it is created. To succeed in their staging of the instantaneous and random while at the same time managing sponsor agreements and advertising, influencers must navigate many different technologies, aesthetics, algorithms, contracts, cultures, and genres. When they appear effortless, it is because the expertise in staging is consciously hidden or simply taken for granted (Abidin, 2016). To return to the meme *Instagram vs. reality*, it is worth noting that the meme is not just used against internet celebrities as a critique of excessive glamour but also positions the person making/sharing the meme as someone who is conscious of this divide—and by sharing it, they show how they are not like the "others" who are inauthentic.

In sum, influencers have taught us that authenticity is something that is created and that requires specialist knowledge about online aesthetics and the marketing of the self. Influencers must carefully and masterfully balance representations that are idealized yet relatable, and they actively use various platforms, filters, algorithms, and more to achieve this goal.

While both selfies and influencers are concerned with the visual (as both amateurs and professionals), in the third and final example, we will examine self-representation as numbers through the *quantified self (QS)*. The QS is a movement that focuses on the quantifiable and how statistical analysis of your life can make you a better person, yet questions of authenticity are still central. What is really being counted—is it your "real" you?

12.6 The Quantified Self: Believing in a Countable and Optimized Self

"The quantified self" (QS) describes a social movement that uses digital technology for self-measurement with the goal of self-development (Lupton, 2016). With the motto "self-knowledge through numbers," the idea of QS is that by counting, measuring, and registering data on your own life, you can generate a knowledge base that helps you improve yourself. Many of the technologies and practices that QS enthusiasts have established are now mainstream, like counting your steps through wearables or mapping your sleeping habits through an app. For enthusiasts, mapping can include counting the number of steps walked, the number of calories consumed, measuring blood pressure, hours slept, blood sugar levels, pulse, and/or oxygen uptake. Such measurements are often combined with interest-based or specialized log entries, such as registering which books you read, when you drink coffee, your productivity level, mood, or level of creativity. As an exploration of identity in the face of digital technology, the movement begs the question: can you count yourself to a better life—and what is "better" in this context?

Digital technology is central to QS because it is through digital technologies like wearables, dedicated apps, and social media that it becomes possible to generate and analyze data about yourself and your everyday life. QS enthusiasts log many different everyday aspects of their lives and put together different data sets to "research" their own lives. Which data are gathered depends on what information is available, which data are easy to get, and what someone wants to improve. If someone wants to learn what causes a rash on their hand, eating habits could be useful to register, while those who wish to find out when in the day they are most effective at work might need to collect information on their sleeping habits, eating habits, productivity, and self-esteem. As an example, one QS enthusiast chose to compare logs of his coffee purchases with data he had gathered on his mood throughout the day. He discovered that too much caffeine made him stressed after lunch, so he switched out his lunchtime coffee for tea (Spiller et al., 2018).

It is not a new phenomenon to log information about our daily lives. Diaries have historically been used to register what happened that day, recording events, visitors, or just mundane things like the weather or what was for dinner. Diaries were then sent home to families after long journeys or inherited between generations so that the family could take part in their relatives lives. Later, the diary developed the personal form we recognize today, where we document heartbreak and our inner thoughts. The diary's origin, however, was a partially public record of normal people's lives. As such, it is not the documentation of our everyday lives that is new with QS but rather the automation of registering the data and information we gather. With digital technology, the logging of data is something that often occurs in the *background* without being noticed, and it requires relatively little effort to create a data point.

Take exercise, for example. Logging exercises are popular in the QS milieu and are an example of a self-measurement practice that has become mainstream. Keeping track of exercise (when, where, how long, how far, etc.) requires a good deal of work if all the measurements are done using a stopwatch, logbook, and measuring tape. Without digital tools, making data takes time. It takes time to log results in neat tables and calculate progress or lack of progress since our last workout—and afterward, we have to look after the book so that the data is not lost. In comparison, it requires little work to install an exercise app on your phone that automatically logs when, where, and how long you have been active and presents these data with the help of simple analytical tools that visualize your averages and progress. Digitalization changes the ways in which exercise data is collected, which types of data are collected, and how they are analyzed. So even if QS has clear non-digital roots, there are some essential differences between the old almanacs, which are filled with descriptions of weather or dinner menus, and the forms of self-measurement that QS advocates.

QS is interesting from an identity perspective because, through self-measurement, it creates an intricate data set about individuals we can understand as "digital twins." The digital twin offers new information about the user's everyday life, and this knowledge is used to make decisions and evaluate situations. The digital twins that are created through measurement delight users but also potentially make QS enthusiasts vulnerable in that large amounts of personal data are gathered on them without their necessarily having control over where these data end up.

However, we should not think of the digital twin as simply information that is passively gathered. Knowing that we are making data to log our lives affects how we live our lives: logging our moods affects how we feel, and if we want every step to be registered, we might skip runs on the days our Fitbits are out of battery (Kristensen & Prigge, 2018). As such, QS demonstrates how our self-representations are not just ways of showing ourselves to the world; the creation and use of digital representations of ourselves also shapes how we think about ourselves and the world.

A clear challenge for QS enthusiasts is the fact that many things in life cannot be (easily) quantified. They are aware that not everything can be measured and that not all measurements provide useful information. They nonetheless find joy in generating and analyzing data about themselves, which contrasts with "normal users," who apply technology to meet specific goals, such as losing weight (Kristensen & Prigge, 2018). As such, QS is an interesting nexus of (1) excessive data registration practices by private individuals, (2) a zeitgeist in which the quantifiable is highly valued, and (3) an identity project that is inextricably linked to the use of digital technology.

All technology expands or limits our agency. For QS enthusiasts, the emphasis is on how digital technology can give users new "senses": senses that can perceive precisely how many steps have been taken or how many calories have been consumed (try this yourself in Box 12C exercise). For QS enthusiasts, the cyborg is not an abstract theory but a way of life. The technology is experienced as an extension of the body that shapes how they experience themselves and how they understand the world around them. What is considered healthy, valuable, effective, or useful will thus also be characterized by how technology registers (or does not register) data.

Box 12C.   Exercise: Count Yourself for a Week

Download a step-counting app (or find one on your phone, since they are often standard programs), and let it run in the background for a week.

Then, get better acquainted with your "digital twin":
- Experiment with different ways the data can be visualized for you, and reflect on which visualization you prefer and why. Do you like detailed descriptions or "the big picture"? Numbers or graphs? Why?
- Explore to what degree your digital twin is representative of your activity in the past week. To what degree does the digital twin give an accurate image of you and your activities? Are all your steps registered, or are some missing (e.g., did you leave your phone somewhere while you walked around your home)?
- Do you believe that these data are useful and that they could improve your everyday life?

12.7 Discussion: The Cyborg's Expanded Toolbox

What happens when identity is digitalized? In the selfie example, both how we communicate and how we express ourselves are digitalized. High spirits at a party are expressed not just through text or speech but by taking a picture of ourselves *at* the party to be shared with friends and acquaintances. For influencers, both production and distribution of content are characterized by digitalization, and this could not have been done in the same way without digital technology. Because smartphones and digital platforms are widely accessible, influencers are not dependent on studios, expensive cameras, or professional editors. While we must not underestimate the amount of expertise required to create digital content on a daily or weekly basis (and that this also requires a great deal of specialist equipment), private individuals' opportunities to broadcast from their living rooms are greater than ever. In QS, digitalization has also caused major changes, as the transition from bodily experiences to digital twins affects both how users interpret themselves and how they act in the world. QS is an expression of a society concerned with the measurable and quantifiable, and enthusiasts' eagerness is strengthened by a belief that quantified information provides important insights (Porter, 1995).

Even if a lot has changed, there are also elements that remain stable in the digitalization of identity. Selfies are an example of how digitalization has shifted communication toward the visual and how self-representation is done through digital networks. But even if the work of giving a specific impression has changed format and form, the need to appear in a specific way in order to make a desirable impression on others has remained the same. For influencers, digitalization has affected who can become famous as well as what content can be created, but it is worth noting that the intimate details and interactions that characterize influencer content still have a great deal in common with "celebrity gossip" magazines. In QS, the process of making a digital twin is entirely dependent on digital technology, including logging, creating, and processing data materials. Nonetheless, neither eating food nor going jogging are done by machines, even if the experience of eating or jogging changes through digital measurement.

If we return to the cyborg as a framework for thinking, we see that digitalization expands our metaphorical toolbox for identity work: we can express ourselves in many new ways, we do this in an increasing number of places, we have access to larger audiences, and we can use a variety of formats. The self is expressed through spontaneous and stylized selfies, in private and professional contexts, and as images, posts, and data. At the same time, these examples show how this identity work is highly ambivalent; there is community, creativity, and self-expression as well as worry, pressure, and insecurity linked to how we appear and are perceived. Digitalization does not only provide new ways of thinking about ourselves but also causes us to create many versions of ourselves. Our identity work leads to representations in the form of social media profiles, edited and curated selfies, digital twins, and personal data shifting hands— representations that we must engage with because they are important parts of the interactions we have with other people and society more broadly.

It is also worth noting that the cyborg's toolbox has clear limitations. The technological and cultural guidelines for selfies and general self-representation in social media and QS emphasize some values, motives, and bodies at the expense of others. We cannot ignore that selfie and influencer cultures highlight and idolize beauty ideals that are rooted in racism, sexism, heteronormativity, and ableism. These norms are strengthened through technologies like photo filters that make the user "more beautiful" by manipulating images to make the person look thinner and lighter-skinned (Rettberg, 2014). Similarly, QS Technologies place a high value on productivity and efficiency and presumes that being more productive is self-improvement. Even if the methods that QS advocates can be useful for those with illnesses or disabilities who may need detailed information about their everyday lives, the high value place on optimization is not necessarily compatible with an inclusive work life and can thus lead to the further exclusion of those who are ill or disabled.

In closing, let us return to the meme from the beginning of this chapter that compared Instagram with "reality" and thus argued that we are not "real" enough on social media. The meme is a good example of how we *normalize* each other's use of technology by pointing out what "correct use" includes. Even if you are sympathetic to the meme's critique, the division it sets up between "real" and "fake" is problematic. Consequently, in this chapter, we have used quotation marks around words like "real," "true," "false," and "fake." This is to make it clear that what we consider authentic cannot be reduced to how glamorous or idealized one appears or how often one uses photo filters. In the meme *Instagram vs. reality*, the images that show people "in reality" can be just as staged as the Instagram images, albeit in a different way. Our three examples also show how authenticity is not an inherent quality but rather something that is created; it is a conscious aesthetic expression we choose for our visual or data-based communications with each other.

While digital technology is in many contexts considered to be logical, effective, and modern, digital technology that is used to express the self has more often been seen as dangerous; this includes a fear that technologies provide more opportunities to edit and change the self and thus make possible and normalize an identity that is not "real." Thinking through and with the cyborg makes it less important to think about "real" versus "false" because the cyborg does not have the capacity for such categories—it is already a hybrid in which the technical and the human have melted together, and, as such, it rejects the existence of "real" and "fake" and instead embraces the compound, hybrid, and complex.

12.8 Conclusion

In this chapter, we have examined how digital technologies create new ways of understanding, exploring, and expressing ourselves and our identities. We have looked at three different ways to be ourselves digitally: through selfies, influencers, and the Quantified Self. These invite us to think about ourselves as cyborgs rather than humans who appear "real" or "fake" on digital surfaces. As cyborgs, we are in a constant process of linking ourselves to new technology. This is not just about our identities' being formed by technology; we are inextricably linked to digital technology, and digitalization of the self thus includes a transformation of the self.

References

Aalen, I. (2015). *Sosiale medier*. Fagbokforlaget.

Abidin, C. (2016). "Aren't these just young, rich women doing vain things online?" Influencer selfies as subversive frivolity. *Social Media + Society*, 2(2). https://doi.org/10.1177/2056305116641342.

Abidin, C. (2017). #familygoals: Family influencers, calibrated amateurism, and justifying young digital labor. *Social Media + Society*, 3(2). https://doi.org/10.1177/2056305117707191.

Abidin, C. (2018). *Internet celebrity: Understanding fame online*. Emerald Publishing.

Bishop, J. (2014). Dealing with internet trolling in political online communities: Towards the this is why we can't have nice things scale. *International Journal of E-Politics*, 5(4), 1–20. https://doi.org/10.4018/ijep.2014100101.

Cambre, M. C., & Lavrence, C. (2019). How else would you take a photo? #Selfieambivalence. *Cultural Sociology*, 13(4), 503–524. https://doi.org/10.1177/1749975519855502.

Case, A. (2010, December). *We are all cyborgs now* [Video]. TED Conferences. https://www.ted.com/talks/amber_case_we_are_all_cyborgs_now?language=en.

Caunt, J. (2019). "Instagram vs. Reality" exposes the truth about those unrealistically "perfect" pics. *Boredpanda*. https://www.boredpanda.com/instagram-vs-reality-truth-behind-pictures/.

Chui, R. (2014). A multifaceted approach to anonymity online: Examining the relations between anonymity and antisocial behaviour. *Journal of Virtual Worlds Research*, 7(2). https://doi.org/10.4101/jvwr.v7i2.7073.

Goffman, E. (1978). *The presentation of self in everyday life.* Harmondsworth.

Haraway, D. (1987). A manifesto for cyborgs: Science, technology, and socialist feminism in the 1980s. *Australian Feminist Studies*, 2(4), 1–42. https://doi.org/10.1080/08164649.1987.9961538.

Hess, A. (2015). The selfie assemblage. *International Journal of Communication, 9*(1), 1629–1646. https://ijoc.org/index.php/ijoc/article/view/3147

Ingram, M. (2014, 4 April). Mark Zuckerberg's views on anonymity seem to be evolving, and that's a good thing. *GigaOm Blog*. https://gigaom.com/2014/04/04/mark-zuckerbergs-views-on-anonymity-seem-to-be-evolving-and-thats-a-good-thing/

Instagram vs. Reality (2019). *Know Your Meme.* https://knowyourmeme.com/memes/instagram-vs-reality

Kristensen, D. B., & Prigge, C. (2018). Human/technology associations in self-tracking practices. In B. Ajana (Ed.), *Self-tracking: Empirical and philosophical investigations* (pp. 43–59). Springer International Publishing.

Leary, M. R., & Tangney, J. P. (2011). *Handbook of self and identity.* Guilford Press.

Lupton, D. (2016). *The quantified self.* John Wiley & Sons.

Mariabelli, M., & Page, X. (2018). Performing identity through social media: A sociomaterial perspective. *Social Science Research Network, 8*(2). https://doi.org/10.2139/ssrn.3134979.

Moser, I. (1998). Kyborgens rehabilitering. In K. Asdal, A. J. Berg, B. Brenna, I. Moser, & L. M. Rustad (Eds.), *Betatt av viten, bruksanvisninger til Donna Haraway* (pp. 39–74). Spartacus Forlag.

Phillips, W. (2019). It wasn't just the trolls: Early internet culture, "fun," and the fires of exclusionary laughter. *Social Media + Society, 5*(3). https://doi.org/10.1177/2056305119849493.

Pinch, T. (2010). The invisible technologies of Goffman's sociology from the merry-go-round to the internet. *Technology and Culture, 51*(2), 409–424. https://doi.org/10.1353/tech.0.0456.

Poole, C. (2010, February). *The case for anonymity online* [Video]. TED Conferences. https://www.ted.com/talks/christopher_moot_poole_the_case_for_anonymity_online?language=en

Porter, T. M. (1995). *Trust in numbers: The pursuit of objectivity in science and public life.* Princeton University Press.

Rettberg, J. W. (2014). *Seeing ourselves through technology: How we use selfies, blogs and wearable devices to see and shape ourselves.* Palgrave Macmillan.

Schreiber, M. (2017). Audiences, aesthetics and affordances: Analysing practices of visual communication on social media. *Digital Culture & Society, 3*(2), 143–163. https://doi.org/10.25969/mediarep/13519.

Senft, T. (2008). *Camgirls: Celebrity and community in the age of social networks.* Peter Lang.

Shulman, D. (2016). *The presentation of self in contemporary social life.* SAGE Publications.

Spiller, K., Ball, K., Bandara, A., Meadows, M., McCormick, C., Nuseibeh, B., & Price, B. A. (2018). *Data privacy: Users' thoughts on quantified self personal data.* In B. Ajana (Ed.), *Self-tracking: Empirical and philosophical investigations* (pp. 111–124). Springer International Publishing.

Şot, İ. (2022). Fostering intimacy on TikTok: A platform that 'listens' and 'creates a safe space'. *Media, Culture & Society, 44*(8), 1490–1507. https://doi.org/10.1177/01634437221104709

Taylor, T. L. (2006). *Play between worlds: Exploring online game culture.* MIT Press.

Turkle, S. (1995). *Life on the screen: Identity in the age of the internet.* Simon & Schuster.

PART 4
Conclusions and Handouts

CHAPTER 13

Digitalization Summarized

In the introduction of this book, we used "a deep Norwegian forest"—disorienting, bountiful, and filled with possible dangers and rewards—as a metaphor for how we experience digitalization. By presenting a range of theoretical perspectives and empirical examples, we have provided you with tools for you to navigate this "forest" on your own and make critical reflections about where to go next. Being critical is not about being negative but rather being able to capture the complexities that digitalization involves, so your assessment of digitalization and its consequences is as accurate as possible. In this final part of the book, we will summarize and link together the themes of *social change*, *user perspective*, and *critical thinking*, as well as give advice about how you can use these concepts actively in your own studies and research. First, we will summarize the most important content from the earlier chapters in this book.

DOI: 10.1201/9781003289555-17

13.1 Part 1: A Critical Perspective on Digitalization

This book started by describing digitalization as a phenomenon and discussing the need for critical perspectives.

13.1.1 Chapter 1: Welcome to the Digital Forest

In Chapter 1, we presented digitalization as a forest that is easy to get lost in. That digital technology is ubiquitous (everywhere at all times), making the experience of navigating it similar to walking deep in the forest—an experience that can be both liberating and limiting. We introduced the concept *it could be otherwise* (ICBO) to address how technological development is not predetermined and how we need awareness of other possible trajectories if we want to understand how things turned out the way they did, as well as how we can affect them. We need such critical perspectives because digitalization often ends up being *solutionism*, where technology is presented as a frictionless solution to the world's problems. Digitalization is then treated like a black box where we only see what goes in (a problem) and out (a digital solution) with little awareness of how things actually change inside. Opening black boxes is something the academic field of Science and Technology Studies (STS) is well equipped to do. An STS perspective argues for an approach to digitalization that includes both technological and social changes (a sociotechnical process) and that the process should be *critically* examined.

13.1.2 Chapter 2: What Is "Digitalization," Exactly?

In Chapter 2, we probed the term *digitalization*, and learned that it could not be easily defined as it is used actively and differently by various actors based on their own interests, for example, as a political tool. We also introduced our own definition of digitalization, used throughout this book:

Digitalization describes social and technological changes related to the development, implementation, and/or use of digital technology. Digitalization includes both technological changes in the form of digitization (through which the world is translated into a machine-readable format) and social change, where society, groups and individuals are reorganized around and with new technology.

We then presented four questions to help you understand *what* happens in a digitalization process: (1) How is digitalization justified? (2) What is being digitized? (3) What is changed by digitalization, and (4) what remains the same despite digitalization? These questions will help you to open the black boxes of digitalization so you may understand *how* and *why* the consequences of digitalization took a specific form and how digitalization can be affected. We argued that understanding this requires more nuanced analyses—something a *sociotechnical perspective* can help provide.

13.2 Part 2: Analytical Tools

Part 2 of this book presented a range of theoretical terms that function as a "mental toolbox" for navigating the digital forest and support your critical thinking about digitalization.

13.2.1 Chapter 3: A Sociotechnical Perspective on Digitalization

In Chapter 3, we argued how a *sociotechnical perspective* on digitalization can contribute to critical thinking about digitalization. Three central concepts were provided: *interpretive flexibility*, that technology is open to different interpretations and forms of use; *delegation*, how we can understand interactions between humans and technologies as an exchange of responsibilities and tasks; and *actor network*, that technologies work in networks comprising both humans and nonhumans.

Because a single technology can be used in different ways, the consequences of a digitalization process are not predetermined. A critical perspective on digitalization, based on insights from sociotechnical research, is thus about understanding how a technology is subject to negotiation, formed by interpretations, and is part of a complex actor-network made up of other users, technologies, systems, and institutions. We also saw how the term *technology* has referred to different phenomena throughout its history, as well as how the term is still subject to change. Finally, we considered how sociotechnical perspectives reject all forms of determinism, instead embracing digitalization processes as complex, contradictory, and sensitive to context.

13.2.2 Chapter 4: Domestication: A User Perspective on Technology

In Chapter 4, we introduced *domestication* theory. This theory explains how technologies must go through a "taming process," in which interpretation and negotiation between the technology and the user are seen as necessary for the technology to be usable. Domestication emphasizes three dimensions that are decisive for how technologies are appropriated: (1) *practical*, how the technology is being used; (2) *symbolic*, what meaning it holds; and (3) *cognitive*, how users learn to use the technology. Domestication theory provides a nuanced understanding of the role of users and *non-users* in technology appropriation. Through the concepts of *re-domestication* and *dis-domestication*, we also showed how technologies, throughout their lifetimes, can take on different roles and functions in everyday life. Finally, we highlighted how the domestication of technology is formed by norms, rules, and moral evaluations—and, as a result, how technology use must also be understood as a *moral practice*.

13.2.3 Chapter 5: Script: Technology's Manuscript for Use

Chapter 5 introduced the theory *script* to understand how technologies hold and communicate values through material expectations about use and users. A central contribution of script theory is linking the developer's preconceptions about use, users, and the world to how technology is designed. The materialization of these preconceptions does not necessarily "come true," since users can interpret and use the technology in other ways than intended. The technology's functionality, aesthetic, and customization possibilities are made with intended end users in mind, and through script analyses, we can open the black box of technology more closely to examine who the intended users of a technology are as well as what ways it is intended to be used.

Script theory builds on three central assumptions: (1) that the developers' understandings of society and users are written into the technologies they make, (2) that technologies communicate values in addition to carrying out jobs, and (3) that intended and actual use are not necessarily the same. To describe how this happens in nuanced ways, we also listed some component parts of the script, such as *in-scription, de-scription, sub-scription, anti-program*, and *co-scription*.

13.2.4 Chapter 6: Technologies as Normality Machines

In Chapter 6, we considered how the development and implementation of digital technologies can strengthen or counteract injustice and inequality. The main point argued in this chapter is that technologies are normality machines, that is, that they form what we see as normal (as well as abnormal), since they are a central infrastructure in our everyday lives. Chapter 6 criticizes conceptions of technology as neutral or objective and uses the development of a student app as a thought experiment to make clear that no technology can be designed without an imagined user, and that stereotypical or simple ideas of who users are can make the design discriminatory. This chapter also emphasizes the concept of the *digital divide*, which describes differences in access to, and opportunities for, the use of digital technology by different groups.

13.2.5 Chapter 7: Digital Technology in the Past and Present

To give you an idea of how digital technology has had different interpretations throughout history (its *interpretative flexibility*), Chapter 7 started with Barlow's internet manifesto from 1996. Through a short review of computing history, we considered how the *control society* and *information society* led to what we can call the *communication society*, which describes a society centered on communication and interaction between users in digital networks. This chapter also offered some possible ways to conceptualize the present based on how society is impacted by digitalization, such as *cyborg theory*, *network society*, *platform society*, and *acceleration society*, among others. The aim was to encourage reflection about what you believe characterizes our present relationship with digital technology and to consider the grand narratives created about digitalization.

13.3 Part 3: Empirical Cases

In Part 3 of this book, we presented empirical examples of digitalization and showed how digitalization shapes health, work, control, culture, and identity.

13.3.1 Chapter 8: Digitalization of Health: Networks of Care and Technology

This book's first empirical chapter, Chapter 8, detailed how the digitalization of health creates new ways to think about our bodies and senses. How we define "good health" is influenced by technologies and is, as such, also a technological concern. This chapter gives three different examples of the digitalization of health.

First, we examined how so-called welfare (or "wellbeing") technology, especially technologies aimed at elderly populations (gerontechnologies), makes it possible to live at home for longer. The example we used was the social robot Tessa, a "talking" flowerpot that gives reminders to its primary users (people with dementia) and alerts to its secondary users (care workers and family). Sensors and sensor systems can create safer environments for the elderly, their relatives, and healthcare professionals, but they also raise ethical questions. We also examined how *exergaming*— workout games aiming to improve health—provides new constellations of play, exercise, and technology. However, exergames also individualizes large, complex problems, shifting focus from the societal barriers of active lifestyles to whether you can make exercise "fun enough." Finally, we considered how support groups on social media create communities for mental health. The support groups gave users feelings of belonging and acceptance as well as useful information, and such groups can provide an important link to professional help. The examples make visible how health is produced by an *actor network*, as the technologies examined never work alone. What has the digitalization of health taught us about digitalization?

- That we must understand digital technology as part of an actor network and that the introduction of new technologies does not remove the need for institutions or professionals like healthcare workers. However, digitalization can require them to take on new roles.
- Health technologies have important social impacts, including ethical issues that should be considered when a new health technology is being implemented.

13.3.2 Chapter 9: Digitalization of Work: Automation, Responsibility, and Reskilling

In Chapter 9, we examined how work is being digitalized and how automation is changing our work lives. We saw how different visions for the future of work can be linked to historical changes in humans' relationships to work, from *animal laborans* (the working animal) to *homo faber* (the creating human).

This chapter provided three examples of how new digital technology is changing how we think about work, how we carry out work, and where we work. In the example of self-service checkouts, we saw supermarkets replacing human cashiers with machines. This leads to new responsibilities both for the customer (to scan goods) and for the employee (to oversee customers' use of the checkout). Our second example showed how digital stopwatches, which aim to automate the organization of care work, put high pressure on employees' use of time and created unrealistic expectations regarding how effective care work can be. Our third example focused on how tradespeople on construction sites relate to digital control systems like control robots. The robots were expected to find construction errors made by ailing communities of practice, but in doing so, they may further weaken those communities. What has the digitalization of work taught us about digitalization?

- That digitalization includes the transfer of responsibilities and tasks between humans and technologies. Even if streamlining is the goal, it is rare for work to be fully automated, and even automated solutions are likely to require new forms of work since automation technology also requires oversight.
- That digitalization provides increased opportunities for control, as digital technology makes it easier for activities, interactions, and transactions to be logged. When a large proportion of work is subject to registration, this results in increased surveillance and control.

13.3.3 Chapter 10: Digitalization of Control: Surveillance, Automation, and Algorithms

In Chapter 10, we explored the use of digital technology in the surveillance and control of both animals and people. This chapter introduced four terms that describe different networks of control: *surveillance*, *sousveillance*, *metaveillance*, and *panopticon*. This chapter emphasizes how digitalization makes surveillance technologies widely available and that they are used in an increasing number of contexts and sectors. Since surveillance with digital technology is dependent on digital tracks, the data we create by using technologies also plays an important role in increased surveillance. Information about where we are, what we do, and when we do it is valuable to companies that collect and sell big data, as it can illuminate consumption and other trends to be used in advertising or other marketing campaigns.

Three examples illustrated the digitalization of surveillance: control of animals with digital fences, which made visible how users can meet surveillance with *antiprograms*; virtual fences for children, which are much more ethically problematic, especially considering the amount of personal data gathered about children; and predictive police algorithms, a form of surveillance created by data sets, where machine learning and algorithms are used to predict the future—that is, to predict who has the highest chance of committing a crime. An important critique arising from this last example is the idea of *algorithmic bias,* that is, that algorithms can learn biases from us and strengthen them. What has the digitalization of control taught us about digitalization?

- That digitalization includes transforming the world into data points. Data is a resource that many actors want, particularly in the form of big data, which can allow actors to better understand behavioral trends among large groups of people.
- That digitalization leads to ethical and social challenges when surveillance technologies become widely available and allow new, previously impossible modes of surveillance and control of people (and animals).

13.3.4 Chapter 11: Digitalization of Culture: Remix, Community, and Prosumers

In Chapter 11, the digitalization of cultural expressions is investigated. Starting with a focus on *remix culture*, this chapter considers user-driven creative expressions and practices in which copying, transforming, and combining are central. Instead of thinking of users as passive consumers of culture, this chapter emphasizes *prosumers*, who consume and produce simultaneously. The empirical examples (memes, fan fiction, and live streaming of gaming) therefore focus on cultural expressions that have emerged from online user communities and that are dependent on digital technology for creation, sharing, and use. Memes make visible how one can build collective identities through sharing and imitation, fan fiction emphasizes how user-driven creativity can provide alternative stories about the world, and the streaming of games on Twitch.tv shows how users are active coproducers—not just of content but also of platforms. What has the digitalization of culture taught us about digitalization?

- That digitalization has made possible new ways of producing, using, and transforming culture in which the border between producers and consumers has shifted
- That the digitalization of culture is a process of change characterized by remix and formed by participatory culture and the material preconditions for networked publics

13.3.5 Chapter 12: Digitalization of the Self: Selfies, Influencers, and the Quantified Self

Starting with Goffman's concepts of *frontstage* and *backstage*, this chapter explores our work of appearing in desired ways to others, both with and without digital technology. Chapter 12 emphasizes authenticity as an important dimension of self-representation because digital technology challenges the relationship between frontstage (where we are observed) and backstage (where we don't have to manage others' impressions of us). The meme *Instagram vs. reality* illustrates that we have a tendency to think about what is presented in social media (e.g., selfies or influencer posts) as less "real." However, the empirical examples of selfies, influencers, and the quantified self illustrate that our ideas about what is real and fake are both constructed and changeable. We argue that *cyborg theory* is a more productive way to think about self-representation, as the cyborg is less concerned with what is real and more concerned with what it can do. As such, this chapter argues for a move away from a moral evaluation of authenticity to an interest in how cyborgs can create expressions we experience as "real" or "fake."

Selfies are an example of self-representations made for communication. It requires both knowledge and hard work to appear as one wishes on social media, something that becomes clear when we consider influencers. Influencers are experts at balancing the idealized and the messy, and they use strategic glimpses of their backstage lives to appear authentic. The quantified self, on the other hand, shows how new technologies can make new representations of the self possible in the form of numbers (so-called *digital twins*), and they shape how we understand ourselves and influence how we act in everyday life. What has digitalization of the self taught us about digitalization?

- We are all cyborgs, both humans and machines, and through digital technology, we can exist in many places at the same time
- That digitalization has increased and complicated the ways we can communicate and represent ourselves. This also means that our identities are increasingly formed by digital technologies, and our relationships with technology are often intimate
- That digitalization challenges our ideas of what is "real." Since digital technology allows more opportunities for manipulation and social media has norms that drive expression toward an ideal, new ways of producing authenticity have arisen

13.3.6 Chapter 13: Digitalization Summarized

To conclude, we wish to address this book's three main themes. We will summarize which social changes have been shown to be central in digitalization, what user perspectives have been made visible in the study of digitalization, and how critical thinking through the lens of sociotechnical theories is a potent way to reject simple explanations and faulty premises regarding digitalization. We are not attempting to make a complete summary of what happens in all digitalization processes the world over, but rather want to bring together different lessons from this book's theoretical and empirical chapters.

These main themes are followed by analytical (Chapter 14) and methodological (Chapter 15) cheat sheets, which we hope you will find useful. These cheat sheets are intended to provide pragmatic questions that are useful in the study of digitalization, whether you are writing an assignment as a student or you are evaluating a digitalization process at work. The analytical cheat sheet summarizes the central theoretical concepts that are presented in this book and links them to analytical practices, while the methodological cheat sheet gives tips on data collection. With them, we hope that you will be better able to analyze digitalization as a form of social change, where user perspectives are a necessary starting point for critical analysis.

13.4 Digitalization as Social Change

This book's first theme—*social change*—is both a description of digitalization (since digitalization is social change) and a justification for why we wished to write this book. The world is undergoing rapid change, and digitalization encourages (and sometimes hinders) transformation in a number of areas. Students need a broad and thorough introduction to social change in order to understand how digitalization affects both individuals' everyday lives and society at large. It is particularly important to question who experiences these social changes and which changes they are subjected to, as benefits (or problems) as a result of digitalization are not equally distributed. It is also important to be able to understand *why* and *how* the changes happen. In this book, three concepts are central to understanding digitalization at the social level.

13.4.1 Digitalization Is Ubiquitous

Digitalization is not a single process that happens in one specific place for one specific person. Instead, digitalization happens at many levels and in many places simultaneously: from the individual to the global, from the local to the international. That digital technology is everywhere affects how we relate to it. This makes digitalization a diverse phenomenon that includes a number of different technologies, services, users, and actors. Whether you pay for food at a self-service checkout, have your health data registered and used without your consent, or work somewhere that introduces new requirements for registration and production, digitalization is a part of your life. Digital technology is not something we need to seek out; it is something we have to fight to escape—if we do not wish to have it in our life.

Because digitalization is a ubiquitous process, there will be many examples of digitalization improving people's lives, but also many examples of digitalization causing problems and concern. The same technology that makes one user feel trapped will make another user feel liberated. If you are able to see both possibilities and problems, it will be easier for you to navigate the digital forest.

13.4.2 Digitalization as Cyborgification of Society

We are all cyborgs who wear digital technology on our bodies and use it at work, in our spare time, and for self-expression. We express engagement through online communities, learn in virtual reality, and talk with flowerpot robots. Digitalization melts together arenas, actors, and technologies. Exergames are an example of a new hybrid technology that combines computer games' ability to motivate with the health benefits of physical activity. The cyborgification of society is not just a question of users' identities but a way to describe a society that is increasingly intertwined with technology—to the point that distinguishing between the human and the technical is simply creating a false boundary.

13.4.3 Digitalization as an Institutional Transformation of Society

Digitalization changes the ways in which we organize society, and it is clear that these transformations represent both possibilities and limitations for institutions. Health services are searching for digital tools that will make care work easier, stores are replacing employees with self-service checkouts, and robots are taking over jobs that were previously inextricably linked to humans' skills. Together, they all point to how institutions, both big and small, are changing. Roles that were previously seen as deeply human are now being delegated to machines, while we in turn have to take on new roles in response to digital solutions, and organizations are shaped by the tools they use.

In the face of these transformations, registration and control have unfortunately become central; our interactions and actions are increasingly traced and quantified. This doesn't simply create problems for personal data security; when an increasing number of institutions are digitalized, this also creates new forms of control and surveillance in the sectors in which these institutions operate, like health, culture, and work.

13.5 A User Perspective on Digitalization

This book's second theme, *user perspectives*, centers users in digitalization processes. We employ user perspectives to open the black boxes of technology and reject simple explanations about how technology is becoming part of our everyday lives. Throughout this book, we have focused on how users take part in *actor network*, how they *delegate* tasks to and are delegated tasks by technology, as well as how differences in use are due to technology's *interpretive flexibility*. We wish to emphasize the following themes regarding users in particular.

13.5.1 Users Are Prosumers

Technology users in the twenty-first century are not passive consumers of developers' *scripts* but active participants and cocreators of how technology affects their own lives. This can be seen as a melting together of the producer and the consumer into a *prosumer*. We have seen how authors of fan fiction want to take part in developing their own stories, how Twitch.tv users cocreated an opportunity to broadcast their passion for games, and how farmers provide feedback on how grazing technology should be improved when their goats "hack" the technology. Not only does digital technology in many cases allow for user modification, but we are also increasingly seeing an expectation that users should be part of development processes.

13.5.2 User Communities of Different Users

It is important to acknowledge that there is no single standard user and that users make communities to learn together and from each other; tradespeople who need to learn from more experienced specialists, mental health support groups that offer acceptance and necessary information, and fan fiction writers who want feedback. Consequently, we should always consider how users interact and if they are part of a network with other users who together interpret technologies' *scripts* and affect each other's *domestication* of technologies.

13.5.3 Unexpected Use

A particularly important aspect of the user perspective is how it captures unexpected interpretations and practices of technology. We have seen goats who risk being shocked because they want the grass that is greener on the other side of the virtual fence and stopwatch regimes that healthcare workers ignore because they want care to be measured by quality, not minutes. User practices define what technology can and will do, meaning we should never take for granted how a technology is appropriated.

13.6 Critical Thinking about Digitalization

This book's last major theme, *critical thinking*, is probably the most important. If digitalization is to result in better lives for everyone, not just the powerful and privileged, we must ask critical questions about what the technology entails, where it comes from, and who it benefits. To conclude, we therefore wish to bring up three key reasons to think critically about digitalization.

13.6.1 A Critical Perspective on Technological Fix

Technology is often presented as the solution to societal problems, but we must be alert and critically examine the premises of what is being suggested. As we have seen, health technology has been presented as a solution to loneliness, construction robots as a solution to construction errors, and predictive police algorithms as a solution to crime. Such solutions appear promising because they address complex and diffuse problems with specific and concrete technologies. However, if implemented uncritically, they can just as easily end up strengthening the problems at hand. The above technologies are presented as solutions to problems, but all of them treat the symptoms of the problems, not the causes. At the very least, the problems deserve more holistic solutions. Loneliness, a job market with few permanent positions, and criminality cannot be solved by one new robot, service, or algorithm—at least, not alone.

13.6.2 A Critical Perspective on the Impossible "Neutral"

Technology is not neutral; all technology contributes to inclusion and exclusion because all technology carries values and preferences for use and users. Consequently, we have a particular responsibility for understanding and assessing the values and preferences of technology, as well as for whom they have consequences. Presuming that technology represents something neutral, that because it's a technology instead of a human doing the task, it is objective, mostly leads to further discrimination against groups who are already marginalized. For example, predictive police algorithms will flag people with dark skin as high risk, while hiring algorithms rank men as better than women. We cannot leave these decisions to technology if we don't know what values the technology is built on and which rationales inform its decision processes. With the increased interest in AI, this is a particularly salient point, as AI systems are often characterized by no one (including the developers) truly understanding how the system produces its output.

13.6.3 It Could Be Otherwise (ICBO)

This book starts and ends with the gold standard for critical thinking, with the phrase: *it could be otherwise*. Knowing that the world didn't need to be the way it is, and that the path to the future is not yet laid, invites reflection about why things are the way they are and acknowledges that we actually have the power to shape the future. By reading this book, we hope that you will see the value of asking critical questions about the technologies in your life. How did they become the way they are? How could they have been developed differently? Who was in a position to make decisions when the technology was developed, and who was left out? What can you do with digital technology in your life so that its use matches your own values and desires? Last but not least, what can *you* do so that digitalization effects changes for the better in the future? Think critically; think ICBO.

CHAPTER 14

Analytical Cheat Sheet

A Guide for Thinking Critically about Digitalization

To understand what happens in a digitalization process, you must be able to answer four questions: (1) How is the digitalization process justified? (2) What is being digitized? (3) What stays the same, and (4) What is changed? Answering these questions requires a nuanced understanding of the interactions between a technology, its users, and society. This guide presents useful questions to ask when you study digitalization processes, and the answers will give you a

DOI: 10.1201/9781003289555-18

relatively good basis for answering the questions above. They are sorted by the five main theoretical concepts shared in this book: *interpretative flexibility*, *delegation*, *actor network*, *script*, and *domestication*.

14.1 Interpretative Flexibility

Interpretative Flexibility

To explore technologies' interpretative flexibility is to welcome and seek out different interpretations of what a technology is, has been, and should be.

14.1.1 Which Different Interpretations of the Technology Exist among Different Users?

One technology can be interpreted in many different ways. Explore how different groups of users think about the same technology and where these interpretations come from. A police officer can have different thoughts about predictive police algorithms than those who are affected by their discriminatory effects (Chapter 10). The benefits for some can lead to disadvantages for others.

14.1.2 Which Different Interpretations of the Technology Existed in the Past?

In order to denaturalize technology's place in in society, compare today's interpretations with a historical perspective. The reasons why a technology turned out as it did can be investigated by looking back in time. Technological development rarely (if ever) involves radical transformations coming out of the blue; more commonly, technologies go through small, incremental changes and technological systems are replaced in bits and pieces.

14.1.3 How Do Different Actors' Interpretations Relate to Each Other?

Who decides which interpretations of a technology become dominant? How are the relationships between the different actors and their interpretations? How do some interpretations become dominant and not others?

14.1.4 How to Undertake Your Own Investigations of Interpretive Flexibility

When you wish to investigate interpretive flexibility, it is important to map different understandings of the technology or digitalization process you're exploring.

- Search your data for different understandings and descriptions of your chosen technology/digitalization process, and make a note about who says what. For example, it is likely that different actors in the digitalization process will emphasize different aspects of the technology.
- Have a particular focus on marginalized voices. Who, both in the past and in the present, couldn't express themselves on the themes you're exploring? Which interpretations are hidden away because the majority rules? Historically, there are a number of examples of how the voices of women, people of color, and LGBTQ+ individuals have been suppressed, hidden away, or concealed, so you should make extra effort to make sure they are heard.
- Which narratives exist about the future? You cannot predict the future, but you can analyze who gets to decide how the future is formed and what visions are allowed to become dominant. It is also important to consider different sources to gain a variety of narratives. Throughout this book, we have referenced fictional

works, which might seem limitless in scope, but science fiction is also limited by context and contemporary culture.

14.2 Delegation

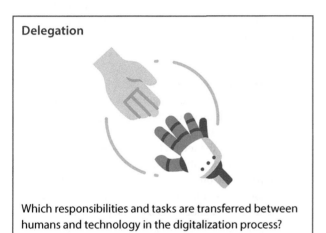

Delegation

Which responsibilities and tasks are transferred between humans and technology in the digitalization process?

14.2.1 Which Tasks Are Transferred to and from Technology?

Delegation characterizes all interactions between humans and technologies. Using delegation as an analytical tool in the study of digitalization is useful for understanding which changes digitalization actually causes, beyond what is conjured up in visions. Delegation is particularly concerned with how tasks and responsibilities are distributed between people and technology. In the digitalization of grocery stores, the work of scanning goods was delegated from employees to customers via self-service checkouts (Chapter 8), while in the digitalization of the construction industry, controls were delegated to robots, who are expected to have oversight over construction defects (Chapter 8).

14.2.2 How to Do Your Own Investigation of Delegation

When you explore delegation processes around technology, we recommend that you consider them together with the actor network perspective by mapping different actors. To understand what is delegated, it can help to compare how the situation was before the digitalization process started as well as to explore which people and technologies are involved—and which jobs they have.

- When digital technologies and people cooperate, who does what? Start by considering how the technology is used and focus on who are performing what tasks and where responsibility is placed.
- Consider what the technology is tasked to do: which duties and responsibilities are given to the technology? Who had these duties and responsibilities before technology was introduced? And what needed to change so that the technology could do the job? Remember, delegation goes both ways, so make sure to also consider how people adjust to the technology to take advantage of its functions (see, for example, how people needed to adjust to welfare technologies in Chapter 8).

14.3 Actor Network

Actor Network

Actor network is about understanding technological agency as distributed in a network of different actors, both human and nonhuman, and the negotiations that take place between them.

14.3.1 Which People Other Than Users Are Involved in the Digitalization Process?

End users are not the only people that matter, as they are not the only people using the technology or influencing how it is used. There are examples of many secondary users of technologies, such as elderly people's relatives (Chapter 7) or the boss at a work (Chapter 8), who can affect how they are used. In the study of networked technologies, such as social media, it is also relevant to study how user communities shape how the technology is used (Chapter 11).

14.3.2 Which Other Technologies Are Involved in the Digitalization Process?

Digital technology is often dependent on other technologies and technological systems, and how these relate is important to understand. Examples include cloud services where data is saved, wearables that collect digital footprints, and sensors, to name a few. In addition, analog technologies, like selfie sticks (Chapter 10) and exercise bikes (Chapter 7), can also be decisive in how we, for example, take selfies or take part in exergaming.

14.3.3 Which Other Nonhuman Actors Are Involved in the Digitalization Process?

There are other actors than people and technology involved in digitalization, even if our main focus is precisely on how people use technology. For example, animals are also a user group that has influence, such as goats that don't want to adjust to the control of a collar (Chapter 10). Other nonhuman actors include legislation (or the lack of legislation) regarding the sale of personal data (Chapter 10), local politics (such as the use of digital stopwatches in home care, Chapter 8), or a fictional story (like those fans rewrite, Chapter 11). These nonhuman actors should also be considered when mapping an actor network.

14.3.4 How to Do Your Own Investigation of an Actor Network

Investigating an actor network can be done using different methods. What is important is that the exploration of digitalization does not limit itself to considering only the app, service, or device that is your main interest. You must include contextual factors surrounding the technology. Both observation of use and qualitative interviews about use are good ways to map a network. Be sure to pay attention to how actors (both human and nonhuman) become part of/are included in/are excluded from digitalization processes.

14.4 Script

Script

Script describes developer's vision for use and users that are materialized through the design of a technology and can be understood as a technology's manuscript for how the technology should be used.

14.4.1 How Is the Technology Intended to Be Used Based on the Design?

Investigate the technology's preferences regarding use and users by studying its functionality, aesthetics and default settings/customization options. Together, these three aspects of design will tell you what the technology "considers" to be important forms of use, qualities the user has, and what it considers standard use.

14.4.2 How Is the Technology Intended to Be Used Based on Information from Producers, Designers, and/or Developers?

Technology doesn't develop in a vacuum. It is made by people with motivations and agendas for what they want to make and who, like all humans, are limited by experience and bias. Developers imagine how users should use a technology, but it is far from certain that this is how it will be used by the end user. To understand which visions shaped the design of a technology, look for statements made by producers, designers, and/or developers (or perhaps interview them if you have the chance) regarding what visions they have for their design.

14.4.3 How to Do Your Own Investigation of a Script

To gather data about design, you need to use the technology (or watch demonstrations of the technology being used if you don't have access to it yourself) to identify what it does and how. Concretely, you need to open/start the program, tool, or application you plan to study and map how it functions by testing it out and describing its functions, aesthetics, and settings. While testing it, you should take notes on what you observe, preferably with the help of screen captures or photos, so that you have a visual representation of the design that you can reference later. It is also worth noting down any reflections you have about the design while testing it out. How did it feel to try the technology out? Was it easy to navigate? Were you afraid to press any buttons?

In addition, you should consider which narratives and visions are linked to the technology and how they are created by more than the technology itself. Relevant secondary sources that inform scripts are:

- *Promotional materials*: adverts, slogans, flyers, offers
- *Instruction materials*: manuals, instruction books/videos, courses, tutorials
- *Media coverage*: press releases or other reporting about the technology

- *Producer presentation:* business plans, strategy documents, or self-descriptions from the producer, e.g., "about us"

Secondary sources, like those listed above, are gathered through strategic internet searches. Search for advertisements (both images and videos) made for the product as well as media coverage and reviews on social media. Go to the product's website and read what the producer has written. Search for places where the product is sold, e.g., the App Store or Amazon, to read descriptions and reviews of the product.

14.5 Domestication

Domestication

Domestication describes technology appropriation as a "taming process." The term captures how users shape technology through their use.

In domestication analysis we consider three important dimensions of the domestication process—*practice, symbolic,* and *cognitive*—with questions for each below.

14.5.1 Practice: How Is the Technology Used?

What practices is the technology part of, and how are existing practices being changed by the implementation of a new technology in everyday life? Appropriating technology usually involves some form of rearrangement of daily routines or spaces for use; pay particular attention to these when investigating how, when, and with whom the technology is being used. Take the flowerpot robot Tessa (Chapter 8) as an example, where distance to the TV and a new setup for cables had to be fixed before it could function.

14.5.2 Symbolic: What Does Digitalization Symbolize for the User?

What does a given technology mean in users' lives? Which values and opinions do we express by using technology? What does the technology represent to the user? Is the use voluntary, a luxury, and a way of expressing creativity (Chapter 11), or does the technology symbolize something forced, unwanted, or outside of our control (Chapter 10)? Be open to contradictory meanings, as technologies can hold multiple meanings. In short, it can be both fun and scary at the same time, and users may feel both concern and excitement regarding its use.

14.5.3 Cognitive: How Do Users Learn to Use the Technology?

All technology requires knowledge, and we learn new skills through use. We can see this, for example, in how influencers have mastered presenting themselves as both glamorous and approachable, as needed (Chapter 12). To investigate the cognitive dimension, ask how they learned to use the technology and what skills/knowledges they have to enact in order to use the technology.

14.5.4 How to Do Your Own Investigation of Domestication

There are many ways to study use. Independent of the methods you use, the following points are relevant to examine and could be a useful starting point for an interview guide or observation guide:

- What does use consist of? When was the technology used? Is it used often or rarely?
- Do they use the technology alone or with others? With whom?
- Do they use the technology together with other technologies? Which?

- Why do users use the technology? What is the motivation (or lack thereof) for using it? Is there any force involved, or is the use voluntary?
- What meaning does the use have? What does the technology symbolize to the user? Which feelings are involved?
- How did the user learn how to use the technology? What has technology use taught the user?

CHAPTER 15

Methods Cheat Sheet

How to Study Digitalization

In the previous chapter, we presented analytical questions that will help you unravel the messy reality that digitalization represents. In this chapter, you will get some tips on how you can collect data material that can provide answers to your questions. This guide is intended as an *addition* to the instruction in methods you have received in your program of study and should not be considered an introduction to qualitative methods (see Box 15A). The aim of this chapter is to link established methods such as interviews, observations, and document analysis to the study of digitalization processes. It therefore assumes that you already have basic training in qualitative methods. This guide can be used as a toolbox with tips and tricks to help you better explore digitalization

DOI: 10.1201/9781003289555-19

in practice, and it is particularly aimed at students who are planning to write a paper, report, or exam about digitalization.

Box 15A.   What Are Qualitative Methods?

Qualitative methods are well-suited to the study of digitalization processes because they allow for nuanced and contradictory descriptions of technological meaning and practice. As such, they enable us to understand both the "how" and "why" of digitalization. There are many books and texts that provide introductions to qualitative methods. If you haven't been able to take a methods course, you might wish to consider taking a free online course, like a MOOC (Massive Open Online Course), on qualitative methods, such as "Qualitative Research Methods" (University of Amsterdam) or "Qualitative Research Methods: Conversational Interviewing" (MIT).[1]

15.1 Research Question: What Are You Going to Find Out?

We take it for granted that you know which digitalization processes and/or digital technologies you plan to study. To get the most out of your analysis, you need to be clear about which aspects of digitalization you are interested in. Do you want to understand what has gone wrong in a process or how the technology could be improved? Or are you more generally interested in how digitalization forms phenomena like learning, self-understanding, inclusion, or work? While broad, open questions are a lot of fun to explore, it can be challenging to undertake such investigations in practice. Even simple technologies with few users are part of complex actor networks, and you can easily get lost in the complexity if you don't have a thematic "guiding star" that lights the way to the answers you are seeking. Especially for undergraduates, it is usually smart to select small and clearly limited cases for study, as qualitative methods favor deep analysis of something small rather than a shallow analysis of something big.

To understand what you are most interested in, try making a mind map. Place your thematic guiding star in the middle, and then explore what it relates to and which connections are most interesting. In a similar way to how crime shows visualize how clues relate to each other by having the detective pin them on a big wall, you can map out an *actor network* that shows different actors and how they relate to each other, and think about the different human–technology relationships that are relevant to your study.

If you are a student, you will presumably have a paper assignment or a learning outcome that sets boundaries for what you will be doing, for example, by defining some theoretical terms or perspectives you should use. This framework should be kept in mind when designing your project. If an exam question asks you to use *domestication*, it requires good data about use, while an exam question asking you to use *script* will depend on a thorough analysis of design.

15.2 Choosing a Method: How Are You Going to Find It?

When you know *what* you will explore, the next step is to decide *how* you will explore it. The table in Box 15B presents three common methods you can use.

Box 15B.	Three Common Data Collection Methods		
	Interview	**Observation**	**Document Analysis**
What?	Semi-structured conversations with interview participants about technology.	Observation of one's own and others' use of technology.	Interpretation and summary of relevant documents about technology.
Why?	Suitable for gaining insights into patterns of use and users' experiences that you might not have thought of yourself. Takes relatively little time and gives data that can easily be used in analyses.	Well-suited to understand where technology fits within an actor network, that is, how the technology relates to other technologies, humans, systems, knowledges, and ideologies.	Aims to see which frameworks shape digitalization processes. Particularly useful for understanding visions and technological discourses. Also important is identifying nonhuman actors (e.g., laws, structures, and nature) that affect digitalization. Can provide oversight over a theme/field.

	Interview	Observation	Document Analysis
How?	Set up an interview guide to support conversations with participants. Make notes during the interview or record the discussion and transcribe it later.	Use the technology like a "normal user," but systematically observe what happens and take notes for later analysis (a field diary). This includes testing out functions that you might not otherwise have tried and speaking with other users about what they do when they use the technology.	Search for or ask for copies of relevant documents, like project descriptions, product descriptions, adverts, training materials, media coverage, and government or other reports. Read the documents and highlight the sections that are relevant for your project.
Ethics	Inform the participants that the interview is voluntary and exploratory. Formal interviews require informed consent.	If the study includes observations of other users, they must be informed about the study, their personal data must be protected, and consent must be given.	Check the status of the documents (are they public or private?) and share them only if you have permission.

15.3 Tips for Getting Good Data

15.3.1 Interview

Be an active listener. That means nodding approvingly to encourage your interviewee and asking follow-up questions when topics emerge that you didn't expect but find interesting. In addition, questions like "To confirm, do you mean...?" are useful for ensuring you understand the answer and can lead to interesting elaborations. Descriptions of events rather than general considerations of the technology are more likely to capture nuances, and it is often here that the complex and important answers lie. If the interviewee only gives general and diffuse answers, you can try to phrase your questions more directly toward their experiences: "When you last used technology X, what happened?" This will encourage them to describe situations.

Good opening questions are "how did you start using this technology?" as it gives the interviewee a chance to give context for their use, whereas asking the interviewee to compare the technology to alternatives (for example, other platforms or services) will help tease out the meaning the technology holds.

15.3.2 Observation

Be present: listen, look, and reflect. Observation is a flexible method, but it can often include dead periods during which little happens, so be prepared that it can take time to get the answers you are looking for and that you need to remain focused. Nonetheless, be aware that when "nothing happens," you are likely observing a practice or use of technology that is black-boxed. Use the opportunity to ask people what they are doing, why they are doing it, and why they are doing it the way they are doing it. Use your field diary actively and be particularly careful to write down all situations that occur, including complications during installation or the pleasure you feel when a feature works, so that you can later analyze them in depth.

If you are doing observation of online communities or users online, make sure that you are adhering to ethical guidelines. Just because something is posted online does not mean users intend for it to be researched.

15.3.3 Content Analysis

When reading elaborate and complicated texts, such as government reports and white papers, it is easy to be persuaded by the report's perspective. Remember that the text is not a "fact," even if it has authority; it is rather one of several stories about a technology. Remain critical in your appraisal of how technological solutions are framed, what visions of the future they are drawing on, and who stands to benefit from the solutions proposed.

Another important question to ask when analyzing reports or policy briefs is what context the document is made in. As we remember from the discussion of how digitalization is defined (Chapter 2), it is a term that is used in different ways depending on who is speaking and to what audience. Who made the report, and what goals do they have for digitalization?

15.3.4 Take Lots of Notes

Be sure to write down observations and reflections during the entire research process, regardless of your chosen method. Our interpretations of technologies change through both use and study, so the notes you make (especially if you are using observation) are crucial to making clear what was important during the data collection process—and not just in retrospect. If you make notes, much of the analysis will already be done by the time you finish collecting your data, and no matter what, you will need to interpret your sources— your notes will save your "future self" time and work by borrowing a little bit of time from your "present self."

Another important aspect of taking notes *during* the research process is to ensure that you are reflecting on the work you do. All these theories and methods are, after all, tools to help you think, and thinking by writing is a great way to help the mind focus.

15.3.5 Take Screenshots or Make PDFs

Make copies of relevant websites (and date them!) for later use. They may not remain as they are and may even become inaccessible during data collection and analysis. (If you forget, you may be able to access a copy of the website on the Wayback Machine at web.archive.org.) It is also easier to develop an overview of your own data materials when you have a defined collection of files rather than a jumble of files, links, and documents. If you plan to save URLs, write down a description of the content of the website and take screenshots of important materials rather than just saving a long list of links. This will save you time later and will provide proof of what you observed if the website is updated or deleted.

15.3.6 Store Data Safely and Ethically

Universities have regulations regarding the collection and storage of data, and as such, they often offer digital services that can help store data. Check whether you are following the practical and ethical guidelines at your place of study. It is particularly important if you are doing interviews or observations, where you gather information about human subjects, that your data is stored in safe and ethical ways (hint: your usual cloud solution may not be sufficient).

15.4 From Data to Analysis

After the data have been collected, the next step is to get an overview of what they say. Since analytical work is a directed form of interpretation, *you* are the most important research instrument during an analysis, and you need to know your data inside out. To gain an overview of your data materials, you should (1) create summaries of your sources (whether they are interviews, observations, or documents), (2) read through the summaries you have written, and (3) read through the notes you have made. The aim here is to become so familiar with your data that you know what it says (and doesn't say). Before you bring in theory, you should be able to identify some general features of the data materials:

- What are the recurring themes in the data?
- What is the dominant discourse (the most common and most obvious way to discuss/interpret the phenomenon you are studying)?
- Which actors are involved, and which are central?
- What is expected? What is surprising?

If it is impossible for you to answer these questions, it is an indication you should spend more time familiarizing yourself with the data or that you chose a data collection method that was less than ideal (or perhaps just unlucky; we never know what we will find) and should supplement it with another one.

15.4.1 Applying Theory to Data

Qualitative analysis is a systematic yet creative process where you gain a deeper insight into the data. This means that you should weave your sources together (whether they are interviews, observations, documents, or a combination of all three) into a single, cohesive explanation that answers your research question(s) with the help of theory.

Another way to explain analysis is to "apply theory to the data," where you ask questions of the materials based on the chosen theory. The questions presented in the analytical cheat sheet (Chapter 14) attempt to operationalize the theories presented in this book into questions you can ask of your material. If some questions don't make sense, or if some don't seem relevant, that's okay. Trying to force an unsuitable theory on data usually results in a weak analysis, and we seek a good match between research question, data, and theories. In this sense, theories are like glasses that allow you to see different things, and you choose glasses depending on your situation: if you plan to explore a dark ruin, you would wear night-vision goggles, not sunglasses. The point of asking questions of the data is to reveal connections that lie beneath the surface of seemingly simple phenomena and to ensure that the questions you are asking are helping you get the answers you need.

15.4.2 Writing an Academic Text about a Digitalization Process

To write texts in academic genres is a difficult task: it requires precise language, evidence for claims made, and many genre-specific features, not to mention local variations between fields, courses, and instructors. Accounting for these variations is far outside the scope of this book, but we do wish to give one piece of advice: use writing resources when writing academic texts (see Box 15C for examples).

Experienced researchers with many publications don't walk around with all the rules of academic writing in their heads; they check them when they need to. Using writing resources and tools is not "training wheels" for students; it is representative of how actual researchers work. As such, you should think of the writing process as an actor network in which both humans (peers, instructors, the writing center) and nonhuman actors (books, citation guides, referencing software, templates, and guides) take part.

Box 15C.   Recommended Resources for Academic Writing

Books on academic writing	Craswell, G. (2004). *Writing for academic success*. SAGE. Swales, J., & Feak, C. (2012). *Academic writing for graduate students: Essential skills and tasks*. Michigan University Press.
Websites on citation	The Purdue OWL is user-friendly and comprehensive. In addition, most universities and colleges have their own websites about academic writing that are quite useful.
Citation tools	Zotero, Mendeley, and EndNote are examples of programs that (1) organize your references, (2) help format your references in your text, and (3) automatically generate a references list based on the references you have used.
"Phrase banks"	"Phrase banks" include phrases and sayings that are often used in academic writing and are particularly useful for starting a new paragraph. See, e.g., phrasebank. manchester.ac.uk and ref-n-write-com/trial/academic-phrasebank/
Local writing resources	Many universities and colleges have their own academic writing centers/groups/forums. Find them, join them, and use them!
Peers	Set up a "shut up and write" session with some peers. Meet each other to work hard for 20–30 minutes at a time and take shared breaks.

15.4.3 A Methodological Challenge: Using Yourself!

Digitalization processes can be challenging to research because they change so quickly—what was "hot" yesterday can quickly be "not" tomorrow. New technological trends hit fast, and most assuredly faster than the average pace of academia. Consequently, there is a need for students and researchers who have grown up and lived in the digital world and are already familiar with different technologies and practices. What might seem completely natural and obvious to you, such as the norms and customs of use for a digital platform, might take someone else weeks—if not months—of study in order to grasp. So, don't be afraid to use your own experiences and interests when you form your project and analyze the data!

Note

1 You can find these courses on Coursera: https://mitxonline.mit.edu/courses/course-v1:MITxT+21A.819.1x/

Index

303